ANCIENT ISRAEL'S WOMEN OF FAITH

A Survey of the Heroines of the Old Testament

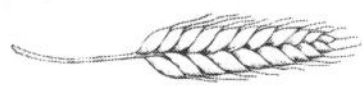

Claude F. Mariottini

Ancient Israel's Women of Faith: A Survey of the Heroines of the Old Testament

Published by Kregel Academic, an imprint of Kregel Publications, 2450 Oak Industrial Dr. NE, Grand Rapids, MI 49505-6020.

Library of Congress Cataloging-in-Publication Data

Names: Mariottini, Claudemiro Francisco.
Title: Ancient Israel's women of faith : a survey of the heroines of the Old Testament / Claude F. Mariottini.
Description: First edition. | Grand Rapids, MI : Kregel Academic, [2025] | Includes bibliographical references and index.
Identifiers: LCCN 2025029857 (print) | LCCN 2025029858 (ebook)
Subjects: LCSH: Bible. Old Testament—Biography | Women in the Bible—Biography | LCGFT: Biographies
Classification: LCC BS575 .M336 2025 (print) | LCC BS575 (ebook)

ISBN 978-0-8254-4950-5

Printed in the United States of America

25 26 27 28 29 / 5 4 3 2 1

"Claude Mariottini's *Ancient Israel's Women of Faith* reminds us of the importance of the many and often-overlooked women of the Old Testament, both their significance within Israel's story and as models of faith for believers today. Drawing on his own careful study of the relevant biblical texts and the scholarship on those texts and on the larger ancient Near Eastern world, Mariottini brings to life the women of the Old Testament, allowing modern readers to discover the challenges these women faced as well as the ways they served God and Israel in their contexts. One cannot fully appreciate the work of God through Israel without knowing the stories of these women of God, and *Ancient Israel's Women of Faith* provides a wonderful entry into the study of these important characters."

—Phillip G. Camp
Professor of Bible, Hazelip School of Theology
Lipscomb University

"The Old Testament features more than one hundred named women within its pages, as well as countless unnamed women. Many were Israelite; a number non-Israelite. Some were mothers; others, prophets. Several were abused, while a few attained great distinction. Most of these women, however, have remained virtually unknown to even the most devoted Bible readers, not only in the pew but even in the seminary. In *Ancient Israel's Women of Faith: A Survey of the Heroines of the Old Testament*, Claude Mariottini presents the stories of many of these remarkable women and also deals with some of the issues they faced. With the clarity and accessibility that are so characteristic of his writing, he explores the ways in which God's plans were accomplished in the world through their lives. In reading *Ancient Israel's Women of Faith*, contemporary women (and men) will no doubt discover new ways that they, too, can be part of the realization of God's plans today."

—Ralph K. Hawkins
Professor of Religion
Averett University

"If a woman asks, 'Can God use me? Do I have a role to play in his kingdom?,' point them toward this book! *Ancient Israel's Women of Faith* is a solid scholarly work that focuses on biblical history, uncovering insights that are often overlooked by casual readers of the Bible. Pragmatically, this text will encourage women who may have wrestled with their roles in God's kingdom, while challenging others who have failed to affirm a woman's calling. This text might focus on the 'ancient,' but it has implications that remain powerful today!"

—Charles Moore
Former Pastor and President
Northern Seminary

"For those who desire to go beyond the frequently mentioned heroes of the Old Testament and meet extraordinary women who are frequently overlooked, Dr. Mariottini is a valuable and able guide. Sympathy and admiration will be felt for these new friends as your understanding of their stories deepens by way of Mariottini's analysis of Hebrew terms and cultural context. May the faith of these heroes of old inspire new heroes today."

—Jeff Griffin
Senior Pastor
The Compass Church

"The inclusion of women in the Old Testament has long been taught as a rarity, sometimes causing us to miss the audacity of an ancient religious text from a patriarchal time to include such amazing narratives of women. Mariottini's *Ancient Israel's Women of Faith* captures a fresh look at how often powerful men in the ancient text encounter equally powerful women. Together, all have a role in God's faithful plans to set the world right again. This book invites us to tell the whole story of God's people, named and unnamed."

—Joy J. Moore
President, Professor of Homiletics
Northern Seminary

"Who can find an ʾēšet-ḥayīl [amazing woman]? . . . Many women have done admirable things."
(Prov 31:10, 29 author's translation)

To my great-granddaughters,
Sophie and Millie,
God's precious gifts
and a never-ending source of joy

"A man can die without bitterness
if he can see his children's children."
Stanley Brice Frost

"Job lived one hundred and forty years, and saw his children, and his children's children, four generations.
And Job died, old and full of days."
(Job 42:16–17)

Unnamed or Named: Women in the Hebrew Scriptures Are Amazing

I

No one taught me that Moses was alive
to lead his people, help them to survive,
to bring them out of Egypt to be free
because some nameless midwives held the key
to keeping Hebrew babies all alive.
And I wonder how a slave girl had the drive
to help her captor heal, keep him alive.
And yet her name has been withheld from me.
No one taught me.
Looking now for nameless women, now I dive
into the text to learn of many wives
and daughters—some sad stories, you'll agree,
and some who lived and died with dignity,
though no one taught me.

II

Such awesome women in those ancient days—
the matriarchs whose roles we reappraise
and Hagar whose deep prayers the Lord God heard—
their stories are preserved in God's Holy Word.
Their deeds and words and faith still can amaze.
True prophets are deserving of our praise.
Thus we name Miriam; it will not faze
us that Deborah and Huldah spoke God's word.
Such awesome women.
The courage of Vashti and Esther we praise
along with Abigail and with Ruth who stays
with Naomi. The less-loved wife God heard
when she prayed for sons and Tamar who blurred
the role of harlot and others who blaze.
Such awesome women.

Wilda Morris

Contents

PART 4: ABUSED WOMEN

PART 5: WOMEN OF DISTINCTION

PART 6: NON-ISRAELITE WOMEN

List of Abbreviations

AB	Anchor Bible
ABD	*Anchor Bible Dictionary*. Edited by David Noel Freedman. 6 vols. New York: Doubleday, 1992.
ABRL	Anchor Bible Reference Library
BBE	The English Bible in Basic English
BBR	*Bulletin for Biblical Research*
BDB	F. Brown, S. R. Driver, and C. A. Briggs. *Hebrew and Lexicon of the Old Testament*. Oxford: Oxford University Press, 1907.
BibSem	The Biblical Seminar
BLS	Bible and Literature Series
BSac	*Bibliotheca Sacra*
CBQ	*Catholic Biblical Quarterly*
CC	Continental Commentaries
CSB	Christian Standard Bible
DOTTE	*Dictionary of Old Testament Theology and Exegesis*. 5 vols. Grand Rapids: Zondervan, 1997.
ESV	English Standard Version
GW	God's Word Translation
HTR	*Harvard Theological Review*
IEJ	*Israel Exploration Journal*
Int	Interpretation: A Bible Commentary for Teaching and Preaching
JAAR	*Journal of the American Academy of Religion*
JAJSup	*Journal of Ancient Judaism Supplement Series*
JBL	*Journal of Biblical Literature*
JBQ	*Jewish Bible Quarterly*
JETS	*Journal of the Evangelical Theological Society*
JNES	*Journal of Near Eastern Studies*
JSNT	*Journal for the Study of the New Testament*
JSOT	*Journal for the Study of the Old Testament*

JSOTSup	Journal for the Study of the Old Testament Supplement Series
KJV	King James Version
LHBOTS	Library of Hebrew Bible/Old Testament Studies
LXX	Septuagint
MDB	*Mercer Dictionary of the Bible*. Edited by Watson E. Mills. Macon, GA: Mercer University Press, 1990.
NAB	New American Bible
NCB	*New Century Bible*
NET	New English Translation
NICOT	New International Commentary on the Old Testament
NIV	New International Version
NJB	New Jerusalem Bible
NLT	New Living Translation
NRSV	New Revised Standard Version
OBT	Overtures to Biblical Theology
OTL	Old Testament Library
RevExp	*Review and Expositor*
RSV	Revised Standard Version
TNK	Jewish Publication Society TANAKH 1985
VT	*Vetus Testamentum*
WBC	Word Biblical Commentary
WO	*Die Welt des Orients*
WW	*Word and World*
ZAW	*Zeitschrift für die alttestamentliche Wissenschaft*

Foreword

In my early years as a Christian young woman, I was in a church system that required women to be silent in the church—and by silent, I mean we could only sing from our seats. Even a woman getting an education beyond the legal requirement was considered a waste of time. Women were expected to marry, have children, and help make their husbands look good no matter what their husbands did or how they treated their wives. And of course, modesty was the highest virtue: to wear long dresses, no makeup, no jewelry, and plain hair because we wouldn't want to be a stumbling block to a man!

In this system, and many religious ones like it, preaching and teaching were all about what the men in the Bible and the church did for God: They preached about the male heroes, leaders, and role models and about women's obedience and chastity.

Life was unsafe. Vibrant girls and women lost their voices and character. God became small.

After breaking out of versions of the "shepherding" movement,[1] I embarked on a slow journey to restore a trusting relationship with God and to study Scripture for myself, outside of the rigid box that put a firm lid on the lives of girls and women. Even during my early graduate work in theological and biblical studies, I heard similar messages of submission from fellow students and occasionally faculty or administration that promoted keeping women silent in Scripture and in the church.

Recovering from a "Whack-a-Mole" mentality—the mentality that causes a woman to duck reflexively every time she dares to lift her head (or her voice)—takes time.

1. The "shepherding movement," also known as the "discipleship movement," emphasized discipleship and accountability of believers involved in a Christian community. The movement began when Bob Mumford, Derek Prince, and others began teaching a model of church leadership and discipleship that emphasized authority and submission. The main teaching of the movement was that every Christian should be under the spiritual care of a personal shepherd (or pastor) who would provide guidance, accountability, and protection.

As I grew more confident in biblical Greek and Hebrew, read deeply, and engaged in conversations with scholars, pastors, teachers, and friends from a wide variety of backgrounds and cultures, I grew to enjoy questioning and searching Scriptures for God's perspective on many topics, including the role of women in culture and ministry.

Along the way, teaching Biblical Hebrew and Exegesis to master's and PhD students at different seminaries continued to bring new questions and insights. I also taught most of the books of the Old Testament, Old Testament theology, and other topical classes, which continued my quest to know God and Scripture.

For the last four years, I've had the privilege of continuing the legacy of teaching a class at Northern Seminary on women in the Old Testament, which my colleague, Emeritus Professor Claude F. Mariottini, previously taught.

Ancient Israel's Women of Faith reflects more than thirty-five years of his research in the Hebrew Bible, with a keen attention to all the women, named and unnamed, who are so commonly overlooked. There are more than one hundred named women, most of whom even the avid Bible reader has never heard mentioned in church, Bible studies, Sunday school, or seminary.

Claude Mariottini is out to change that by providing a highly accessible and scholarly account of a large selection of the women of the Old Testament. But this book is not just for women! It is for all who want to learn more about how God works through both men and women to accomplish his purposes. When men *or* women miss the many ways that God works through women, they will fail to know what God is doing in the world.

Mariottini encourages the reader to observe the message from Scripture that women have significant roles in Scripture; they challenge unjust laws and persons in power and risk their lives to save others. In Mariottini's words, the Bible is rich with "women who make a difference . . . who refuse to quit whenever confronted with adversity. . . . God is working in partnership with these women to accomplish his work on earth."

He also invites the reader to consider that Israelite culture grew in its understanding of the necessity of dignifying and valuing women from Exodus to Deuteronomy.

While telling the stories in a manner that's easy to read, he includes scholarly perspectives on the biblical text and cultural circumstances that include some controversial topics. Let the reader be alert to hear debated viewpoints—Mariottini invites the reader into the conversation! Hopefully, if something controversial or disagreeable is found, you will return to the biblical text itself and consider studying to explore these issues further.

One of the many chapters I found especially interesting is Mariottini's construction of the matrilineal genealogy of Jesus according to Matthew. He calls this "The Genealogy of Jesus According to His Great-Grandmothers." In this lineage, he includes all the named and unnamed mothers (e.g., the mothers of kings David, Jehoram, and Ahaz are never given in Scripture). He also points out the three missing kings in Matthew's genealogy—those affiliated with Queen Athaliah. One of the many overlooked topics is that Queen Athaliah, the mother of King Ahaziah, is in the Messiah's lineage.

God is not afraid of controversy or questions. Scripture itself draws us in to observe and discuss the hard questions along with the simple ones, the beautiful topics along with the tough, for "All Scripture is God-breathed and is useful for teaching, rebuking, correcting and training in righteousness, so that the servant of God may be thoroughly equipped for every good work" (2 Tim 3:16–17 NIV).

Most readers will find many surprises in *Ancient Israel's Women of Faith*. The first is realizing how many women are in the biblical text. Women are not mere accessories to stories about men, as some suppose, but often initiators of new narratives. Mariottini prompts the reading and rereading of scriptures that preachers and others have often wrongfully used to exclude, vilify, or overlook women through mistranslations or misunderstanding the culture or laws of the ancient world—and the heart of God.

I trust this book will inspire and enhance your appreciation for both the amazing women of our Bibles and those around us.

—Ingrid Faro
Professor of Old Testament
Northern Baptist Seminary

Preface

During my tenure as professor of Old Testament at Northern Baptist Seminary, I taught a course called "The Women of the Old Testament." The course emphasized that the women of the Old Testament played an active role in the formation and transmission of Israelite faith. Put another way, the women of the Old Testament were much more than accessories for the men or bit players in God's grand narrative.

Readers, however, sometimes miss the active and influential role women played in Israelite society because women's roles are largely invisible in the Old Testament—which was the work of Israelite men who, in general, wrote to men. Further, most of the Old Testament was written by an elite religious group composed primarily of male leaders in the community. Thus, we should not be surprised to find that the Old Testament perspective is mostly male-oriented. However, these male authors do not portray women unsympathetically. In many places, women speak with their own voices, and their stories and words help us understand the formal and informal power women exercised in the community.

In her article "Names and Naming in the Biblical Word," Karla Bohmbach said that there are 2,900 men and 170 women whose names appear in the Hebrew Bible and in the New Testament.[1] Another study calculates that there are 1,315 names of men in the Hebrew Bible.[2] Despite these scholars' certainty, we cannot cite a definite number of named men or women in the Bible because some names can refer to men or women.

We can be certain, though, that there are more than one hundred named women in the Hebrew Bible, along with hundreds of nameless women. Though nameless to readers today, these women made vital contributions to Israelite society. Many of them served in professional roles.

---

1. Karla Bohmbach, "Names and Naming in the Biblical Word," in *Women in Scripture*, ed. Carol Meyers, Toni Craven, and Ross Shepard Kramer (Boston: Houghton Mifflin, 2000), 33–39.
2. See citation in Bohmbach, "Names and Naming in the Biblical World," 33.

Some women served as prophets in ancient Israel leading their communities and being in demand as proclaimers of good news. Some were professional singers and members of an association of women singers. Professional lamenters worked at funerals, and professional weavers prepared garments used in religious settings. Some women were professional diviners, professional instrumental players, professional dancers, and professional midwives. A few wise women advised kings and the leaders of their communities.[3] The Old Testament mentions several other influential women, such as one who built cities, one whose city was named after her, a woman who led her clan, and another who ruled Israel.

We cannot assume that all women in early Israel experienced a common lifestyle. The specifics differed in how a peasant, a noblewoman, or any other woman lived. But a set of expectations governed the life of an Israelite woman in any circumstance. Thus, as we study women in ancient Israel, knowing the social, economic, political, and legal conditions of patriarchal society will help us understand the different demands imposed on Israelite women in terms of productive and reproductive labor, in differences of value for women's services, in the range of activities outside the home, and in a woman's authority within the family.

The significant roles women played in Israelite society are found in texts that tell their stories. We know some of these women—such as Sarah, Rebekah, Rachel, and Leah—as the matriarchs of Israel. Others, such as Rizpah, are not well-known, but their stories reveal much about their strong character. Many of the women who lived in ancient Israel remain unknown because their names have never been recorded and their stories never told.

Some women gained recognition because of their relationship with important men in Israel, such as Zipporah, the wife of Moses. Others we know by the functions they performed in Israelite society, such as Huldah the prophetess. The stories of these women come from different places in Israel, different periods in the history of the nation, and different social and cultural situations. Together, these stories show us the important roles women played in Israelite society.

---

3. Claudia V. Camp, "The Wise Women of 2 Samuel: A Role Model for Women in Early Israel," in *Women in the Hebrew Bible: A Reader*, ed. Alice Bach (New York: Routledge, 1999), 195–207.

Some of the laws of the Old Testament indicate that women were subordinate to men in the household. For instance, a wife was considered to be her husband's property (Exod 20:17). A father exerted the right to control his daughter's sexuality (Exod 22:16–17). A single woman was expected to be a virgin at the time of marriage (Exod 22:16). A man could accuse his bride of not being a virgin (Deut 22:13–21). However, the Bible also shows that in many situations women could assume roles traditionally assigned to men. As Frymer-Kensky writes,

> These stories . . . show that beyond the realities of Israel's social structure, the Bible presents a remarkably unified vision of humankind, for the stories show women as having the same inherent characteristics [as] men. The circumstances of their lives are different from those of some men (those with power), but there are no innate differences that preclude women from taking men's roles . . . should the occasion arise, and circumstances warrant it. There is nothing distinctively "female" about the way that women are portrayed in the Bible.[4]

In the following studies on women in Israelite society, I show that the biblical ideal of women as persons of worth and dignity at times is betrayed by the social realities of Israelite society. However, I also demonstrate how the reforms of Josiah and the book of Deuteronomy attempted to improve the status of women in Israelite society during the seventh century BC. Deuteronomy represents the best effort to improve the religious and social problems confronting women in Israelite society. This document was an attempt at developing within every Israelite a special sense of social responsibility to care for the poor, slaves, women, and the underprivileged.

Some chapters deal with remarkable women—prophets and mothers—while others deal with issues women faced in the past and are facing in the present. In all, my goal is to help women today understand and identify with the struggles all women have faced, because the struggles women faced in the past are, in a very real sense, the same struggles women continue to face today.

---

4. Tikva Frymer-Kensky, *In the Wake of the Goddess: Women, Culture, and the Biblical Transformation of Pagan Myth* (New York: The Free Press, 1992), 120.

Acknowledgments

This book fulfills a promise I made to my students a long time ago. Whenever I taught my course on the women of the Old Testament, some of my students encouraged me to publish these studies so that others could benefit from what they had learned in class.

I want to thank all my students who contributed much inspiration to the development of this book. During the quarter in which the course was offered, the women and men in the class exchanged ideas and discussed the problems women faced in ancient Israelite society. The students expressed their feelings and what they had learned by writing research papers in which they selected one of those amazing women of ancient Israel to study in more depth. I must confess that I learned more from the dialogue with my students than they can ever imagine.

I want to express my gratitude to Wilda Morris for writing "Unnamed or Named: Women in the Hebrew Scriptures Are Amazing" at my request. Wendy, as her friends call her, is an accomplished poet. She has served as the workshop chair of Poets and Patrons of Chicago and as past president of both the Illinois State Poetry Society and Poets and Patrons. She has published numerous poems in anthologies and print publications, along with authoring several books of poetry. Wendy has been nominated for both a Pushcart Prize and a Touchstone Award. At the present, Wendy is working on another book of poetry inspired by books and articles on scientific topics.

I want to thank my former colleague Ingrid Faro for writing the foreword for this book. Ingrid Faro is professor of Old Testament at Northern Seminary and the author of *Evil in Genesis*. Professor Faro now teaches the course on women in the Bible at Northern. She is working on a book titled *Redeeming Eden: How Women in the Bible Advanced the Story of Scripture*.

I want to thank Caitlin Naul, Interlibrary Loan Librarian at the White Oak Library in Romeoville, Illinois, for helping me obtain books and articles I needed for research. Caitlin's willingness to help has allowed me to find the resources that were not readily available to me.

I thank Professor Benjamin Forrest for recommending me to Kregel Academic. I also want to express my gratitude to Kristina Vandiver, director of academic and ministry resources at Kregel, to Shawn Vander Lugt, and to Russ Meek, from Kregel's editorial department, for their help in seeing this project to completion.

Finally, I want to thank my wife, Donna, for her editorial help. Donna has served as my editor for more than fifty years. We graduated from seminary together, and she uses her theological education to improve what I write. She has provided valuable input in the development of these studies.

—Claude F. Mariottini
Emeritus Professor of Old Testament
Northern Baptist Seminary

INTRODUCTION

Those Amazing Women of Ancient Israel

Israel's history is filled with women of faith who impacted their society.[1] They served as God's instrument to help people, to be agents of change, and to proclaim God's message to his people. Some of them were ordinary women in the right place at the right time. Sometimes their names are mentioned; they remain unnamed, but their work matters.

Women Who Made a Difference in Israel

People today might think of the Old Testament as a story in which husbands ruled over wives whose primary responsibility was to bear children and take care of their homes. The biblical text, however, reveals women who made significant contributions to the social, political, and religious life of ancient Israel. These women remain unknown to many Bible readers. Their names are only mentioned in passing, and most readers do not notice their accomplishments.

Sheerah, City Builder

Sheerah was an important city builder in Israel. After the sons of Ephraim were killed by the people of Gath, "Their father Ephraim mourned for them many days, and his relatives came to comfort him. Then he made love to his wife again, and she became pregnant and gave birth to a son. He named him Beriah, because there had been misfortune in his family. His daughter was Sheerah, who built Lower and Upper Beth Horon as well as Uzzen Sheerah" (1 Chr 7:22–24 NIV).

1. Carol Meyers, "Women and the Domestic Economy of Early Israel," in *Women in the Hebrew Bible: A Reader*, ed. Alice Bach (New York: Routledge, 1999), 33–43.

According to the Chronicler, Sheerah built three cities: Lower and Upper Beth Horon—located in the hill country of Ephraim (Josh 18:13–14)—as well as Uzzen Sheerah, the location of which is unknown. Nowhere else does the Old Testament refer to a woman building cities, and only a powerful and influential woman would have the means to build one city—much less three!

The book of Joshua mentions several times the cities Sheerah built. The tribal allotment for the two tribes of Joseph went "as far as the region of Lower Beth Horon" (Josh 16:3 NIV). The territory of the tribe of Ephraim went as far as Upper Beth Horon (Josh 16:5). Benjamin's territory went down to Ataroth-addar, on the mountain that lies south of Lower Beth Horon (Josh 18:13). During the war of conquest, Joshua chased the Canaanites by way of the ascent of Beth Horon. As they fled, going down the slope of Beth Horon, "the Lord threw down huge stones from heaven on them as far as Azekah" (Josh 10:11). In the days of Saul, Philistine raiders conquered Beth Horon. Solomon rebuilt Lower Beth Horon (1 Kgs 9:17) and fortified both Upper and Lower Beth Horon with walls, gates, and bars (2 Chr 8:5). Though some find it difficult to believe that an Israelite woman could build cities, the biblical witness is clear that her influence endured through the work she accomplished.[2]

Jehosheba, King Rescuer

Jehosheba saved the life of the future king of Judah, her heroic actions thus preserving the Davidic monarchy. Jehosheba's story begins when a disciple of the prophet Elisha anointed Jehu to fight against the Omride dynasty in the northern kingdom (2 Kgs 9–10). In the southern kingdom, Athaliah had seized David's throne in Jerusalem. The daughter of Ahab and Jezebel, Athaliah was the wife of Judah's king, Jehoram (2 Chr 21:6), and the mother of Ahaziah, who reigned after Jehoram's death (2 Kgs 8:25).

Upon his anointing as king of Israel, Jehu was commissioned to eliminate the house of Ahab and wipe out the worship of Baal. Jehu initiated his mission by killing the members of Ahab's family, including Jezebel, the queen mother. Jehu and his soldiers also wounded

2. See "Sheerah," *The International Standard Bible Encyclopedia*, ed. James Orr, 5 vols. (Chicago: The Howard Severance Company, 1915), 4:2758.

Ahaziah, king of Judah, the son of Athaliah (2 Kgs 9:27–29). Ahaziah fled from Jehu, but he succumbed to his wounds in Megiddo.

When Athaliah saw that Jehu had killed her son, she determined to kill every member of the royal family, which enabled her to seize the throne and rule as queen in Jerusalem for six years. Athaliah could not, however, destroy the monarchical line because Jehosheba, the daughter of King Jehoram and sister of Ahaziah, took the baby Joash, Ahaziah's son and her nephew, and hid him from Athaliah. Jehosheba and young Joash lived in the temple for six years while Athaliah ruled the country (2 Kgs 11:3).

Significantly, Jehosheba was the daughter of Jehoram but not the daughter of Athaliah. Her mother was one of Jehoram's many other wives. Although her father followed the ways of the kings of Israel under the influence of Athaliah (2 Chr 21:6), who worshiped the Canaanite god Baal, Jehosheba did not follow in the ways of her family. Rather, she was a faithful believer in God. She worshiped Yahweh and eventually married the high priest Jehoiada.

Jehosheba was a courageous woman who experienced violence and tragedy in her life, even witnessing Athaliah kill her family. Jehosheba put her own life in jeopardy to save Joash, the Davidic heir. By being faithful to God amid violence and tyranny, Jehosheba saved the life of the future king of Judah and secured the continuance of the Davidic monarchy.

The Women Who Proclaimed Good News

Women who proclaimed good news of victory played a significant role in Israelite society (Ps 68:11).[3] Psalm 68 celebrates a great military victory that occurred because of God's intervention on behalf of the army of Israel.

Israel's victory is associated with the ark of the covenant, which symbolized God's presence with Israel's army when they fought against their enemies. Psalm 68:1 says: "Let God rise up, let his enemies be scattered; let those who hate him flee before him." This verse quotes the Song of the Ark found in Numbers 10:35: "Arise, O Lord, let your enemies be scattered, and your foes flee before you." Here, Moses calls

3. The versions differ in their translation of Ps 68:11. For a detailed study of this verse, see "The Women Who Proclaimed the Good News."

on God to assure the people that whenever they fought against their enemies, they did so with Yahweh's protection. The presence of the ark assured them that their God was the one fighting for them.

The Hebrew word translated "women brought the good news" in Psalm 68:11 (CSB) is *hamebaśśerôt*. Derived from the Hebrew word *bāśar*, which means to proclaim good tidings or to preach, it occurs thirty times in the Old Testament in the context of one who brings news, especially pertaining to military encounters.[4] *Bāśar* is the same word behind the word for "gospel" or "good news" in the New Testament.[5] The word is translated as "tidings" (2 Sam 18:19, 20, 26 NRSV) or "good news" (2 Sam 18:19, 20, 26 CSB).

Hamebaśśerôt is a feminine plural noun with a collective meaning that should be translated as "the bearers [company] of good news." The bearers of the good news are a group of female singers who announced news of military victory. This group probably functioned similarly to the women who greeted Saul and David when they returned home after routing the Philistines (1 Sam 18:6–7).

Mothers Who Deeply Impacted Their Children's Lives

Another group of women who made a difference in Israel were the mothers who nurtured their children and taught them the faith of their ancestors. These women show that it is not power or authority that shapes children's lives. It is the love of a mother willing to make sacrifices; it is the faith of women willing to do everything for their children.

Mothers made a meaningful impact in Israel because they were people of faith. People of faith have the capacity to touch the lives of others and make a difference. Mothers can shape the lives of people and the future of nations, and can be the catalysts for positive transformation in society.

Hannah was barren and unable to conceive, but she was also a woman of prayer. And because she believed in God, God opened her womb and gave her a son, Samuel. Samuel grew up to be a judge, a priest, and a prophet in Israel. He anointed Saul as the first king of Israel and David as the second. Through her faith, this woman became

4. John N. Oswalt, "*bāśar*," *Theological Workbook of the Old Testament*, ed. R. Laid Harris, 2 vols. (Chicago: Moody, 1980), 1:135.
5. The Septuagint (LXX) uses the word εὐαγγελι "good news" to translate the Hebrew word *hamebaśśerôt*.

the mother of a man whom Yahweh called one of the great intercessors in Israel (Jer 15:1).

Rachel was also a barren woman who desperately desired to become a mother. When God opened her womb, she gave birth to Joseph, who saved the people of Egypt and his family from famine. Joseph said: "God sent me before you to preserve for you a remnant on earth, and to keep alive for you many survivors" (Gen 45:7). Rachel was convinced that her prayers would never be answered, but she never stopped praying. People can easily be discouraged when they lack the resolve to persist, but because Rachel persisted in prayer, she impacted the lives of many people through her son.

In part 3, I present the stories of several mothers who, through love, sacrifice, and personal agony, impacted the lives of their children and through them, the nation. These women made a difference because they had within themselves the strength of character and the will to face difficult situations with courage, faith, and determination.

Women Prophets Who Left a Lasting Impact on Israelite History

Prophets were influential men and women whom God called to make a difference in Israel, to present the people with God's will for them: "I raised up some of your children to be prophets" (Amos 2:11). One reason prophetic voices wielded profound authority in Israel was because of their relationship with God. The true prophets stood in the council of Yahweh, heard the deliberations of the members of the divine council, and learned the message they should proclaim to the people. The divine council refers to an assembly over which Yahweh presides. In the council, Yahweh makes decisions alongside angelic beings. Prophets, such as Isaiah (Isa 6:1–13) and Micaiah (1 Kgs 22:19–22), are granted access to this council to witness divine deliberations and receive messages to deliver to the people of Israel. Prophets typically enter the divine council through visions or spiritual experiences rather than physical means.

Jeremiah 23:18 shows how prophets received their messages from God. In describing the failure of the false prophets to proclaim the true word of God, Jeremiah says, "For who has stood in the council of the LORD so as to see and to hear his word? Who has given heed to his word so as to proclaim it?" Yahweh declared that the false prophets failed because they had not been in the divine council, "But if they had stood in my council, then they would have proclaimed my words to my people, and they would have turned them from their evil way, and from the evil of their doings" (Jer 23:22).

The Old Testament mentions several women prophets who were commissioned to proclaim God's message to Israel. These women prophets had a direct encounter with Yahweh. In these encounters with God, the prophetesses heard the word of Yahweh and proclaimed Yahweh's words to the people. Deborah, Huldah, and all the unnamed women prophets in the Old Testament were also in the council of the Lord, for as Amos said, "Surely the Lord God does nothing without revealing his secret to his servants the prophets" (Amos 3:7).

As a person called by God to judge her people, Deborah recognized that she could make a difference in the lives of the people. As a prophet of God, she became an agent of change by influencing how Barak saw the oppressive situation of Israel. The oppression of the Canaanites ceased because Deborah took action to make a difference in Israel. Likewise, Huldah influenced Josiah's reform by identifying and authenticating the document as the word of God. She was able to convince the messengers of Josiah that she was speaking on God's behalf. They accepted her prophetic authority and her leadership. God was accomplishing his work and purpose in the world through the lives of these people whom he called and gifted to accomplish their work.

Thus, these women prophets were called to shape the spiritual destiny of ancient Israel. As soon as these prophetesses heard Yahweh's word, they proclaimed it to the people. Their message was the very word they had received from Yahweh. For the message to have authority, prophets must hear Yahweh speak, and then they must faithfully communicate God's word to the people.

Women Who Make a Difference

Today some women give up whenever they are confronted with opposition or situations they believe are hopeless. Some women live with a sense of resignation because they believe things cannot change. They see the futility of fighting for what they want and need.

Some people are discouraged when confronted with insurmountable situations; others fear the unknown and prematurely end their quest for what they desire. When confronted with challenges and impossible situations, some of us believe we cannot prevail and make a difference in our society. In times of trial, we need people like Deborah—whose faith in God and confidence in his promises made a difference in the life of Israel—because those who make a difference are those who refuse to quit in the face of adversity. The women in these studies teach us that faith in God and a commitment to trust and wait on the Lord are enough to make a difference in the lives of others and in the life of a nation. God was working in partnership with these women to accomplish his work on earth.

God gives each person a gift to be used in a specific situation and in a specific place. When people use their gifts, they make a difference in the lives of others. All of us have a place in the world and in God's plan. God accomplishes his work in the world through the lives of faithful men and women. Faith in God is often forged in the crucible of severe trials. As Ben Zvi writes, "The more a personage seemed to embody the values of loyalty and commitment to YHWH, the more likely candidate she or he will be to stand as the main object of a tradition of a divine test."[6] It is when men and women remain faithful to God in the midst of challenges and trials that God can use them to make a difference in the places where God has placed them.

---

6. Ehud Ben Zvi, "When Yhwh Tests People: General Considerations and Particular Observations Regarding the Books of Chronicles and Job," in *Far from Minimal: Celebrating the Work and Influence of Philip R. Davies*, ed. Duncan Burns and John W. Rogerson, LHBOTS 554 (London: T&T Clark, 2012), 2.

PART 1

ISRAEL'S SOCIAL CONCERN FOR WOMEN

CHAPTER 1

The Status of Women in Israelite Society

The status of women in Israelite society—primarily women's roles and activities outside the family—is a highly debated subject in biblical scholarship. In some texts, the authors of the Old Testament present women as property of their fathers and husbands. This can be seen even in the language used to describe a woman's husband; he was a woman's *baʿal*, a word variously translated as "husband" (Deut 21:13), "owner" (Exod 21:28), or "master" (Judg 19:22). In both the Old Testament and the broader ancient Near East, a man could have many wives (e.g., Gideon, Judg 8:30; Solomon, 1 Kgs 11:3), and multiple wives indicated a man's wealth and power. Few women were independent, for they needed their fathers or husbands to provide for them.

Some Old Testament passages portray women as victims of men's brutality and inhumanity (Judg 19:1–30): women were bought and sold (Exod 21:7), raped (2 Sam 13:19), enslaved (Num 31:9; Deut 21:10–11), murdered (Num 25:6–8), and abandoned (Gen 21:8–14). Fathers could sell their daughters as slaves if forced by greed or compelled by poverty—"When a man sells his daughter as a slave, she shall not be freed as male slaves are" (Exod 21:7 TNK)—though Leviticus 19:29 forbade a man from selling his daughter as a prostitute: "Do not defile your daughter by making her a prostitute, or the land will be filled with prostitution and wickedness" (Lev 19:29 NLT).

Foundational Teachings in Genesis

Other Old Testament texts portray women with inherent dignity as humans. Genesis 1:26–27 affirms that the woman was created in the image of God. Further, woman is the climax of the creation story in Genesis 1–2. Genesis 2:18 describes the woman as her husband's *ʿezer kənegdô*. This Hebrew expression, woodenly translated as "helper beside/opposite him," does not carry the connotation of inferiority or subordination.[1] Instead, God created the woman as a companion to the lonely man, thus giving both humans the possibility of community, commonality, and wholeness.

The biblical view of women as persons of worth and dignity is sometimes betrayed by the social realities present in Israelite society—and every other society. Women's position in Israelite society probably became more difficult as a result of a common misinterpretation of Genesis 3:16: "To the woman he said, 'I will make your your pains in childbearing very severe; with painful labor you will give birth to children. Your desire will be for your husband, and he will rule over you' " (Gen 3:16 NIV).[2] The view that a man should rule over his wife places men in positions of authority and women in submissive roles. The Bible, however, teaches mutual respect in the husband-wife relationship and gives women an important role in the family and in society.

There are other possible ways to translate Genesis 3:16. The Hebrew preposition *b* means "in" and "with."[3] Gafney writes, "If one uses one of the standard lexical tools, one will have to go quite a ways into the entry on the preposition *b* to find occasions when it is translated 'over.' " Thus, according to Gafney, the Hebrew expression translated "over you" can also be translated "with you," as seen in Gafney's translation of Genesis 3:16: "To the woman he said, 'I will greatly increase your pangs in childbearing; in pain you shall bring forth children, yet your desire shall be for your husband, and he shall rule with you.' "[4] This alternative translation reflects the view expressed in Genesis 1:28–30 where God gives sovereignty over his creation to both men and women.[5]

1. Phyllis Trible, *God and the Rhetoric of Sexuality*, OBT (Philadelphia: Fortress, 1978), 90.
2. In the expression "and he will rule over you" (Gen 3:16 NIV), the word "over" has been interpreted as a divine mandate for male authority over women, thus reinforcing patriarchal structures. This interpretation has justified male dominance in familial, religious, and societal roles.
3. BDB, 88.
4. Wilda C. Gafney, *Womanist Midrash: A Reintroduction to the Women of the Torah and the Throne* (Louisville: Westminster John Knox, 2017), 25.
5. John Goldingay, *Old Testament Theology*, 3 vols. (Downers Grove, IL: IVP Academic, 2006), 1:543–44.

Another issue in Genesis 3:16 centers around the Hebrew word *māšal*, which has two meanings in the Hebrew Bible: "to rule" (*māšal* I) and "to be like" (*māšal* II). In his study of the word *māšal* in the Hebrew Bible, Allen H. Godbey concludes that *māšal* in Genesis 3:16 should be translated "to be like" rather than "to rule": "Thy longing shall be toward thy husband; and he shall be likewise toward thee."[6] This alternative translation suggests that men and women will have sexual desires for each other. Jon Berquist likewise adopts *māšal* II in translating Genesis 3:16: "To the woman, God said: 'I will greatly multiply your handiwork and your pregnancy. With work, you can bear children. Your sexual attraction is toward your own man; he will be likewise to you.'"[7]

Genesis 1:26–27 highlights the equality of men and women in creation by emphasizing that both were made in God's image and given dominion over it. The passage states that both share the same divine purpose and inherent dignity. This equality is reinforced by their shared responsibility to rule over the earth, care for creation, and fulfill God's plan together.

Men in Israelite society understood the text to mean a man should rule over his wife, which led them to understand a woman's life as "under the curse." Because of the social limitations imposed upon them, most women in Israel found their sense of worth, fulfillment, and personhood in being a mother and a wife. Rachel felt that her father had sold her and Leah to Jacob (Gen 31:15). As a woman without children, Rachel believed that death would be better than being barren (Gen 30:1).

Empowered Israelite Women

Despite the limitations imposed upon women, such as inheritance laws, restrictions on public roles, and the lack of political power, some women forged important places in Israelite society. Deborah led as a judge, Huldah served as prophet, and Athaliah ruled as a queen. Several women had authority as queen mothers. Thus, many women exercised significant power and authority in Israelite society. Further, centralization of wealth in the hands of a few families elevated the

6. Allen H. Godbey, "The Hebrew Mašal," *The American Journal of Semitic Languages and Literatures* 39 (1923): 105.
7. Jon Berquist, *Reclaiming Her Story: The Witness of Women in the Old Testament* (St. Louis: Chalice, 1992), 35.

status of some women and enabled them to live a life of luxury and exert power over men.

Changing Social Status

Israelite society underwent numerous transformations throughout its history.[8] From a tribal community, in which people had much in common and where few inequalities existed, Israel became a state, with a monarchy and a royal family that consumed a large portion of the goods produced by the average Israelite. The growing number of civil servants forced the state to enact a system of taxation that served to create a class of wealthy citizens at the expense of Israelite farmers and villagers. These social, economic, and political changes in Israelite society impacted the day-to-day lives of Israelite women in significant ways.

In pre-monarchical Israel, women played a significant role in the economic life of the family. Women worked in textile production, agriculture, and animal husbandry. The establishment of the monarchy introduced a system of taxation that forced households to sustain a state-based economy, thus increasing the demand for agricultural production. Women, who already labored in farming and household tasks, likely saw their workload increase. The inability to pay taxes forced some parents to sell their sons and daughters into slavery (Neh 5:5). In addition, the monarchy created a distinction between rural and urban women. The king employed rural women to cook, bake, and make perfumes (1 Sam 8:13). Many women who served the elite became the lower class in Israelite society.

Life Under the Covenant

The people of Israel enacted many laws to provide some relief to the plight of women in Israelite society. The Book of the Covenant, also known as the Covenant Code (Exod 20:22–23:33), is the oldest code of law in Israel. It codified ancient laws and traditions that were practiced among the clans and villages in Israel.

Many laws in the Book of the Covenant deal with social injustice and the plight of the destitute and oppressed in Israel. Some of these

8. Carol Meyers, "The Roots of Restriction: Women in Early Israel," *Biblical Archeologist* 41 (1978): 91–103.

laws attempt to address the religious and social problems of Israelite society and develop a special sense of social responsibility within every Israelite for the poor women, and the underprivileged who did not enjoy the whole benefit of the law.

The Covenant Code contains law protecting Hebrew male (Exod 21:2–6) and female slaves (Exod 21:7–11), regulating the treatment of slaves (Exod 21:20–21; 21:26–27), shielding the poor from exploitation (Exod 22:25–27), affirming the legal rights of the poor (Exod 23:6), providing for the resident aliens (Exod 22:21; 23:9), and safeguarding the widows and orphans (Exod 22:22–24). Mosaic laws recognize women's vulnerability in Israelite society and establish basic rights for female slaves and widows. These laws also address marriage rights and provide sexual protection for unmarried women. The laws in the Covenant Code aim to provide economic security for women and to affirm women's dignity in Israelite society.

CHAPTER 2

The Deuteronomic Concern for Women

In the preface, I wrote that "the status of women as persons of worth and dignity at times [is] betrayed by the social realities present in Israelite society." This chapter introduces how the reforms of Josiah and the book of Deuteronomy tried to improve the status of women and other individuals in Israelite society during the seventh century BC. Deuteronomy seeks to instill a strong sense of concern among Israelites by emphasizing care for the poor, slaves, women, and other underprivileged individuals in Israel.

The book of Deuteronomy is an exposition of the Mosaic law revealed by Yahweh on Mount Sinai. According to the introduction to Deuteronomy, Moses introduced the laws of God to the new generation of Israelites in preparation for their entrance into the promised land. This exposition of the law also invited the people of Israel to dedicate themselves to the demands of the covenant Yahweh had established with them.

As religious and social life degenerated in the northern kingdom in the days of Amos and Hosea, and as religious syncretism rose in Judah in the days of Manasseh, Israelites abandoned the moral values, neglected the demands of the covenant, and their ancient national traditions. In 622 BC, during the renovation of the temple in the days of Josiah, king of Judah (640–609 BC), temple workers found the book of the law (2 Kgs 22:8), likely a version of Deuteronomy. The reading of the book affected Josiah immensely.

In a ceremony in the temple, the king invited the people to renew the covenant and to abide by the demands of the Torah of Moses. In addition to reforming the Israelite religious rituals and traditions, Josiah also desired to improve the plight of the destitute and oppressed in

Israelite society. Deuteronomy reflects the rise of humanism in Israel.[1] Deuteronomy contains additional laws not found in the Book of the Covenant (see previous chapter). These additional laws deal primarily with the oppressed in Israel.

The reintroduction of the Mosaic laws in the days of Josiah called the people who lived in the seventh century BC to hear the words of Yahweh again and to renew their commitment to the God of Israel. Deuteronomy emphasized Israel's experience in Egypt and reintroduced the laws and the demands of the God who had redeemed a people from slavery in Egypt to make them a special people with a universal mission. Israel was called to be a religious community where the justice of God would be manifested to the whole world. Among the many theological emphases of the book, three deserve attention. The first was that Yahweh, the God of Israel, loved Israel with a special love, even when the nation did not deserve his love. Israel was responsible to love God with their whole being (Deut 6:5).

Second, Deuteronomy emphasizes the singularity of Yahweh in the life of Israel. Israel had served other gods, but now Israel had to serve Yahweh exclusively (Deut 6:4). Third, Deuteronomy relates obedience to God to the daily life of each community member. Because Israel was united to God by the demands of the covenant, each community member had to treat other Israelites with justice.

Because they belonged to Yahweh, Israel was a special people separated from the other nations. As such, their daily life and moral conduct had to reflect this relationship with God. The demands of the covenant required personal integrity and social justice of each Israelite. The poor, the slaves, the orphans, the widows, and other destitute persons in Israel became the beneficiaries of the changes introduced by the social reforms of Deuteronomy.

By emphasizing the dignity of women and by bringing them relief from some of the injustices they experienced, Deuteronomy made a real effort to improve the status of women in Israelite society. For example, Deuteronomy 24:1–4 deals with divorce. This law required the man to provide a written bill of divorce, giving the woman a legal

1. Humanism is the effort to emphasize the value, dignity, and potential of human beings; see Moshe Weinfeld, "The Origin of the Humanism in Deuteronomy," *JBL* 80 (1961): 241–47.

document to verify her divorce. The law dealing with the rights of a female slave (Deut 21:10–14) prohibits a man who marries a captive woman from selling her as a slave after the marriage was consummated. The law also required that the woman be set free if the marriage was dissolved. The laws dealing with rape and consensual sex (Deut 22:25–29) say that in case of rape, the man had to marry the woman and was not allowed to divorce her, thus ensuring lifelong financial support for the woman. The law also required capital punishment for the rape of a betrothed woman.

The law dealing with inheritance (Deut 21:15–17) specifies that if a man has two wives and loves the second wife more than his first wife and both give him sons, he cannot treat the son of his second wife as his firstborn. The rights of the firstborn belong to the son of his first wife. This law was designed to protect the rights of the less-favored wife by ensuring that her son would receive a share of the inheritance. The law about the female slave (Deut 15:12–18) requires that the female slave be treated the same as the male slave regarding release in the seventh year of servitude. The law of the newly married woman (Deut 24:5) provided stability for the new wife by helping her and her husband to establish their new home and family. The law about levirate marriage (Deut 25:5–10) gave economic protection to a woman whose husband died without a son. The law required that the brother of the deceased husband provide a son for the widow, and he would continue the deceased's man lineage and inherit his estate.

The laws in Deuteronomy are concerned with the oppressed plight of women in Israelite society. These humanitarian laws provided women with legal protections and rights not found in other societies in the ancient Near East.

CHAPTER 3

The Tenth Commandment

As discussed in the previous chapter, many of the laws in Deuteronomy seek to improve the legal rights of women in Israelite society. One of those laws was the Deuteronomic articulation of the Tenth Commandment. When we study the Tenth Commandment as it appears in Exodus and in Deuteronomy, we can see an important change of attitude toward the status of women in Israelite society.

The Tenth Commandment in Exodus

The Tenth Commandment, as it appears in Exodus, makes clear that the woman is included in what belongs to a man; that it, she is considered part of his property. "You shall not covet your neighbor's house; you shall not covet your neighbor's wife, or male or female slave, or ox, or donkey, or anything that belongs to your neighbor" (Exod 20:17). The "house" is not merely the dwelling of a man but his entire household, as in Genesis 15:2. In Exodus the idea of the "house" likewise includes the wife, the male and female servants, cattle, and whatever else a man may possess: "anything that belongs to your neighbor."

Although the wife was part of a man's house, she was not considered an absolute property of her husband, debased to the level of a slave, as female servants were. The woman had rights as a wife and as a mother. In the home she supervised servants, educated children, and participated in the religious life of the family. The case of Sarah and Hagar illustrates this concept well. Hagar was Abraham's wife (Gen 16:3), but she was Sarah's servant (Gen 16:1). Sarah was the mistress of the household. The Hebrew word *gəbîrâ* (Gen 16:4), a word that means "lady," "mistress," indicates that Sarah had control over Hagar's actions and fate. Sarah may also have had authority over some of the many servants in Abraham's household.

In Israel, most marriages were sealed with the gift of the *mōhar*. There is much question whether the *mōhar*—the bridal price which a man gave to the father of the bride—was actually a purchase by which a woman became the possession of her husband. Whether the *mōhar* was considered the price paid for the bride or a compensation that contributed to the union of two families, it is possible that in many situations the *mōhar* was considered a purchase, which served to promote the idea that the woman was the husband's property.

The idea that the woman was considered the husband's property is implied in a transaction where the woman was purchased at a price. When Boaz decided to redeem the property that belonged to Elimelech, Naomi's deceased husband and Boaz's relative, he came before the elders who were seated at the city gate and sat by them there. When Naomi's other relative who had the right of redemption passed by, Boaz called him to sit with them.

Before the elders of the city, Boaz said to Naomi's relative, "Naomi, who has come back from the country of Moab, is selling the parcel of land which belonged to our kinsman Elimelech. So I thought I would tell you of it, and say, Buy (*qānâ*) it in the presence of those sitting here" (Ruth 4:3–4 RSV).

Then Boaz told his relative, "The day you buy (*qānâ*) the field from the hand of Naomi, you are also buying (*qānâ*) Ruth the Moabitess, the widow of the dead, in order to restore the name of the dead to his inheritance" (Ruth 4:5 RSV). When his relative declined, Boaz turned to the elders of the city and said, "Also Ruth the Moabitess, the widow of Mahlon, I have bought (*qānâ*) to be my wife, to perpetuate the name of the dead in his inheritance, that the name of the dead may not be cut off from among his brethren and from the gate of his native place; you are witnesses this day" (Ruth 4:10 RSV).

The NIV translates the Hebrew word *qānâ* as "buy" in the first instance and as "acquire" in the second: "Then Boaz said, 'On the day you buy (*qānâ*) the land from Naomi and from Ruth the Moabitess, you also acquire (*qānâ*) Ruth the Moabite, the dead man's widow, in order to maintain the name of the dead with his property" (Ruth 4:5 NIV). Even though the NIV uses the word "acquire" to explain how Boaz bought Ruth, it is evident that Ruth was included in the purchase of the land.

According to Exodus 21:7, a man could sell his daughter to another man, but she would become a concubine and not a slave. Rachel and

Leah complained that their father Laban had sold them to Jacob. They said: "Does he not regard us as foreigners? Not only has he sold us, but he has used up what was paid for us" (Gen 31:15 NIV). If they were sold to Jacob, however, then Laban's action may not represent an Israelite practice but rather a Mesopotamian marriage tradition (see Gen 29:26).

The *mōhar*, the bridal price, was paid by Shechem to marry Dinah, Jacob's daughter. When Hamor and his son Shechem went to Jacob and his sons to ask permission for Shechem to marry Dinah, Shechem told Jacob and his sons, "'Do me this favor, and I will pay whatever you tell me. Ask of me a bride-price (*mōhar*) ever so high, as well as gifts, and I will pay what you tell me; only give me the maiden for a wife'" (Gen 34:11–12 TNK).

The versions differ in their translation of the Hebrew word *mōhar* in this passage:

NRSV: "marriage present"
NIV: "price for the bride"
ESV: "bride-price"
CSB: "compensation"
KJV: "dowry"
GW: "price paid for the bride"

Since Shechem had to pay the *mōhar* and give a gift to the family, it is clear that the *mōhar* was the price he had to pay to obtain Dinah to be his wife. Dinah's rape brought shame to her family. The dishonor of Jacob's family led to the violent retribution by Dinah's brothers, Simeon and Levi, who killed Shechem and his family. Although Dinah was given to Shechem as a wife, she was never asked whether she wanted to stay with her husband or return to her family.

In the Covenant Code, the *mōhar* was also the price paid by the man who seduced a virgin. The man who violated the virgin must pay the "bride-price" (*mōhar*) and take the woman as his wife (Exod 22:16–17).

When David planned to marry Saul's daughter, he was told that "the king wants no other price for the bride (*mōhar*) than a hundred Philistine foreskins" (1 Sam 18:25 NIV). Although the request was unusual, David had to pay what Saul requested as a *mōhar* before he could marry Michal. When Abraham sent his servant Eliezer to find a wife for Isaac, Eliezer gave Rebekah's family expensive gifts (Gen 24:53), probably as a *mōhar*, even though the word is not used in the text. The Hebrew term *mōhar* in matrimonial contexts refers to a significant payment made by the prospective husband to the bride's father before marriage consummation. As a result, the woman would be included among a man's property since he had to pay to acquire her as his wife.

The Tenth Commandment in Deuteronomy

Deuteronomy's version of the tenth commandment differs slightly, separating the woman from a man's property to give proper attention to the rights of the woman:

> Neither shall you covet your neighbor's wife. Neither shall you desire your neighbor's house, or field, or male or female slave, or ox, or donkey, or anything that belongs to your neighbor. (Deut 5:21)

Deuteronomy demonstrates more respect for women in general by emphasizing the rights of women as persons of worth, not as mere property of their fathers or husbands. The text clearly distinguishes the wife from a man's property. The text deals first with the man's wife: "Neither shall you covet your neighbor's wife." Then it addresses a man's property: "Neither shall you desire your neighbor's house, or field, or male or female slave, or ox, or donkey, or anything that belongs to your neighbor."

That Deuteronomy placed the woman first indicates that the woman was not to be considered the property of her husband. In addition, while the book of Exodus uses the same Hebrew word, *ḥāmad*, to describe coveting a man's wife and his possessions, Deuteronomy uses two different words for coveting. *Ḥāmad* describes coveting the wife and *ʾawâ* describes coveting a person's property, as if to emphasize that the two desires are completely different: "*covet* your neighbor's wife" (Deut 5:21) and "*desire* your neighbor's house" (Deut 5:21). Further, the word *ḥāmad*, when used in a positive context, expresses the idea of desire. God chose Jerusalem as "the mount that God *desired* for his abode" (Ps 68:16). When used in a negative context, *ḥāmad* expresses something that is forbidden: "The images of their gods you shall burn with fire. Do not *covet* the silver or the gold that is on them and take it for yourself" (Deut 7:25).

Walter Kaiser and others, in *Hard Sayings of the Bible*, argued that since the Ten Commandments were written "by the finger of God" on Mount Sinai (Deut 9:10), the Exodus version of the Decalogue was the original and that the wording of the commandment in Deuteronomy is a free restatement of the Exodus commandment. They write,

> This allowed Moses to present the commandment with some modifications and updating of the situation in light of their pending entrance into the land of Canaan, while still adhering closely to the original form. In fact, these differences are very slight and of very little consequence except as viewed against the challenges that present themselves in entering into the land.[1]

However, it does not seem to me that "these differences are very slight and of very little consequence." As Moshe Weinfeld has pointed out, "The Deuteronomic version inverted the order of these two commandments. Unlike the Exodus version, which has 'house' before 'wife,' Deuteronomy puts first 'wife' then 'house' and devotes to the 'wife' a separate command, which suits the general tendency of this book. Deuteronomy gives special attention to women's rights, and therefore he gives preference to the wife and reserves for her a separate injunction. By the same token she does not join the slave, the animal, and so on, contrary to the arrangement in the Exodus version."[2] The use of two different verbs in Deuteronomy 5:21 regarding coveting a man's wife contributes to the understanding that women in the Old Testament were not merely property but had distinct rights and protections under the law. The Deuteronomic sequence of "wife" and "house" is a radical shift in the view of the status of women in Israelite society. The Deuteronomic change reflects the increased concern for the status of women and the recognition that women had legal rights as members of the covenant community.

1. Walter C. Kaiser Jr. et at., *Hard Sayings of the Bible* (Downers Grove, IL: IVP Academic, 1996), 173.
2. Moshe Weinfeld, *Deuteronomy 1–11*, AB (New York: Doubleday, 1991), 317–18.

CHAPTER 4

The Law of the Hebrew Slave

In addition to showing concern for the status of women in Israelite society, Deuteronomy reformulates the law of the Hebrew slave from the Covenant Code. Exodus 21:2–6 reads,

> When you buy a male Hebrew slave, he shall serve six years, but in the seventh he shall go out a free person, without debt. If he comes in single, he shall go out single; if he comes in married, then his wife shall go out with him. If his master gives him a wife and she bears him sons or daughters, the wife and her children shall be her master's and he shall go out alone. But if the slave declares, "I love my master, my wife, and my children; I will not go out a free person," then his master shall bring him before God. He shall be brought to the door or the doorpost; and his master shall pierce his ear with an awl; and he shall serve him for life.

This law is designed to regulate the treatment of Hebrew slaves in Israelite society. To understand it properly, we must first define two of its terms:

Hebrew slave. The word "Hebrew" is related to the word "Habiru" (also written as Hapiru). The Habiru were not an ethnic group, but the word was used as a pejorative designation to classify a group of people in the ancient Near East who lived on the fringe of society and were considered social outcasts. In the Old Testament, the word "Hebrew" is used to differentiate Israelites from Egyptians (Exod 2:6; 3:18) and Israelites from Philistines (1 Sam 4:6; 13:3). The word is used mainly by non-Israelites to describe an individual Israelite, though Israelites also used the word to describe themselves to outsiders (Jonah 1:9). "Hebrew slave" designated an Israelite citizen who was sold into slavery (Jer 34:9). Many Israelites became slaves because they were unable to pay their debts (e.g., 2 Kgs 4:1; Neh 5:5; Amos 2:6). Poverty in Israel had many contributing factors, much like today: heavy taxation, high interest on loans, bad crops, and natural disasters.

A free person. The word "free person" (Hebrew *ḥopshî*) is a technical term, probably related to a Ugaritic word that means "a free commoner." In the ancient Near East, the *ḥopshî* was an individual whose social status was between a noble and a slave. The word appears sixteen times in the Old Testament and generally refers to a person freed from slavery.

The law of the Hebrew slave in the book of Exodus has several stipulations:

1. A male Hebrew slave shall be released after six years of labor.
2. After six years of work, that is, in the seventh year, he shall go out as a free person, without debt.
3. If the slave comes in single, he shall go out single.
4. If the slave comes in married, then his wife shall go out with him.
5. If his master gives him a wife and she bears him sons or daughters, the wife and her children shall be her master's, and he shall go out alone.

The law stipulates that if the slave's master gave him a wife and children were born of this union, only the male slave was to go free in the seventh year, because the woman and her children belonged to the master. The woman was a perpetual slave and considered to be property of her master. The only way the slave could keep his wife was to renounce his right to go free at the end of his time of servitude and remain a permanent slave in the house of his master.

Deuteronomy reformulates the law of the Hebrew slave from Exodus to allow the woman to be released with her husband. The revised law reads as follows:

> If a member of your community, whether a Hebrew man or a Hebrew woman, is sold to you and works for you six years, in

> the seventh year you shall set that person free. And when you send a male slave out from you a free person, you shall not send him out empty-handed. Provide liberally out of your flock, your threshing floor, and your wine press, thus giving to him some of the bounty with which the LORD your God has blessed you. Remember that you were a slave in the land of Egypt, and the LORD your God redeemed you; for this reason I lay this command upon you today. But if he says to you, "I will not go out from you," because he loves you and your household, since he is well off with you, then you shall take an awl and thrust it through his earlobe into the door, and he shall be your slave forever. You shall do the same with regard to your female slave. Do not consider it a hardship when you send them out from you free persons, because for six years they have given you services worth the wages of hired laborers; and the LORD your God will bless you in all that you do. (Deut 15:12–18)

This passage is a radical revision of the law that appears in the Book of the Covenant. First, as it relates to stipulation five above ("if his master gives him a wife and she bears him sons or daughters, the wife and her children shall be her master's, and he shall go out alone"), the revised law in Deuteronomy allows the female slave to be released together with her husband. Deuteronomy indicates that through marriage, the wife of the slave has now become an integral part of his life. Second, Deuteronomy adds a stipulation that is absent in Exodus. Namely, when the slave was released at the end of his time of service, the master should be generous with his former slave and provide him with provisions to help him and his family to begin a new life after their release.

At the end of the law (Deut 15:17), Deuteronomy again emphasizes that the female slave should enjoy the same benefits as the male slave: "You shall do the same with regard to your female slave." The reason for this injunction is that the female slave is also "your brother," that is, she is kindred of her master. Thus, the Deuteronomic law places the two sexes in a position of equality. In addition, the Deuteronomic law limited a father's power to sell his daughter as a perpetual slave. Above we stopped at Exodus 21:6, but verse 7 reads, "When a man sells his daughter as a slave, she shall not go out as the male slaves do."

Since Deuteronomy explicitly places male and female slaves on the same footing, it supports the rights of women as full citizens in Israel.

The Deuteronomic law appeals to the experience of the oppression in Egypt to motivate the master to be generous in the manumission of the Hebrew slaves. The word “Hebrew” serves to develop solidarity between the master and his slaves since both the master and the servant were slaves in Egypt. These charitable innovations reflect the Deuteronomic tendency to be interested in the plight of the downtrodden. This “social idealism” present in the laws of Deuteronomy is part of the humanitarian concern that became the hallmark of the Deuteronomic reformation during Josiah’s reign.

PART 2

WOMEN PROPHETS

CHAPTER 5

Women Prophets in the Old Testament

Since ancient Israel was a patriarchal society, "which has to do with the centrality of the oldest living male member of the family to the structure of the larger society,"[1] most women who appear in the Old Testament do so in connection with male characters important to the biblical narrative. With a few exceptions, women are minor characters in these stories, and we read little about their lives, their work, or their contribution to society.

In such patriarchal societies, social roles are typically defined according to gender.[2] Men lead in the community and rule over the affairs of the nation. They carry out the duties that maintain and promote the life of the society in which they live. Men serve in politics, fight wars, and oversee the legal and religious affairs of the nation. Women, on the other hand, oversee the household. Their primary responsibilities revolve around caring for the affairs of the house, such as cooking, baking, sewing, and raising children. Although many women play active roles in society, most of their work relates to duties characteristically assigned to women.[3]

The Bible, however, provides a few clues that women also were visibly active in one important position characteristically dominated by males, a significant work in the religious life of Israel. Both men and women served God as prophets. To be sure, most of Israel's prophets

1. Sandra Richter, *The Epic of Eden: A Christian Entry into the Old Testament* (Downers Grove, IL: IVP Academic, 2008), 25.
2. Gerda Lerner, *The Creation of Patriarchy* (New York: Oxford University Press, 1986), 212–13.
3. Carol Meyers, "Women and the Domestic Economy of Early Israel," in *Women in the Hebrew Bible: A Reader*, ed. Alice Bach (New York: Routledge, 1999), 33–43.

were male. While we know of almost thirty men called prophets in the Old Testament, the text reveals only five prophetesses: Miriam (Exod 15:20), Deborah (Judg 4:4), Huldah (2 Kgs 22:14), Noadiah (Neh 6:14), and Isaiah's wife (Isa 8:3), whose name remains unknown to us.

Kingship and the priesthood were kept within traditional families in Israel. To be a king, one had to be born into a royal family. Athaliah was the only woman who became a queen in Judah (2 Kgs 11:1–3). She was married to King Jehoram of Judah because of a political alliance between the kingdoms of Israel and Judah. After Jehoram died from a severe illness (2 Chr 21:18–19), his son Ahaziah became king of Judah (2 Kgs 8:26). Ahaziah was then killed by Jehu (2 Kgs 9:27), and when Athaliah heard of Ahaziah's murder, she killed the members of the royal family, seized the throne of Judah, and declared herself queen. Athaliah ruled in Judah for six years.

To be a priest, one had to be born into a priestly family. Several factors excluded women from the priesthood. The priesthood was assigned to men because Israel was a patriarchal society, and men were considered the primary representatives of the family and community in religious matters. In addition, priests were required to adhere to strict purity laws, and menstruation caused impurity. According to Leviticus 15:19–30, menstruation caused a woman to become ritually unclean for seven days, an uncleanness that would transfer to anything she touched. Ritual impurity, therefore, prevented women from touching the holy vessels in the temple.

A woman, however, *could* be a prophet because in Israel a prophet was a person chosen by God to speak on his behalf. Prophets were endowed with the Spirit of God and sent to proclaim God's message to the community as God's representative. The word "prophet" comes from the Greek word *prophētēs*, which means one who speaks for another, an interpreter of the will of a god, and a proclaimer. The Septuagint uses the word *prophētēs* to translate the masculine Hebrew term *nābî*ʾ, the masculine nominal form of the verb *nāba*ʾ, "to call." As in English, both Hebrew and Greek use feminine forms of the terms to refer to female prophets.

The prophet Micah identified Miriam,, together with Moses and Aaron, as one of the leaders God sent to lead the Israelites in their journey from Egypt to Sinai: "For I brought you up from the land of Egypt, and redeemed you from the house of slavery; and I sent before you

Moses, Aaron, and Miriam" (Mic 6:4). Miriam also led the women of Israel—with tambourines and dancing—in the Song of Miriam: "Sing to the Lord, for he has triumphed gloriously; horse and rider he has thrown into the sea" (Exod 15:21).

In the period of the judges, Deborah was known as both a prophetess and as a judge: "At that time Deborah, a prophetess, wife of Lappidoth, was judging Israel. She used to sit under the palm of Deborah between Ramah and Bethel in the hill country of Ephraim; and the Israelites came up to her for judgment" (Judg 4:4–5). During Deborah's judgeship, the people were oppressed by Sisera, commander of the Canaanite army. Deborah summoned Barak, and together they mobilized the tribal militia to confront their enemy. Although the commander of Israel's army, Barak was reluctant to wage war against the Canaanites. Deborah promised to go with the army, and her leadership inspired the tribal militia to confront Sisera and his forces. With God's help, Israel defeated Sisera and decimated the enemy. The Song of Deborah (Judg 5:1–31) celebrates this victory.

The third named female prophet in Israel, Noadiah, appears in the book of Nehemiah. She and a group of prophets threatened Nehemiah and opposed the construction of the wall, indicating that she was a false prophetess: "Remember Tobiah and Sanballat, O my God, according to these things that they did, and also the prophetess Noadiah and the rest of the prophets who wanted to make me afraid" (Neh 6:14). The name Noadiah also appears as the name of a Levite in charge of the treasure of the temple (Ezra 8:33), leading some scholars to believe that Noadiah was a male prophet.[4] The Hebrew text, however, clearly identifies her as a woman prophet, a *nebîʾâ*.

The fourth prophetess in the Old Testament is Isaiah's wife: "And I went to the prophetess, and she conceived and bore a son" (Isa 8:3). Apart from her marriage to Isaiah, nothing is known about this prophetess, and scholars disagree concerning the role she played in Isaiah's ministry. John Skinner believes she was called a prophetess because she was married to the prophet Isaiah.[5] But most scholars agree that this mysterious woman was a prophet in her own right.[6] The context

4. Rodney H. Shearer, "Noadiah (Person)," *ABD* 4:1122
5. John Skinner, *The Book of the Prophet Isaiah, Isaiah Chapters I–XXXIX*, The Cambridge Bible for Schools and Colleges (Cambridge: Cambridge University Press, 1963), 72.
6. Hans Wildberger, *Isaiah 1–12*, CC (Minneapolis: Fortress, 1991), 337.

in which Isaiah's wife is mentioned indicates that she exercised a prophetic ministry alongside her husband. According to Isaiah 8:16, Isaiah had a group of disciples who preserved his oracles. Perhaps Isaiah's wife was part of this prophetic guild because as a prophetess, "she too was the bearer of the powerful word of the Lord."[7]

The ministry of Huldah, the fifth female prophet named in the Old Testament, is particularly significant. When Josiah sent a group of government officials, all males, to find a prophet who could determine the authenticity of the book of the law found in the temple, they sought out Huldah, a woman (see 2 Kgs 22:11–14). In a society dominated by men, none of them had any problem seeking the counsel of a woman whom God had appointed as his spokesman. In addition to these five named prophetesses, Ezekiel mentions a group of false female prophets who prophesied in his day: "As for you, mortal, set your face against the daughters of your people, who prophesy out of their own imagination; prophesy against them" (Ezek 13:17).

The Old Testament clearly preserves evidence that the prophetic call belonged to men and women alike, a trend continued in the New Testament. Also, Luke tells us about Anna, a prophet who "never left the temple but worshiped there with fasting and prayer night and day" (Luke 2:37). When this prophet saw the baby Jesus in the temple, she "began to praise God and to speak about the child to all who were looking for the redemption of Jerusalem" (Luke 2:38). To this we could add the daughters of Philip (Acts 21:9), and of course the woman known as Jezebel was also a prophet, albeit a false one (Rev 2:20). The presence of women prophets in the Bible demonstrates that God calls both men and women to be proclaimers of the divine word. Women prophets challenge the common assumption about the role of women in the life of the church by demonstrating that gender did not factor into who could receive divine revelation or proclaim God's truth.

7. A. S. Herbert, *The Book of the Prophet Isaiah 1–39* (Cambridge: Cambridge University Press, 1973), 67.

CHAPTER 6

Miriam the Prophetess

A cursory survey of the texts where the women prophets are mentioned reveals that not much information is given about their lives and ministries compared with the many male prophets mentioned in the Hebrew Bible. However, the textual evidence illustrates the remarkable work of these women and the legacy they left in the religious life of ancient Israel. One such female prophet is Miriam, Moses's sister.

Although women's names are rarely mentioned in the Old Testament, Miriam's name appears fourteen times across the books of Exodus, Numbers, Deuteronomy, 1 Chronicles, and Micah. By comparison, Sarah's name appears only once outside of the book of Genesis (Isa 51:2), Rachel twice outside of Genesis (Ruth 4:11; Jer 31:15), Ruth and Esther never outside of the books that bear their names. This fact alone indicates Miriam's significant impact on the historical memory of Israel.

Miriam first appears in Exodus 2:4 as the nameless sister who watched over a basket of bulrushes carrying the infant Moses to see what would happen to him. Miriam is first called by name when the Israelites celebrated their victory against Egypt at the Red Sea, with a song of celebration—the Song of Miriam, one of the oldest poems in the Old Testament.[1]

In the Song of Miriam, Miriam appears leading a group of women in song and dance, praising Yahweh for the victory against their enemies: "Then the prophet Miriam, Aaron's sister, took a tambourine in her hand; and all the women went out after her with tambourines and with dancing. And Miriam sang to them: 'Sing to the Lord, for he has triumphed gloriously; horse and rider he has thrown into the sea'"

1. Frank M. Cross Jr. and David Noel Freedman, "The Song of Miriam," *JNES* 14 (1955): 237–50.

(Exod 15:20–21). This text calls Miriam a "prophet" (NRSV; most translations use "prophetess," see KJV and NIV; the Hebrew term is feminine—*nebî'â*). One issue about Miriam's ministry is whether the word "prophet" should be used to describe Miriam's role in the work of leading the people of Israel. Opponents to the term point to the lack of evidence that Miriam proclaimed oracles or was involved in some form of prophetic ministry as was common in the ministry of the later prophets. Miriam, however, is called a prophet because she led the women in the worship of God during the celebration of Israel's victory over the Egyptians.

We see the association of music and musical instruments with prophecy in the encounter between Saul and the prophets. After Samuel anointed Saul as the first king of Israel, Samuel told Saul to go to Gibeath-elohim, the place where "you will meet a procession of prophets coming down from the high place with lyres, timbrels, pipes, and harps being played before them, and they will be prophesying" (1 Sam 10:5 NIV).

In addition, the Levites responsible for music in the temple were associated with prophetic ministry: "David and the officers of the army also set apart for the service the sons of Asaph, and of Heman, and of Jeduthun, who should prophesy with lyres, harps, and cymbals" (1 Chr 25:1). In Chronicles, singing and playing musical instruments are always combined; this activity is called prophesying because the music used in the worship of God was composed under divine inspiration. As Sara Japhet writes, "Temple music as such, throughout the generations, is depicted as prophecy. Such a view would indicate that 'prophecy' is not ascribed to isolated, unique phenomena, but to the permanent singing establishment, which is part of the cultic framework."[2] Heman, one of the Levitical leaders David selected to oversee temple music, is called the "king's seer" in 1 Chronicles 25:5. Heman had "fourteen sons and three daughters," and they "were all under the direction of their father for the music in the house of the LORD with cymbals, harps, and lyres for the service of the house of God" (1 Chr 25:6). The NIV reads, "All these men were under the supervision of their fathers for the music of the temple of the LORD" (1 Chr 25:6 NIV). The word "men" is not in the Hebrew text. The NRSV reads, "God gave Heman fourteen

2. Sara Japhet, *I & II Chronicles*, OTL (Louisville: Westminster John Knox, 1993), 441.

sons and three daughters. All these men were under the supervision of their father for the music of the temple of the Lord" (1 Chr 25:5–6 NRSV). The NIV excludes Heman's daughters from being involved in music in the temple.

In her study of this passage, Gafney concludes that "the daughters of Heman were musical prophets as were their brothers."[3] Other passages also depict women singing, dancing, and playing musical instruments (e.g., Judg 11:34; 1 Sam 18:6). In short, the Old Testament is clear that women participated both in temple worship and in singing, dancing, and playing musical instruments outside of the cultic context.

Miriam's ministry as a prophetess was associated with her leading the women of Israel to celebrate God's victory over the Egyptians. Although Miriam's song of victory may not be compared to the oracles of the classical prophets, her song of deliverance was divinely inspired, demonstrating her prophetic character. Miriam leads the whole assembly of Israel to join their voices in celebration of God's victory against their enemies. Exodus 15:20–21 clearly shows Miriam leading the women and the congregation of Israel in a song of celebration. The text reveals Miriam's leadership in leading the women in celebration and that "all the women went out after her." It also shows Miriam leading the congregation in worship: "Miriam sang to them."

In addition to the positive portrayals of Miriam, she also played a key role in the conflict that arose between her and her brother Moses. The rebellion of Aaron and Miriam against Moses was over the issue of leadership. Moses's leadership over the people was questioned because he had married a Cushite woman. Hanna Tervanotko writes, "Miriam was known as a character who could make such an inquiry. She could address Moses's personal matters."[4] In her criticism of Moses for marrying a Cushite woman (Num 12:1), Miriam is not identified as a prophet. "Later biblical texts conspicuously omit Miriam's prophetic title—perhaps because in that role she challenges her brother's prophetic authority."[5] For her criticism of Moses, Miriam was punished with an

3. Wilda C. Gafney, *Daughters of Miriam: Women Prophets in Ancient Israel* (Minneapolis: Fortress, 2008), 115.
4. Hanna K. Tervanotko, *Denying Her Voice: The Figure of Miriam in Ancient Jewish Literature*, *JAJSup* 23 (Göttingen: Vandenhoeck & Ruprecht, 2016), 83.
5. Jacob L. Wright, *Why the Bible Began: An Alternative History of Scripture and Its Origins* (Cambridge: Cambridge University Press, 2023), 41.

infectious skin disease (Num 12:10) and was placed outside the camp for seven days. Miriam's esteemed status in the community is reflected in the statement that "the people did not set out on the march until Miriam had been brought in again" (Num 12:15).

Miriam's presence in the Hebrew Bible shows that she played a significant role among the people who left Egypt. Her ministry as a prophet and as a leader in Israel shows that God can call and appoint men and women to do his work in the world. Miriam's life as a prophet and as a leader provided encouragement to many women in Israel. Her ministry as a prophet also challenges God's people today to understand that, notwithstanding discrimination against women in many societies, women have much to contribute to God's work and much to teach those who are willing to listen.

CHAPTER 7

Deborah the Prophetess

At that time Deborah, a prophetess, wife of Lappidoth, was judging Israel" (Judg 4:4). Deborah's Hebrew name, *debôrâ,* is translated as "bee." However, it is rare for Israelites to be named after animals. For this reason, Johannes Cornelis de Moor argues that the name Deborah is associated with the Hebrew word *dābar*, "word," and translates Deborah not as "bee" but as "the woman of the word."[1]

With the exception of Isaiah's wife and Noadiah, music connects the women identified as prophets in the Old Testament. As noted above, Miriam sang the Song of Miriam. Although not directly associated with music, Huldah was the wife of Shallum, the son of Tikvah, the keeper of the wardrobe. This office is only mentioned in 2 Kings 22:14 and 2 Chronicles 34:22 and may indicate that Shallum was in charge of maintaining the Levitical garments of the singers in the temple (also called prophets [1 Chr 25:1–7]), thus associating Huldah with music in the temple. Deborah is credited with the Song of Deborah in Judges 5:1.

The biblical text does not state how Deborah received her call to the prophetic ministry. However, we know that the prophetic word came through dreams (Dan 7:1), visions (Isa 1:1; Ezek 1:1; Amos 7:1), prophetic symbolisms (Jer 1:11–13; 18:1–12; Isa 38:4), ecstasy (1 Sam 10:10), and, in a few cases, through direct communication (Isa 38:4; Jer 1:4; Ezek 24:15; Joel 1:1). God's call to Deborah came in the midst of patriarchal structures. However, the existence of female prophets in other ancient Near Eastern cultures, such as in Mari, indicates that female prophets were not unheard of in that time and space.

1. Johannes Cornelis de Moor, *The Elusive Prophet: The Prophet as a Historical Person, Literary Character and Anonymous Artist* (Leiden: Brill, 2001), 240.

As a woman called by God to the prophetic ministry, Deborah played a significant role in delivering Israel from the oppression of the Canaanites. We see how confidently she wore the prophetic mantle in at least two ways: (1) she demonstrated no doubts that she was called to the prophetic ministry, and (2) acted with authority when summoning Barak to fight against the Canaanites.

Deborah and Barak

Deborah's prophetic mission was to bring God's message to Barak, the leader of Israel's militia, and to all Israel. Barak had no problem acknowledging Deborah as a woman with a mission and a message from God since he recognized that Deborah's message was from Yahweh. Barak was so convinced that God sent Deborah that he refused to go into battle without her, since her presence with the army would ensure the presence of God with Israel and victory against the enemies. Barak's request is comparable to the Israelites' decision to take the ark of the covenant, a sign of God's presence and favor, with them into battle against the Philistines (1 Sam 4:1–3).

Deborah's prophetic words came in the form of a divine oracle summoning Barak to gather the people of Israel to fight against Sisera, the commander of the Canaanite army. Her oracle reveals a strategy for Barak to fight against the Canaanite encroachment.

> [Deborah] sent and summoned Barak son of Abinoam from Kedesh in Naphtali, and said to him, "The Lord, the God of Israel, commands you, 'Go, take position at Mount Tabor, bringing ten thousand from the tribe of Naphtali and the tribe of Zebulun. I will draw out Sisera, the general of Jabin's army, to meet you by the Wadi Kishon with his chariots and his troops; and I will give him into your hand.'" (Judg 4:6–7)

The form of Deborah's oracle reflects a clear awareness of her prophetic status. What Deborah proclaimed to Barak as a person authorized to speak on behalf of Yahweh was what Yahweh had spoken. Deborah even proclaimed Yahweh's message in the first person.

Given Barak's reluctance to go to battle unless she accompanied him, Deborah gave Barak a sign that would authenticate God's presence in the field of battle. Deborah predicted that Yahweh would deliver Sisera into the hands of a woman: "I will surely go with you; nevertheless, the road on which you are going will not lead to your glory, for the Lord will sell Sisera into the hand of a woman" (Judg 4:9). This sign, although unflattering to Barak, would be the evidence of Yahweh's involvement in Israel's victory.

As the time for the battle approached, Deborah told Barak: "'Go! This is the day the Lord has given Sisera into your hands. Has not the Lord gone ahead of you?' So, Barak went down Mount Tabor, with ten thousand men following him" (Judg 4:14 NIV). Deborah was not helping Barak; Deborah was commanding him to go into action. And her words to Barak were not spoken in private but in front of the army to encourage Barak and the fighting men of Israel. Deborah's prophetic words were fulfilled when Sisera was defeated and killed by a woman, Jael, just as Deborah had predicted.

Deborah's greatness came from her accomplishments and character. Although her culture placed constraints on women, she was able to accomplish the mission entrusted to her because she was obedient to God's call.

CHAPTER 8

Isaiah's Wife

The biblical evidence suggests that Isaiah's wife was a prophet who exercised a prophetic ministry alongside her husband. According to Isaiah 8:16, Isaiah had a group of disciples who preserved his oracles. In Isaiah 8:3 the prophet Isaiah calls his wife a "prophetess" (*nebî'â*), a term that could be interpreted in different ways. First, *nebî'â* could simply mean the wife of the prophet, that is, "Mrs. Prophet" or "Mrs. Isaiah."[1] Second, *nebî'â* could indicate that the woman was a prophet in her own right. Third, and most unlikely, the *nebî'â* could refer to a cultic prophet who was not Isaiah's wife.[2] If one accepts this third view, then Isaiah had sexual relations with a woman who was not his wife and had a son born out of this relationship, which runs counter to the ethical values of Israel's prophets. Rejecting this third view leaves only two possible ways to understand *nebî'â* in Isaiah 8:3—either *nebî'â* was an honorific title given to the woman because she was married to a prophet, or Isaiah's wife was a prophet in her own right.

Elsewhere in the Hebrew Bible when prophets' wives are mentioned, they are not called *nebî'â* (see Ezek 24:18; Hos 2:2). Rather, every other usage of *nebî'â* in the Hebrew Bible refers to a woman who exercises the prophetic ministry. Deborah was a *nebî'â* and the wife of Lappidoth (Judg 4:4). Huldah was a *nebî'â* and the wife of Shallum (2 Kgs 22:14). Though both Huldah and Deborah are called *nebî'â* , neither was married to a prophet. Miriam and Noadiah were likewise *nebî'â* , but their marital status is never mentioned. The New Testament

1. "Isaiah's wife is so called, not because she herself possessed the prophetic gift, but because the husband's designation is transferred by courtesy to the wife." John Skinner, *The Book of the Prophet Isaiah, Isaiah Chapters I–XXXIX*, The Cambridge Bible for Schools and Colleges (Cambridge: Cambridge University Press, 1963),, 72.
2. This is the view of Joseph Blenkinsopp, *Isaiah 1–39: A New Translation with Introduction and Commentary*, AB (New York: Doubleday, 2000), 238.

mentions that Anna was a prophet and a widow (Luke 2:36–37). The biblical data, therefore, suggest that a woman was a *nebîʾâ* not because she was married to a prophet but because she exercised the prophetic ministry, because of a divine call, and because she had received the endowment of the Spirit.

Although the Bible provides limited information about Isaiah's wife, several significant clues indicate her active participation in his prophetic work. Her designation as the "prophetess" (Isa 8:3) suggests she possessed prophetic gifts in her own right, making her more than merely the wife of a prophet. In addition, her pregnancy became a powerful prophetic sign foretelling the Assyrian invasion that would soon engulf the region. The Lord directed Isaiah to name their son Maher-Shalal-Hash-Baz ("speeding to the plunder, hurrying to the spoil"),[3] a name that itself proclaimed the coming judgment. Through this act, her motherhood transcended the personal realm to become an integral component of the divine message Isaiah delivered to King Ahaz and the people of Judah. As a prophetess, she likely contributed significantly to their family's prophetic identity. This helps explain why their children receive symbolic names directly connected to Isaiah's prophetic message and ministry.

Isaiah 8:18 offers particular insight into their collaborative ministry when the prophet declares, "See, I and the children whom the Lord has given me are signs and portents in Israel from the Lord of hosts." The use of the plural language, "we" rather than "I," strongly suggests that Isaiah viewed his entire family, including his wife, as a unified witness. Together, they functioned as signs to Ahaz and the people of Jerusalem during a critical historical moment.

3. John N. Oswalt, *The Book of Isaiah, Chapters 1–39*, NICOT (Grand Rapids: Eerdmans, 1986), 221.

CHAPTER 9

Huldah, a Prophet in Israel

Although female prophets are relatively rare in the Old Testament, this was not the case throughout the ancient Near East. In his study "Female Prophets in the Ancient Near East," Jonathan Stökl says that "among the prophetic figures attested in the extrabiblical ancient Near Eastern sources we find considerably more women than in the Bible."[1]

Stökl lists three kinds of female prophets in Mari: *apiltum*, professional female prophets; *muhhutum*, female ecstatic prophets (see 1 Sam 19:18–24); and *qammatum*, "female lay prophets," that is, women employed by the temple who occasionally prophesied.[2] According to Stökl, Neo-Assyrian documents mention thirteen female prophets whose names have survived, and other documents refer to several female prophets without mentioning their names. Stökl concludes his survey of female prophets in the ancient Near East with these words: "In this short survey of female prophets in the ancient Near East I have shown that no difference between men and women can be found with regard to their prophetic function."[3]

The fact that there is no difference between male and female prophets with regard to their prophetic function may be why Josiah sent his embassy to Huldah to inquire of Yahweh rather than sending his men to prominent prophets such as Jeremiah, Zephaniah, or another male prophet, though the biblical text does not tell us. The Bible's silence, however, did not stop the rabbis from speculating, as Tar Ilan explains:

> So why did Josiah approach Huldah on this occasion? In their usual fashion, the rabbis suggest a variety of answers. First,

1. Jonathan Stökl, "Female Prophets in the Ancient Near East," in *Prophecy and Prophets in Ancient Israel: Proceedings of the Oxford Old Testament Seminar*, ed. John Day, LHBOTS 531 (London: T & T Clark, 2010), 48.
2. Stökl, "Female Prophets," 49.
3. Stökl, "Female Prophets," 56.

> they maintain that Huldah was Jeremiah's relative and so he refrained from scolding her. Yet this answer does not satisfy them, for even if she were hanging out in Jerusalem, making a nuisance of herself and no one stopped her, why would a respectable king want her answer to his vital questions? On this they speculate that Josiah had approached Huldah because he knew that women are by nature softer and kinder than men, and he had hoped that her prophecy would spare Jerusalem. As we know, this hope had been dashed. Huldah had proved as tough as Jeremiah would have been in her place. So, a third answer is suggested, by Rabbi Yohanan, who maintains that Jeremiah was not around at the time, for he had gone searching for the ten lost Tribes of Israel in order to bring them back.[4]

How the rabbi knew this remains a mystery. All these answers are highly imaginative speculations, fitting the patriarchal ideology of disbelief in the power of women that the rabbis held.

What we do know is that the scroll found in the temple by the high priest Hilkiah needed authentication. Josiah, following practices common in the ancient Near East, sought a prophetic voice to confirm whether the words in the scroll were indeed the words of God. Josiah consulted Huldah because she was a legitimate prophet of God. When Josiah told his officers to go and inquire of Yahweh on his behalf, his officers went to Huldah, the only woman prophet whose oracle has been preserved in the Old Testament. It is possible that the men of Josiah already knew Huldah and that she had already gained the respect of Josiah and his officers because they did not hesitate to consult her. Ilan speculates that since Jeremiah is not mentioned in the book of Kings, it is possible that Jeremiah and Huldah "represented competing sources of authority" and that Jeremiah did not represent the views of those who were involved in the religious reforms of Josiah.[5]

Josiah became king after a period of great apostasy, which was promoted by his grandfather Manasseh and his father, Amon. Influenced by faithful Yahwists, Josiah began reforming the religious life

4. Tal Ilan, "Huldah, the Deuteronomic Prophetess of the Book of Kings," *Lectio Difficilior* 1 (2010): 7.
5. Ilan, "Huldah," 8.

of Judah by eliminating some of the pagan practices introduced by his predecessors and by commanding the refurbishing of the temple in Jerusalem. During the repairs of the temple, workers discovered a scroll and brought it to Hilkiah, the high priest serving in the temple. Hilkiah told Shaphan, the king's secretary: "I have found the book of the law in the house of the LORD" (2 Kgs 22:8). Shaphan read the scroll, then brought it to King Josiah and read it to him.

The book had a profound effect on the king. Josiah tore his clothes in great despair. In his desire to determine whether the book was authentic, Josiah sent Hilkiah, the high priest, Ahikam, son of Shaphan, Achbor, son of Micaiah, Shaphan, the secretary, and Asaiah to Huldah to determine whether or not the scroll was authentic. When Josiah's men came to Huldah to validate and authenticate the content of the book found in the temple, she gave Josiah's officer a message of doom. She said to them:

> Thus says the LORD, the God of Israel: Tell the man who sent you to me, Thus says the LORD, I will indeed bring disaster on this place and on its inhabitants—all the words of the book that the king of Judah has read. Because they have abandoned me and have made offerings to other gods, so that they have provoked me to anger with all the work of their hands, therefore my wrath will be kindled against this place, and it will not be quenched. But as to the king of Judah, who sent you to inquire of the LORD, thus shall you say to him, Thus says the LORD, the God of Israel: Regarding the words that you have heard, because your heart was penitent, and you humbled yourself before the LORD, when you heard how I spoke against this place, and against its inhabitants, that they should become a desolation and a curse, and because you have torn your clothes and wept before me, I also have heard you, says the LORD. Therefore, I will gather you to your ancestors, and you shall be gathered to your grave in peace; your eyes shall not see all the disaster that I will bring on this place. (2 Kgs 22:15–20)

Huldah introduces her message using the traditional prophetic formula. She begins her speech, just like male prophets, by claiming that her words were the words of God: "Thus says the LORD, the God of Israel." Huldah clearly saw herself as a messenger of God set apart to speak in God's name. Further, her oracle shows that she had an intimate relationship with God and knew that God had a purpose for his people and that he cared enough that he wanted to communicate his will through her.

Huldah's oracle mentions events that will happen in the future. Although many false prophets claimed to speak for God, Huldah spoke concerning what God was about to do to Judah because she knew the character of God, the nature of sin, and the rebellion of the people of Judah. She, as a prophet, proclaimed God's judgment because of the wickedness and idolatry of the people.

As a true prophet of God, Huldah told the king's servants that the message of the book was indeed authentic and that God's wrath—and therefore his judgment—was set against the people because they had abandoned God, disobeyed his teachings, and worshiped other gods. She also proclaimed that because Josiah had humbled himself before Yahweh, he would not see the terrible events that would come upon the nation.

Huldah stated that Josiah would die in peace: "Therefore, I will gather you to your ancestors, and you shall be gathered to your grave in peace; your eyes shall not see all the disaster that I will bring on this place" (2 Kgs 22:20). Josiah, however, died fighting against the army of Neco, king of Egypt. In his attempt to prevent Egypt from helping Assyria in its struggle against Babylon, Josiah joined his army at Megiddo to fight Neco. During the battle, Josiah was mortally wounded. His servants brought his body from Megiddo to Jerusalem in the king's chariot. Josiah was buried in his own tomb as the people lamented his death (2 Kgs 23:30).

The Chronicler, in trying to explain how Josiah, a good king who followed the Lord with all his heart, died at a young age, said that Josiah failed to obey the word of God in the mouth of Neco:

> But Neco sent envoys to him, saying, "What have I to do with you, king of Judah? I am not coming against you today, but against the house with which I am at war; and God has commanded me to hurry. Cease opposing God, who is with me, so that he will not destroy you." But Josiah would not turn away from him but disguised himself in order to fight with him. He did not listen to the words of Neco from the mouth of God, but joined battle in the plain of Megiddo. (2 Chr 35:21–22)

Josiah's violent death does not mean that Huldah was a false prophet. Rather, Huldah's oracle that Josiah would die a peaceful death means that he would not see the manifestation of God's anger against Judah in his lifetime. Josiah's death, however, does show the beginning of the fulfillment of Huldah's prophecy. Josiah's death brought about the events that would culminate with the destruction of the temple and the exile of Judah. As Baruch Halpern writes, the death of Josiah was

> not as a postponement of Yhwh's punishment, but rather as its onset. Despite a loyalty to Yhwh comparable only to that demanded by Moses (with all his heart, soul and strained fabric of his being: 2 Kgs xxiii 25), the text takes Josiah's killing as Yhwh's affirmation of his intention to reject Jerusalem and the temple by means of exile (xxiii 26–7, 29–30). The consequences were the captivity of Jehoahaz (xxiii 33–4), invasions under Jehoiakim paving the way for an exile promised by Yhwh's "servants, the prophets" (2 Kgs xxiv 1–4), the deportation of Jehoiachin (xxiv 10–16), and the destruction of the temple and exile of the population under Zedekiah (xxiv 20, xxv 21, 26). Josiah's death is the milestone marking the start of the road to exile.[6]

The impressive insight Huldah demonstrated in evaluating the message of the book found in the temple provided a powerful incentive for the religious reforms of Josiah.

Little else is known about Huldah. After giving her oracle to Josiah's men, she disappears from the pages of Scripture. Her role in the story ends with these words, "They took the message back to the king" (2 Kgs 22:20). Although nothing else is said about Huldah, it is evident that her words had a profound impact on Josiah and provided prophetic approval to the religious reforms that attempted to bring Judah back to the worship of Yahweh and to eliminate the syncretistic elements in the religion of Israel.

---

6. Baruch Halpern, "Why Manasseh Is to Blame for the Babylonian Exile: The Evolution of a Biblical Tradition," *VT* 48 (1998): 499.

CHAPTER 10

Noadiah the Prophetess

Most people who read the Bible are not familiar with Noadiah the prophetess. She is mentioned only once in the oft-overlooked book of Nehemiah, in one of the prayers Nehemiah prayed against his enemies: "Remember Tobiah and Sanballat, O my God, according to these things that they did, and also the prophetess Noadiah and the rest of the prophets who wanted to make me afraid" (Neh 6:14). Although Nehemiah's prayers indicate that the prophetess Noadiah and the other prophets were attempting to make him afraid, what Nehemiah meant by these words is not clear. In addition, the text does not give any information about Noadiah except that she and the nameless prophets somehow were threatening Nehemiah's life.

Several issues in the text make it difficult to understand Noadiah's role in Nehemiah's work. The first issue is her sex. The Hebrew Bible calls Noadiah *hannabîʾâ*, "the prophetess," indicating clearly that she was a woman. However, the Septuagint—the Greek translation of the Hebrew Bible—calls Noadiah *prophētē*, "the prophet," and "Noadiah" appears as a male name in Ezra 8:33. The Septuagint likely translated *nabîʾâ* with the masculine *prophētē* because of the Levitical name in Ezra 8:33 and because they believed that the "him" of Nehemiah 6:12 referred to Noadiah rather than to Shemaiah. Thus, we should follow the Hebrew tradition in understanding Noadiah to be a woman.

The second issue is the role Noadiah played in the conspiracy against Nehemiah. A summary of the text found in Nehemiah 6:10–14 will help clarify the problem. The text begins when Nehemiah went into the house of a man named Shemaiah. Shemaiah told Nehemiah: "Let us meet together in the house of God, within the temple, and let us close the doors of the temple, for they are coming to kill you; indeed, tonight they are coming to kill you" (Neh 6:10). But Nehemiah was not willing to run away. Nehemiah said: "Should a man like me run away?

Would a man like me go into the temple to save his life? I will not go in!" (Neh 6:11).

Then Nehemiah realized that Shemaiah was lying to him. Nehemiah said, "Then I perceived and saw that God had not sent him at all, but he had pronounced the prophecy against me because Tobiah and Sanballat had hired him. He was hired for this purpose, to intimidate me and make me sin by acting in this way, and so they could give me a bad name, in order to taunt me" (Neh 6:12–13). The text does not provide any clue as to how Nehemiah realized that Shemaiah was not a prophet sent by God but was instead a false prophet hired by his enemies to intimidate him, something they had done in the past (Neh 6:8–9). Nehemiah probably realized that to run away from his enemies and hide himself in the temple would give a victory to his enemies and demoralize him in the eyes of the people working with him. As a result, Nehemiah prayed: "Remember Tobiah and Sanballat, O my God, according to these things that they did, and also the prophetess Noadiah and the rest of the prophets who wanted to make me afraid" (Neh 6:14).

From these words we may arrive at the following conclusions: First, because Nehemiah named her, we can conclude that Noadiah was likely an influential prophetess who had an important role in opposing Nehemiah. The other prophets are mentioned as a group. Second, Noadiah and the other prophets opposed the political and religious work of Nehemiah. Third, the threat posed to Nehemiah was so real that Nehemiah was afraid for his life and prayed to God to vindicate him.

Another issue that arises in the opposition between Nehemiah and Noadiah is the reason Nehemiah feared her and the other prophets of Jerusalem. The context seems to indicate that Noadiah and the other prophets opposed the construction of the walls of Jerusalem, as he also experienced from local officials: "When Sanballat the Horonite and Tobiah the Ammonite official heard this, it displeased them greatly that someone had come to seek the welfare of the people of Israel" (Neh 2:10).

Although the context of the confrontation between Nehemiah and the local leaders is the rebuilding of the wall, Wilda Gafney offers a different reason for the conflict between Noadiah, the prophets, and Nehemiah. Gafney writes: "I suggest that [Noadiah] was opposed to [Nehemiah's] policies, which included breaking apart families and leaving women and their children as persons without status or identity, with neither shelter nor sustenance."[1] Gafney argues that the walls of Jerusalem were designed to protect the people and that the prophets of Jerusalem would not oppose their rebuilding because such a project would have the support of all citizens of Jerusalem. Instead, Gafney believes that Nehemiah was continuing the process of ethnic purity began by Ezra. When Nehemiah saw that many Jews had married foreign women and many of their children were unable to speak Aramaic, the language spoken in Judah after the people returned from Babylon, Nehemiah "contended with them and cursed them and beat some of them and pulled out their hair; and made them take an oath in the name of God, saying, 'You shall not give your daughters to their sons, or take their daughters for your sons or for yourselves'" (Neh 13:25).

Gafney's theory has merit. The mention of Noadiah together with Tobiah and Sanballat reinforces her theory. Tobiah is identified as an Ammonite (Neh 2:10). Although he was a foreigner, he was related by marriage to the high priest Eliashib, who prepared accommodations for him in the temple precincts (Neh 13:4–5). Sanballat was a Horonite (Neh 2:10). According to Torrey, the expression "Horonite" was a contemptuous epithet given to Sanballat by Nehemiah.[2] Sanballat was the governor of Samaria and opposed Nehemiah on political grounds. Sanballat tried to prevent the rebuilding of the wall because he feared that Samaria would lose control of Judea. Since Tobiah and Sanballat had hired the prophets of Jerusalem to discourage Nehemiah, we can infer that the prophets opposed him on political, religious, and economic grounds. Nehemiah decided not to meet with them because he believed Tobiah and Sanballat had plans to harm him. If Noadiah and the false prophets hired by Sanballat opposed Nehemiah because of his policies on mixed marriages, the marriage of Sanballat's daughter to the grandson of the high priest Eliashib (Neh 13:28) may be one evidence for this opposition.

From the meager evidence the biblical text provides about Noadiah, it is clear that Noadiah was a leader among the prophets of Jerusalem who opposed Nehemiah. The biblical text does not explain why

1. Wilda C. Gafney, *Daughters of Miriam: Women Prophets in Ancient Israel* (Minneapolis: Fortress, 2008), 111–12.
2. Charles C. Torrey, "Sanballat 'The Horonite,'" *JBL* 47 (1918): 387.

Noadiah opposed Nehemiah. Nehemiah's words indicate that Noadiah appears to have been working alongside other prophets in opposition to Nehemiah's rebuilding efforts and that Tobiah and Sanballat were Nehemiah's opponents who used various tactics to discourage and prevent the reconstruction of the wall.

Noadiah was a woman of great influence since Nehemiah had to pray to God to help him in his struggle against her.[3] Much about Noadiah and her work as a prophet, however, remains unknown. If she was a false prophet or a prophet who took the side of the women who had to leave their husbands, we will never know.

3. Tamara C. Eskenazi, "Out from the Shadows: Biblical Women in the Postexilic Era," *JSOT* 54 (1992): 41.

CHAPTER 11

The Nameless Prophetesses in Ezekiel

In addition to the five women prophets whose names appear in the Old Testament, Ezekiel refers to a group of female prophets who remain nameless. This is what Ezekiel had to say about these nameless prophetesses:

> As for you, mortal, set your face against the daughters of your people, who prophesy out of their own imagination; prophesy against them and say, Thus says the Lord GOD: Woe to the women who sew bands on all wrists, and make veils for the heads of persons of every height, in the hunt for human lives! Will you hunt down lives among my people, and maintain your own lives? You have profaned me among my people for handfuls of barley and for pieces of bread, putting to death persons who should not die and keeping alive persons who should not live, by your lies to my people, who listen to lies.
>
> Therefore thus says the Lord GOD: I am against your bands with which you hunt lives; I will tear them from your arms, and let the lives go free, the lives that you hunt down like birds. I will tear off your veils, and save my people from your hands; they shall no longer be prey in your hands; and you shall know that I am the LORD. Because you have disheartened the righteous falsely, although I have not disheartened them, and you have encouraged the wicked not to turn from their wicked way and save their lives; therefore you shall no longer see false visions or practice divination; I will save my people from your hand. Then you will know that I am the LORD. (Ezek 13:17–23)

The work of these nameless women is different from that of other female prophets in the Old Testament in that these "prophesy out of their own imagination" (Ezek 13:17). Ezekiel's words resemble those of Jeremiah when he described the false prophets: "They speak visions of their own minds, not from the mouth of the LORD" (Jer 23:16). These women are called false prophets,[1] female sorcerers,[2] women soothsayers,[3] and fortune-tellers[4] because they use magical arts and do not proclaim a true word from God.

Daniel Block identifies these female prophets as witches. "These are not prophets as Ezekiel understands the office; they are witches, black magicians, charlatans."[5] Block's identification of these female prophets as witches and black magicians is problematic because Ezekiel calls them prophets and says that they had a religious role in the community. These female prophets use their magic incantations to cure diseases.[6] They are denounced because they speak without divine authorization from Yahweh and proclaim messages originating from their own imagination rather than from God.

Nancy Bowen writes that the activities Ezekiel ascribes to these female prophets resemble incantations associated with childbirth. "This comparative material therefore suggests the possibility that the role of the female prophets in the community was to deal with the issues of pregnancy and childbirth. This understanding of the activity of the female prophets would explain why Ezekiel would view these women as powerful."[7] These women used magical elements to prophesy to the people. Their work is so different from the classical prophets of the Old Testament that their prophecy cannot be compared to the prophecies of the other Old Testament prophets nor their work to the work of the other women prophets mentioned in the Hebrew Bible. Their work differs drastically from the true

1. Ronald E. Clements, *Ezekiel*, Westminster Bible Companion (Louisville: Westminster John Knox, 1996), 59.
2. Leslie C. Allen, *Ezekiel 1-19*, WBC (Waco, TX: Word, 1994), 204.
3. Walther Eichrodt, *Ezekiel: A Commentary*, OTL (Philadelphia: Westminster, 1970), 168.
4. Moshe Greenberg, *Ezekiel 1–20*, AB (New Haven, CT: The Anchor Yale Bible, 1983), 239.
5. Daniel I. Block, *The Book of Ezekiel, Chapters 1–24*, NICOT (Grand Rapids: Eerdmans, 1997), 417.
6. Eichrodt, *Ezekiel*, 169.
7. Nancy R. Bowen, "The Daughters of Your People: Female Prophets in Ezekiel 13:17–23," *JBL* 118 (1999): 427.

prophets of Yahweh, male and female, whose words we read in the Old Testament.

In fact, when Yahweh tells Ezekiel to prophesy against these women, he calls them "the daughters of your people, who prophesy." They are not called "prophetess," *nebî'â*, like the other women prophets who spoke to the people on behalf of God. It is possible that Ezekiel avoids the word *nebî'â* to describe these nameless women in a deliberate attempt to show contempt for their work.

Ezekiel opposes the work of these nameless women in part because they put in danger the lives of many Israelites who believed their words and work. Some of the expressions Ezekiel uses to describe their work are unclear, possibly because some of the rituals he describes probably reflect magical rituals that were practiced in Babylon. We can, however, make several assertions from the text.

First, these women demanded payment for their oracles: "You have profaned me among my people for handfuls of barley and for pieces of bread." Saul refers to the practice of paying prophets for oracles: "Then Saul replied to the boy, 'But if we go, what can we bring the man? For the bread in our sacks is gone, and there is no present to bring to the man of God'" (1 Sam 9:7). In addition, the prophet Micah condemned the false prophets because they gave oracles according to the payment they received: "Thus says the LORD concerning the prophets who lead my people astray, who cry 'Peace' when they have something to eat, but declare war against those who put nothing into their mouths" (Mic 3:5).

Second, these women prophets did their work using magical incantations: "Woe to the women who sew bands on all wrists, and make veils for the heads of persons of every height, in the hunt for human lives." The NIV describes these bands as "magic charms" (Ezek 13:18). It is difficult to know whether these bands and the veils were used by the prophetesses or by their clients. These items were likely amulets used to ward off evil spirits. Since the veils were made "for the heads of persons of every height," we may infer they were used as a covering to protect the clients with their magical power.

Third, these women were "in the hunt for human lives." They were actively pursuing people to become their clients and to use their services. They needed more "customers" because their livelihood depended on people paying for their services: "Will you hunt down lives among my people, and maintain your own lives?" Fourth, Ezekiel accuses these women of having profaned the name of Yahweh by their practices Ezekiel says that these female prophets profaned Yahweh "for handfuls of barley and for pieces of bread" (Ezek 13:19). Zimmerli writes that in these actions "lay their specific crime, in that they dispensed life and death according to the size of the payments which were given to them . . . thereby dishonoring the name of Yahweh among his people. They brought his majesty down to the level of their ungodly human decisions."[8]

The expression in 13:19 is difficult to explain: "Putting to death persons who should not die and keeping alive persons who should not live, by your lies to my people, who listen to lies." Walther Eichrodt explains what these false prophetesses were doing:

> There can be no doubt that Ezekiel took for granted that these prophetesses could and did produce solid results. When he accuses them of deceiving Yahweh's people and says they gain credit with the people, because they are so afraid of the truth as to turn away from it, he is not suggesting that all they do is a mere ineffective fraud; what he is pointing to is the falsehood of their claim to be acting with God's commission or according to his will. We see at this point what dangerous rivals they are to genuine prophecy.[9]

Eichrodt goes on to describe their work:

> Under the appearance of devoutness, they bring about the death of some who were destined to life, by misleading them to their ruin, or by frightening them to death by gloomy suggestions of coming destruction. Others, delivered over to death by sickness or accident in accordance with God's will, they preserve alive by exercising their powers. Such evil doings serve to lead the whole people astray, by obscuring for them the clear will of God which they ought to obey and by enslaving them to uncon-

8. Walther Zimmerli, *Ezekiel 1: A Commentary on the Book of the Prophet Ezekiel, Chapters 1–24*, Hermeneia (Philadelphia: Fortress, 1979), 297.
9. Eichrodt, *Ezekiel*, 171–72.

> trollable forces. Genuine prophecy finds itself caricatured and ousted by demonic soothsaying, which seems to work within a very limited sphere, and yet poisons the whole atmosphere.[10]

Because of their deceit, Yahweh declares judgment upon the nameless prophetesses: "Because you have disheartened the righteous falsely, although I have not disheartened them, and you have encouraged the wicked not to turn from their wicked way and save their lives; therefore you shall no longer see false visions or practice divination; I will save my people from your hand. Then you will know that I am the LORD" (Ezek 13:22–23).

The prophets of Israel had to contend with the work of the false prophets and their work against the eternal purposes of God. On the one hand, Yahweh accuses these female prophets of troubling the spiritual lives of the righteous by shaking their confidence in God and by making them doubt his power. On the other hand, Yahweh also accuses them of having "encouraged the wicked not to turn from their wicked way and save their lives" (Ezek 13:22). Ezekiel says that God wants to save wicked people if they turn from their evil ways and turn to God. These false prophetesses, however, encouraged the evildoers not to abandon their evil ways and be saved.[11]

Thus, the ministry of the many women called by God to become messengers of God's love to all Israel was marred by the ministry of a few women who wanted, by deceit, to join their ranks. These false prophetesses, like all the false prophets mentioned in the Old Testament, deceived the people by preaching a message they never received from God: "They speak visions of their own minds, not from the mouth of the LORD" (Jer 23:16). These false prophets were never called to proclaim God's word: "I did not send the prophets, yet they ran; I did not speak to them, yet they prophesied" (Jer 23:21). The problem of counterfeit prophets was not a phenomenon unique to Israel in the Old Testament. Indeed, false prophets will plague God's people to the end of time. Jesus said: "Beware of false prophets, who come to you in sheep's clothing but inwardly are ravenous wolves" (Matt 7:15).

---

10. Eichrodt, *Ezekiel*, 172.
11. Horst D. Preuss, *Old Testament Theology*, OTL, 2 vols. (Louisville: Westminster John Knox, 1996), 2:86.

Faced by a myriad of voices claiming to speak on behalf of God, believers must depend on a faith that has been disciplined through fellowship with God, a faith that can see through a vision that comes not from God, but out of the prophet's own mind. Only faith and the knowledge of God's word can judge the truth and falsehood of prophecy. When Christians have their faith focused on Jesus, "they will not follow a stranger, but they will run from him because they do not know the voice of strangers" (John 10:5).

CHAPTER 12

Women Who Proclaim the Good News

Psalm 68 has been difficult for scholars to analyze because they continue to debate its genre. The psalm celebrated a great military victory in which God had intervened on behalf of the army of Israel. The psalm's author used words and phrases found in other songs that were composed to celebrate Israel's military victories. The opening verse of Psalm 68 is a quotation from the Song of the Ark found in Numbers 10:35. Psalm 68:1 reads: "Let God rise up, let his enemies be scattered; let those who hate him flee before him." This verse echoes Numbers 10:35, which says: "Arise, O LORD, let your enemies be scattered, and your foes flee before you." Here, Moses calls on God in order to assure the people that whenever they fought against their enemies they did so with the protection of Yahweh. The ark's presence assured them that their God was fighting for them.

The author of Psalm 68 also alluded several times to the Song of Deborah found in Judges 5, as pointed out by Shoshana Sussman, who shows several parallels between Psalm 68 and the Song of Deborah in Judges 5.[1] For instance, Psalm 68:12 says, "The kings of the armies, they flee, they flee! The women at home divide the spoil." The leader of the army fleeing is a reference to Sisera in Judges 4:17, "Sisera had fled away." The women dividing the spoil refer to Sisera's mother imagining her son and his soldiers dividing the spoils after defeating the army of Israel (which they did not): "Are they not finding and dividing the spoil?—A girl or two for every man; spoil of dyed stuffs

1. See Shoshana Sussman, "Psalm 68: Echoes of the Song of Deborah?" *JBQ* 40 (2012): 238–40.

for Sisera, spoil of dyed stuffs embroidered, two pieces of dyed work embroidered for my neck as spoil?" (Judg 5:30).

According to Michael Coogan, the similarity of language and thought between Judges 5 and Psalm 68 "suggests that the author of the latter [Psalm 68] was deliberately alluding to the song in the composition of his hymn."[2] Coogan writes:

> It seems more likely to us that we may have here a rare biblical example of direct literary relationship, that the author of Psalm 68 knew the Song of Deborah (quite possibly in written form) and used it as a source for his own composition. The process of borrowing was not simply a mechanical one, however; it has an analogy in one composer's use of another's theme in a series of variations: echoes of the original recur through such a piece but they are often not exact quotations; rather they are more complex and reflect the borrower's own ideas and time.[3]

Psalm 68 should be understood as a song composed to celebrate a great military victory by the army of Israel. It is in this context that I want to study the expression that appears in 68:11. English Bibles differ on how to translate the verse, as seen below.

- NRSV: "The Lord gives the command; great is the company of those who bore the tidings."
- RSV: "The Lord gives the command; great is the host of those who bore the tidings."
- NIV 1984: "The Lord announced the word, and great was the company of those who proclaimed it."
- NIV 2011: "The Lord announces the word, and the women who proclaim it are a mighty throng."
- TNK: "The Lord gives a command; the women who bring the news are a great host."
- CSB: "The Lord gave the command; a great company of women brought the good news."

2. Michael D. Coogan, "Structural and Literary Analysis of the Song of Deborah," *CBQ* 40 (1978): 162. Coogan also includes a complete list of Psalm 68's allusions to the Song of Deborah.
3. Coogan, "Structural and Literary Analysis," 161.

- ESV: "The Lord gives the word; the women who announce the news are a great host."
- KJV: "The Lord gave the word: Great *was* the company of those that published *it*."

The above is only a sample of how English translations have understood Psalm 68:11. Some translations (NRSV, RSV, NIV 1984, KJV) translate the Hebrew word *hamebaśśerôt* as "company" while others (NIV 2011, TNK, CSB, ESV) translate the same word as "the women."

To understand why the versions differ in their translation of this Hebrew word, it is important to understand how the word is used in the Hebrew Bible. The word *hamebaśśerôt* is derived from a Hebrew word *bāśar* which means to proclaim good tidings, to preach. The word occurs thirty times in the Old Testament, and it is used in the context of "to bring news, especially pertaining to military encounters."[4]

The use of the word *bāśar* in the report of the death of Absalom in 2 Samuel 18:19–27 provides a good example of its meaning. *Bāśar* appears several times in these eight verses and is typically translated as "tidings" (2 Sam 18:19, 20, 26 NRSV) or "good news" (CSB). *Bāśar* is the same word behind the word for "gospel" or "good news" in the New Testament.[5]

Martin Tate devotes much space to translating this word in his commentary on Psalms 51–100. Tate writes that instead of translating the word *hamebaśśerôt* as a *piel* participle feminine plural, translators have understood the word to be a collective plural and translated it as "the bearers [company] of good news."[6] Tate argues that when interpreting the word as a collective plural, "the feminine element may be omitted." The traditional interpretation of the feminine participle as referring to a group of women proclaiming victory news, however, remains most compelling, particularly since in ancient Israel, battle victory announcements were typically the domain of women.[7] Schilling argues that "the use of *bsr* in Ps 68:12 (Eng. V. 11), which speaks of 'female messengers of victory in great number,' represents a definite

4. John N. Oswalt, "*bāśar*," *Theological Workbook of the Old Testament*, ed. R. Laid Harris, 2 vols. (Chicago: Moody, 1980), 1:135..
5. Millar Burrows, "The Origin of the Term 'Gospel,'" *JBL* 44 (1925): 21–33.
6. Marvin E. Tate, *Psalms 51–100*, WBC (Dallas: Word, 1990), 164.
7. See Exod 15:21; Judg 11:34; 1 Sam 18:6–7; cf. Ps 68:26.

transition from secular news of victory to news of victory in the sphere of salvation history grounded in Yahweh."[8]

The use of feminine language in Psalm 68:11 emphasizes the distinctive liturgical role of women in Israelite worship. Women's victory celebrations, with tambourines, dancing, and responsive singing, as seen with Miriam in Exodus 15 and Deborah in Judges 5, became ritualized reports of sacred proclamation, making women not just casual announcers but official interpreters of Yahweh's salvific acts in history. Thus, the feminine participle preserves this specialized religious function where women are presented as declaring Yahweh's faithfulness to his people.

These women who proclaimed the good news of God's salvation probably acted similarly to the women who greeted Saul and David when they came home victorious after defeating the Philistines. "As they were coming home, when David returned from killing the Philistine, the women came out of all the towns of Israel, singing and dancing, to meet King Saul, with tambourines, with songs of joy, and with musical instruments. And the women sang to one another as they made merry, 'Saul has killed his thousands, and David his ten thousands'" (1 Sam 18:6–7). Several other passages in the Old Testament show that women celebrated great military victories with music, songs, and dancing (e.g., Exod 15:19–21; Judg 11:34).

The most amazing lesson from Psalm 68:11 is that when "the Lord announced the word," it was a group of women who proclaimed it. And what they proclaimed was the good news of what God had done for his people. There are many people today who deny that God calls women to proclaim the good news. The Bible reveals that, when God calls, women are ready to proclaim his good news. God called Deborah, and she answered the call and preserved the story of the great deliverance in a song. God gave Huldah a message to teach and she taught that message to Josiah's men who came to her to know the word of God. In Psalm 68:11 the Lord announced the word and many women, "a great host," proclaimed that word to the people of Israel. Therefore, when the Lord announces his word, women have the right to proclaim it, just as the women in Psalm 68 proclaimed the good news of what God had done for his people.

8. O. Schilling, "*bsr*," *Theological Dictionary of the Old Testament*, 17 vols. (Grand Rapids: Eerdmans, 1975), 2:315.

CHAPTER 13

The Daughters of Heman

According to Chronicles, the three daughters of Heman, a seer and Levitical leader selected by David to be in charge of temple music, were prophets in the same ways that his sons were prophets: "All these were the sons of Heman the king's seer, according to the promise of God to exalt him; for God had given Heman fourteen sons and three daughters. They were all under the direction of their father for the music in the house of the Lord with cymbals, harps, and lyres for the service of the house of God" (1 Chr 25:5–6).

But not all Bible translations hold this view. A few exclude Heman's three daughters from the prophetic ministry of music. Below is a sample of how some English translations exclude Heman's three daughters from participating in the music ministry of the temple. The sections of the verses where the translations differ are emphasized in bold letters.

> NRSV: All these were the sons of Heman the king's seer, according to the promise of God to exalt him; for God had given Heman fourteen sons **and three daughters. They were all under the direction of their father for the music in the house of the Lord** with cymbals, harps, and lyres for the service of the house of God.
>
> NIV 1984: All these were sons of Heman the king's seer. They were given him through the promises of God to exalt him. God gave Heman fourteen sons and three daughters. **All these men were under the supervision of their father for the music of the temple of the Lord**, with cymbals, lyres and harps, for the ministry at the house of God."
>
> CSB: All these sons of Heman, the king's seer, were given by the promises of God to exalt him, for God had given Heman fourteen

> sons and three daughters. **All these men were under their own fathers' authority for the music in the Lord's temple,** with cymbals, harps, and lyres for the service of God's temple.

Both the New International Version and the Christian Standard Bible exclude Heman's three daughters from the music ministry of the temple by saying that "All these men were under the supervision of their fathers for the music of the temple of the LORD." The translation of the NIV and the CSB are based on the words of 25:1 "David and the officers of the army also set apart for the service the *sons* of Asaph, and of Heman, and of Jeduthun, who should prophesy with lyres, harps, and cymbals" (1 Chr 25:1, emphasis added).

The word "father" in the Hebrew text of 1 Chronicles 25:6 is singular: the Hebrew word *ʾabîhem* literally means "their father." The NIV 1984 has "their fathers," but the plural word for father is not in the Hebrew text. The NIV 1984 has to use the plural "fathers" in a collective sense in order to include the men mentioned in verse 1 and to exclude the three daughters mentioned in verse 6. The CSB also has the plural "fathers" even though the biblical text has a singular word "father."

The translations reflect two different theological positions about the role of women in the work of God in the world. One view, popularly known as the egalitarian position, affirms that both men and women are created equal and that both share responsibility in having dominion over God's creation. This view also affirms that although sin created a distortion of this mutuality, the gospel of Jesus Christ has abolished this distortion and that now both men and women are equally called to serve God.

The other view, popularly known as the complementarian position, affirms that in ancient Israel, the political and religious structures of Israelite society were focused on male leadership. Therefore, God has set apart men to hold political and religious leadership in Israel. Those who hold this view believe that the three daughters of Heman were not part of the music ministry of the temple.

Commentators take different positions on this issue. Ralph Klein writes, "The three daughters seem irrelevant in a description of Heman as the father of singers unless it hints that there were also female singers in the temple."[1] But Knoppers writes: "Each of the fourteen sons

1. Ralph W. Klein, *1 Chronicles*, Hermeneia (Minneapolis: Fortress, 2006), 482.

[of Heman] is mentioned, but the three daughters go unnamed. Nevertheless, both sons and daughters sing at the Temple."[2]

The addition of the word "men" in the NIV and the CSB is unwarranted because it is not found in the Hebrew text and alters its straightforward meaning. Women musicians played a significant role in the temple of Yahweh, with the daughters of Heman in 1 Chronicles 25:5–6 serving as a notable example of this practice. God gave Heman fourteen sons and three daughters. The text explicitly mentions that Heman's three daughters participated in temple music alongside his fourteen sons. Like their brothers, they served under their father's direction. They probably played instruments including cymbals, harps, and lyres, suggesting formal musical training. In addition to the daughters of Heman, the Bible mentions other women musicians in the temple. In a procession of temple functionaries into the temple of Yahweh, Psalm 68:25 mentions the singers in front, the musicians last, and young women playing musical instruments between them. Ezra 2:65 mentions two hundred male and female singers returning from exile to serve in the rebuilt temple.

There are several references in the Bible to women playing and singing in a cultic setting as mentioned above. Although most of these women appear in the early history of Israel, Carol Meyers has demonstrated that the absence of any mention of women musicians in the later period of Israel's history is not evidence that women were not involved in the music of the temple.[3] Thus, the biblical evidence goes against the NIV and the CSB in their view that the word "father" in 1 Chronicles 25:6 should be interpreted collectively in order to include Asaph, Heman, and Jeduthun and his sons and to exclude the daughters of Heman from the music ministry of the temple.

2. Gary N. Knoppers, *1 Chronicles 10–29*, AB (New York: Doubleday, 2004), 850.
3. Carol Meyers, "Of Drums and Damsels: Women's Performance in Ancient Israel," *Biblical Archaeologist* 54 (1991): 25.

CHAPTER 14

"Your Daughters Shall Prophesy"

We have already seen that God calls both men and women to the prophetic ministry. True prophets were sent to speak a divine message in the name of God and empowered by God's Spirit. Micah, for example, identifies himself as a prophet because he is filled with the Spirit of God: "But as for me, I am filled with power, with the spirit of the LORD, with authority and with might; To declare to Jacob his crimes and to Israel his sins" (Mic 3:8 NAB).

Although Micah explicitly connected his ministry with the Spirit, not all prophets did so. Amos and Jeremiah, for example, never associated the Spirit with the message they proclaimed, likely in an effort to distance themselves from the raving prophets who were active in the religion of the Canaanites (see 1 Kgs 18:28–29). Rather, they emphasized the divine word communicated to them directly by Yahweh. The Spirit also worked through people anointed to do God's work. These people were charismatic leaders because they were endowed with the Spirit of God, the *rûaḥ* of Yahweh. Their work was attributed to the Spirit of the Lord. Thus, it is said that the Spirit of the Lord came upon Othniel (Judg 3:10), that the Spirit of the Lord took possession of Gideon (Judg 6:34), and that the Spirit of the Lord used Jephthah (Judg 11:29) and Samson (Judg 13:25) to defeat Israel's enemies. But the gift of the Spirit was limited to a few individuals whom God called and endowed with the Spirit to do a special work in Israel, as is clearly seen in the story of the elders of Israel (Num 11:25–29).

The story of the elders comes in the context of the Israelites complaining to Moses in the wilderness that they did not have enough food to feed themselves. Moses lamented to the Lord that the burden he was carrying was too much for him. In order to help Moses with the leadership of the people, the Lord told Moses to appoint seventy elders to assist him: "The LORD said to Moses, 'Is the LORD's power limited? Now you shall see whether my word will come true for you or not.' So Moses went out and told the people the words of the LORD; and he gathered seventy elders of the people, and placed them all around the tent. Then the LORD came down in the cloud and spoke to him, and took some of the spirit that was on him and put it on the seventy elders; and when the spirit rested upon them, they prophesied" (Num 11:23–25).

Moses was the leader of Israel, and he had the fullness of the Spirit. Once the leadership of the people was divided among the seventy elders, the endowment of the Spirit was shared with the elders when they were installed into their offices. This sharing of the Spirit means that the elders' authority was derived through Moses. The prophesying of the elders confirmed to the community that they were chosen to assist Moses in his responsibilities.

Two elders, Eldad and Medad, had not joined the other elders around the tent of meeting when the Spirit came upon the group: "Two men remained in the camp, one named Eldad, and the other named Medad, and the spirit rested on them; they were among those registered, but they had not gone out to the tent, and so they prophesied in the camp" (Num 11:26). When Eldad and Medad began prophesying, Moses's helper Joshua was concerned and told Moses to halt their prophesying. Moses responded, "Do you think you need to stand up for me? I wish all the LORD's people were prophets and that the LORD would put his Spirit on them" (Num 11:29 GW).

The story of Eldad and Medad parallels contemporary tendencies where some people attempt to confine the work of the Spirit by claiming that prophetic gifts belong exclusively to a selected group of people rather than acknowledging God's freedom to distribute spiritual gifts as he chooses. Joshua is concerned that their activity would restrict or limit the work of Moses, so he asks Moses to stop them from prophesying. Moses's response reflects the attitude of an individual who believed that God's work was not limited to a few individuals. Moses rejects Joshua's request by expressing the desire that the spirit of prophecy would come upon all of God's people.

Moses's desire that all of God's people would receive the Spirit and become prophets had to wait hundreds of years before it became a reality. Moses's wish becomes a prophetic oracle in the mouth of the prophet Joel: "Then afterward I will pour out my spirit on all flesh; your sons and your daughters shall prophesy, your old men shall dream dreams, and your young men shall see visions. Even on the male and female slaves, in those days, I will pour out my spirit" (Joel 2:28–29). Joel's apocalyptic oracle reflects the hope that, someday in the future, the Lord will come and deliver his people from the hands of their enemies. On that day, all of God's people will receive the fullness of the Spirit, and every one of them, men and women, young and old, slaves or free, will prophesy. Significantly, "all flesh" here refers specifically to God's people rather than to humanity as a whole.

When Joel spoke of "your sons and daughters," the prophet was speaking about God's people. The spirit that is poured out on all people is the spirit of prophecy. This spirit of prophecy will lead people to dream dreams and see visions. In the Old Testament, the manifestation of the Spirit of God was selective; it came upon a few individuals. But according to Joel's promise, God's Spirit will be given to all God's people, not just to a select group of people as it was done in the past. From the least to the greatest, all those endowed with the Spirit of God would become prophets.

According to Peter, what happened on the day of Pentecost fulfilled Joel's prophecy (Acts 2:14–18). Those gathered in Jerusalem were Jews and proselytes who had come to celebrate the Feasts of Passover and Pentecost. Although initially only Jewish believers received the Spirit, eventually the Spirit of God also fell upon Gentiles: "The gift of the Holy Spirit had been poured out even on the Gentiles" (Acts 10:45).

When Joel prophesied about the pouring of the Spirit, Israelite society tended to exclude some people and had a limited view of the role of women in the religious life of Israel. As Smith writes: "With few exceptions, the Israel of Joel's time was narrow and exclusive, hating and hated by other peoples."[1] According to Joel, though, even slaves will share in the democratization of the gift of the Spirit, and no one will be able to restrict or limit the ability of men and women, young and old, bound or free, to proclaim God's word to a lost world. Joel's inclusion of slaves is extraordinary, for nowhere in the Old

---

1. George Adam Smith, *The Book of the Twelve Prophets* (New York: A. C. Armstrong and Son, 1902), 418.

Testament is it said that a slave received the gift of prophecy. This view is so unique that the translators of the Septuagint could not accept that slaves also would become prophets, so they translated the text as "my servants," thus interpreting slaves of men to mean "servants of God." The implication of Joel's prophecy is immense. As Nogalski writes, "Given the patriarchal structures of the time, this promise to include women, children, and slaves, as well as men and elders, in the work of YHWH is unparalleled in Old Testament texts."[2]

To prophesy, to have dreams, and to see visions are the work of the prophets and evidence of the fullness of God's Spirit. So, according to Joel and according to Peter's interpretation of Joel's prophecy, the Day of Pentecost was the day when all of God's people became prophets. Now, people everywhere, men and women, can proclaim the gospel of God's love and offer a message of hope and salvation in the name of Christ. To be sure, the calling of women to be prophets was not a fluke. It was part of God's plan to save humanity. With the outpouring of the Spirit on the Day of Pentecost, the idea of gender, age, and social status is eliminated; now both men and women can prophesy. This is what Paul meant when he wrote: "There is no longer Jew or Greek, there is no longer slave or free, there is no longer male and female; for all of you are one in Christ Jesus" (Gal 3:28). Joel's prophecy and the outpouring of the Spirit reveal that God is no respecter of persons. God calls men, women, the old, the young, and slaves to the prophetic ministry. Moses said, "I wish all the Lord's people were prophets and that the Lord would put his Spirit on them" (Num 11:29 GW). On the Day of Pentecost, God granted Moses's wish.

---

2. James D. Nogalski, "Joel," in *The Book of the Twelve: Hosea–Jonah*, Smyth & Helwys Bible Commentary (Macon, GA: Smyth & Helwys, 2011), 238.

PART 3

THE MOTHERS OF ISRAEL

CHAPTER 15

Sarah: A Mother in Her Old Age

When God called Abraham, God told him to leave his father's household and go to a land he would show him (Gen 12:1). The call included God's promise to bless Abraham and make him into a great nation. Abraham departed from Haran and took his wife, Sarah, and his nephew Lot with him.

According to Genesis 20:12, Sarah was Abraham's half-sister. She was the daughter of Terah, but she was not the daughter of Abraham's mother. When Terah left Ur, Abraham and Sarah went with him (Gen 11:31). God promised Abraham that he would be a blessing to "all the families of the earth." God's promise, "I will make of you into a great nation" (Gen 12:2), implies that Abraham would have many descendants—that is, Sarah would give a son to Abraham. Abraham's children then would become the agents through whom God's purpose for the world would be accomplished.

But they had a problem that jeopardized the fulfilment of the promise: Sarah was barren (Gen 11:30). In ancient Israel, conception was seen as a blessing from the Lord, as the reward for faithful observance of the covenant: "Blessed shall be the fruit of your womb" (Deut 28:4). Likewise, barrenness was considered to be a curse by God (Deut 28:18) and a source of shame for the woman.

The Problem of Old Age

The promise was further complicated by Abraham's and Sarah's old age (Gen 18:11). Abraham was seventy-five years old when God called him (Gen 12:4), and Sarah was sixty-five years old. As is well known, conception becomes increasingly difficult with age. When the Lord appeared to Abraham saying that he would bless and protect him,

Abraham responded, "O Sovereign Lord, what good are all your blessings when I don't even have a son?" (Gen 15:2 NLT). Abraham knew that God could give him and Sarah a son in their old age, for he knew that sons are a gift from the Lord (Ps 127:3). God hammers this truth by delaying Isaac's birth.[1]

Sarah had the same problem. She knew it was impossible for her to become a mother at the age of ninety (Gen 17:17). When Sarah heard God's promise to Abraham, that he would become a father in less than twelve months, Sarah laughed silently to herself and said, "How could a worn-out woman like me enjoy such pleasure, especially when my master—my husband—is also so old?" (Gen 18:12 NLT). But when the Lord heard Sarah's laughter, he said to both, "Is anything impossible for the Lord?" (Gen 18:14 CSB).

The Promise in Peril

In addition to the problem of Abraham's and Sarah's advancing age, Abraham himself imperils God's promise not once, but twice. Abraham endangers the promise for the first time early in his story when he traveled to Egypt because of a famine in the land of Canaan (see Gen 12). When he was about to enter Egypt, Abraham said to Sarah, "I know well that you are a woman beautiful in appearance; and when the Egyptians see you, they will say, 'This is his wife'; then they will kill me, but they will let you live. Say you are my sister, so that it may go well with me because of you, and that my life may be spared on your account" (Gen 12:11–13).That is precisely what happened, but God afflicted Pharaoh and his house with great plagues because of Sarah. Seeing the great affliction within his household, Pharaoh called Abraham and said, "What is this you have done to me? Why did you not tell me that she was your wife? Why did you say, 'She is my sister,' so that I took her for my wife?" (Gen 12:18–19). Fretheim writes that Abraham's decision to give Sarah as Pharaoh's wife compromised her honor and dignity.[2]

Pharaoh's statement that he had taken Sarah as his wife implies that the marriage had been consummated. Fretheim writes, "The reference to 'wife,' as well as the time that passes [Gen 12:17], makes it possible,

1. Leon R. Kass, "Educating Father Abraham: The Meaning of Wife," *First Things* 47 (November 1994): 20.
2. Terence E. Fretheim, *Abraham: Trials of Family and Faith* (Columbia: The University of South Carolina Press, 2007), 50.

even likely, that the marriage is consummated." This truth becomes more apparent by the fact that when Abraham gives Sarah to become Abimelech's wife, Genesis 20:6 explicitly says that Abimelech did not have sexual relations with Sarah.[3] Sarah, however, did not become pregnant with Pharaoh's child because God intervened to save Sarah from a potential pregnancy.

The second threat to the promise came when Abraham repeated his deception with Abimelech, the king of Gerar (Gen 20). Once again, God intervened to protect Sarah. That night Abimelech had a dream in which God told him that Sarah was a married woman. The marriage was not consummated because Abimelech "had not approached her" (Gen 20:4).

Sarah and Hagar

In her desperation to become a mother, Sarah took matters into her own hands and gave her maid Hagar to Abraham so that she could become a mother through her. "Now Sarai, Abram's wife, bore him no children. She had an Egyptian slave-girl whose name was Hagar, and Sarai said to Abram, 'You see that the LORD has prevented me from bearing children; go into my slave-girl; it may be that I shall obtain children by her'" (Gen 16:1–2). Hagar's marriage to Abraham posed a real threat to God's promise because Hagar was a foreigner, an Egyptian, and a slave. This story of the conflict between Sarah and Hagar shows how dysfunctional Abraham's family was.

Sarah blamed God for preventing her from conceiving. A. H. Konkel, in his study of the word *ʿṣr* ("prevent"), says that the word carries the idea of restraint, such as restricting a person's movement (1 Chr 12:1), placing a person in prison (2 Kgs 17:4), or withholding a womb from conception (Gen 16:2).[4] Sarah holds God responsible for her infertility. She told Abraham plainly that "the LORD has prevented me from having children" (Gen 16:2). So Sarah, eager to have a son, remembered the laws of her old country and adopted the common Mesopotamian. For example, documents found at Nuzi specify that a childless woman could give her slave girl to her husband so that the mistress could obtain children by her.[5]

3. Fretheim, *Abraham*, 50.
4. A. H. Konkel, "*ʿiṣr*," *DOTTE*, 3:501.
5. John Van Seters, "The Problem of Childlessness in Near Eastern Law and the Patriarchs of Israel," *JBL* 87 (1968): 401–8.

Hagar was a personal maid to Sarah, and as such, Sarah had the power to give her to Abraham as a secondary wife. Sarah believed that God would accept her action because Abraham would have a son who would become the heir of the promise that God had given to him. In other words, Sarah sought to build her own family through Hagar (the Hebrew of Gen 16:2 reads, "perhaps I will be built through her").

The Announcement of Isaac's Birth

One of the fundamental problems with the birth of Ishmael, Hagar's son through Abraham, was that Ishmael became Abraham's firstborn son. According to the custom in Israel, the firstborn son received the inheritance from his father. In Genesis 17:19, however, God told Abraham that "your wife Sarah shall bear you a son, and you shall name him Isaac. I will establish my covenant with him as an everlasting covenant for his offspring after him." Isaac, not Ishmael, was heir to the covenant promise.

The covenant was made with both Abraham and Sarah, as is indicated by God's changing her name from Sarai to Sarah in Genesis 17:15, just as he had earlier changed Abraham's name from Abram to Abraham.[6] As a covenant partner with Abraham, Sarah also received God's blessing (Gen 17:16), though God's promise to Sarah is different from the promises God gave to Abraham. Sarah's blessing consists in the opening of her womb so that she will be able to conceive a son. In addition, what God said about Sarah's future is significant in a patriarchal society.

Having heard God's announcement that she would indeed bear her own son, Sarah's response was to laugh: "So Sarah laughed to herself, saying, 'After I have grown old, and my husband is old, shall I have pleasure?'" (Gen 18:12). God responded to Sarah's attitude by addressing Abraham. "Why did Sarah laugh, and say, 'Shall I indeed bear a child, now that I am old?'" (Gen 18:13). Sarah's laugh seems to indicate that Abraham never told Sarah that God had promised she would bear a son (Gen 17:5). God reaffirmed his promise: "Is anything too wonderful for the Lord? At the set time I will return to you, in due season, and Sarah shall have a son" (Gen 18:14). Nevertheless, Sarah spoke to God and denied that she laughed at the announcement of her

6. Ralph W. Klein, "Call, Covenant, and Community: The Story of Abraham and Sarah," *Currents in Theology and Mission* 15 (1988): 126.

upcoming pregnancy. "But Sarah denied, saying, 'I did not laugh'; for she was afraid. [God] said, 'Oh yes, you did laugh'" (Gen 18:15).

Twice God said he would bless Sarah. Twice God said that Sarah would give birth to a son. God also said that nations and kings will come through her. These promises indicate that Sarah was not just the wife of Abraham; she was a full partner with Abraham in God's mission to bring the nations unto himself.

Sarah Becomes a Mother

In due time Sarah became pregnant just as God had promised. Sarah was sixty-five years old when she came to Canaan with Abram. She was ninety years old when she gave birth to her son (Gen 17:17). After twenty-five years of waiting, of doubting, and anticipation, Sarah became a mother: "The LORD dealt with Sarah as he had said, and the LORD did for Sarah as he had promised. Sarah conceived and bore Abraham a son in his old age, at the time of which God had spoken to him" (Gen 21:1–2).

Why did it take so long for Sarah to conceive? Terence Fretheim, in his study of the life of Abraham, offers an excellent explanation. He writes, "A possible reason for the long delay in the fulfillment of the promise relates to the developing response of Abraham and Sarah (including their lack of trust). The texts would thus be a witness to divine perseverance in the face of human mistrust and resistance." According to Fretheim, "God's will is able to be frustrated in view of human response."[7]

Sarah laughed with joy at Isaac's birth: "God has brought laughter for me. . . . Who would ever have said to Abraham that Sarah would nurse children? Yet I have borne him a son in [my] old age" (Gen 21:6–7). Sarah's conception was miraculous because God opened the womb of an old woman and blessed her by allowing her to become a mother in her old age. Throughout the whole ordeal, God's promise that Sarah would become a mother of kings was in danger because of Abraham's foolishness and Sarah's scheming, but Sarah did become mother of the son who would inherit the promise given to Abraham and without whom "there is no Israel, there is no fulfillment of the promises of Genesis 12:1–3."[8]

---

7. Terence E. Fretheim, *Abraham: Trials of Family and Faith* (Columbia: The University of South Carolina Press, 2007), 118.
8. Wendell W. Frerichs, "The Birth of Isaac: Genesis 21:1–7," *WW* 14 (1994): 155.

CHAPTER 16

Rachel: The Struggles of a Barren Woman

"When Rachel saw that she bore Jacob no children, she envied her sister; and she said to Jacob, 'Give me children, or I shall die'" (Gen 30:1).

Ancient Israel honored women who had many children. The community saw them as blessed by God, as we see in the blessing spoken to Rebekah when she left her family to become Isaac's wife: "May you, our sister, become the mother of many thousands of children" (Gen 24:60 GW). It is in light of this view of motherhood that one should understand the pathos of Rachel's words, the desperate heart they reflect. The story of Jacob and Rachel is a beautiful love story of how Jacob fell in love and of how the seven years he worked for Rachel were "to him but a few days because of the love he had for her" (Gen 29:20).

Jacob loved Rachel, but the cunning Laban (Gen 29:22–23)—Jacob's father-in-law—tricked the trickster Jacob into marrying Leah first. Leah's position as a wife was affirmed by the children she bore Jacob. Rachel, unable to have children, became jealous of her sister. Rachel's harsh words—"Give me children, or I shall die"—offer insight into the tension caused by the rivalry between the two sisters.

Rachel's desire to become a mother was natural. Rachel's desperate cry was that of a childless woman who desperately wanted to become a mother and, through motherhood, fulfill her destiny as a woman and as a wife. In the Hebrew Bible, women praised the Lord when he gave "the barren woman a home, making her the joyous mother of children" (Ps 113:9). This was the case of Hannah, who, after giving birth to Samuel, said: "My heart exults in the Lord. . . . The barren has borne seven" (1 Sam 2:1, 5).

Rachel's suffering became more grievous every day as she saw her sister enjoying the love and the affection of her sons. Further, the barren wife in Israel had no prospect for the future and was believed to be cursed by the Lord (Gen 20:18). Rachel expressed her frustration as a childless wife by her outburst against her husband. Jacob's reply likewise expressed his frustration at the situation because he recognized that his wife was asking the impossible from him. Jacob asked, "Am I in the place of God, who has withheld from you the fruit of the womb?" (Gen 30:2). When Rebekah was unable to have children, her husband Isaac prayed for her for twenty years before his prayers were answered (Gen 25:21). Hannah also prayed to God for a son (1 Sam 1:10). But there is no evidence that Jacob ever prayed for Rachel, but he did remind his wife that the power of conception was not in his hands, that it belonged to God. Out of her despair, Rachel invoked a custom common in the ancient Near East, the same custom invoked by Sarah when she was unable to give Abraham a son (Gen 16:2). Rachel gave her maid Bilhah to Jacob as a wife so that the maid could conceive a son on her behalf (Gen 30:3). Adoption was common in Mesopotamia in the days of the patriarchs. According to documents from Nuzi, barren couples could adopt a son or a daughter and give them the legal rights and duties of a natural-born child. In the process of adoption, the child of the servant was placed upon the mistress's knees and declared to be her own child.[1]

Rachel told Jacob: "Here is my maid Bilhah; go into her, that she may bear upon my knees and even I may have children through her" (Gen 30:3). Later, Jacob adopted Joseph's two sons by placing them on his knees (Gen 48:12). The children of Machir, the son of Manasseh, were likewise born upon Joseph's knees (Gen 50:23).

Despite having children through her maid, Rachel herself remained barren, and the rivalry between the sisters continued for many years. One day when Reuben, Leah's son, found some mandrakes in the field, the rivalry flared again. Mandrakes, also known as "love apples," were considered aphrodisiacs that also aided in conception.[2]

---

1. John Van Seters, "The Problem of Childlessness in Near Eastern Law and the Patriarchs of Israel, JBL 87 (1968): 401–8.
2. John H. Walton, *The Minor Prophets, Job, Psalms, Proverbs, Ecclesiastes, Song of Songs*, vol. 5 of *Zondervan Illustrated Bible Backgrounds Commentary* (Grand Rapids: Zondervan Academic, 2009), 529.

Rachel, hoping that the mandrakes would help her conceive a child, offered Leah a night with Jacob in exchange for the mandrakes that Reuben had found. When Jacob returned home from the field, Leah told him: "I have hired you with my son's mandrakes" (Gen 30:16). After spending the night with Jacob, Leah became pregnant and gave him another son, whom Leah named Issachar. Then Leah gave birth to a sixth son, leading her to say, "'God has endowed me with a good dowry; now my husband will honor me, because I have borne him six sons;' so she named him Zebulun" (Gen 30:20). Then Leah gave birth to a daughter and named her Dinah.

The rivalry between Leah and Rachel increased as Leah gave birth to more children and Rachel continued to be barren. The situation became even worse as Rachel saw the hand of God behind this situation. According to the narrator of the story, at the beginning of the rivalry between Leah and Rachel, it was the Lord who allowed Leah to conceive: "When the LORD saw that Leah was hated, he opened her womb; but Rachel was barren" (Gen 29:31). And Jacob told Rachel that it was the Lord "who has withheld from you the fruit of the womb" (Gen 30:2).

Finally, the Lord had compassion on Rachel and harkened to her desperate prayers: "Then God remembered Rachel. God answered her prayer and made it possible for her to have children" (Gen 30:22 GW). Rachel became pregnant and gave birth to a son whom she called Joseph. After becoming a mother, Rachel said: "God has taken away my disgrace" (Gen 30:23 GW). The biblical text clearly credits God for opening Rachel's womb. Rachel became pregnant, but not because of the mandrakes she acquired from Leah. It was an act of grace in answering a desperate woman's prayer that allowed the barren one to bear a son.

The Bible contains many stories of barren women who desperately wanted to become mothers, women who sought a future for their families: Sarah (Gen 11:30), Rebekah (Gen 25:21), Rachel (Gen 29:30), Hannah (1 Sam 1:2), Manoah's wife (Samson's mother; Judg 13:2), the Shunammite woman (2 Kgs 4:8–17), and Elizabeth (Luke 1:7). All these barren women conceived and gave birth to children because of the gracious intervention of God, who opens wombs and "gives the barren woman a home, making her the joyous mother of children" (Ps 113:9).

The birth of children to barren women cannot be explained apart from the powerful and marvelous work of God who creates something new when all seems to be hopeless and lost. Rachel was blessed by God because he answered her prayers and allowed her to become a mother. The blessing of Rachel is reflected in the words of the women of Bethlehem when Ruth bore her son: "May the Lord make the woman who is coming into your house like Rachel and Leah, who together built up the house of Israel" (Ruth 4:11).

CHAPTER 17

Moses's Two Mothers

The book of Exodus opens with the birth of a baby boy who grew up to deliver his people from their oppressive situation in Egypt. But first, baby Moses endured a unique hardship that required his birth mother to relinquish him to an adoptive mother.

The book of Exodus in the Hebrew Bible is called *shemôt*, "the names." And yet the author withholds the names of Moses's two mothers in these first two chapters, as if concealing the identities of the people involved in Moses's birth to maintain the safety of the child. The name of Jochebed, Moses's birth mother, is only mentioned later in the book, when the genealogy of her husband is given.

Moses was born at a time when "a new king arose over Egypt, who did not know Joseph" (Exod 1:8). This pharaoh was afraid of the Hebrews because they had become a multitude of foreigners that he feared would join the enemies of Egypt and take control of their land. So Pharaoh ordered that all boys born of Hebrew women be thrown into the Nile so that they could die (Exod 1:22). Killing the baby boys was an effort at killing the nation, for as Siebert-Hommes writes, "Without sons, the history of a nation has no future."[1]

With the future of Israel thus threatened, several women acted to provide a future for Israel by saving the life of one baby boy: (1) the two midwives; (2) Moses's sister, Miriam; (3) Moses's birth mother, Jochebed; and (4) Pharaoh's daughter. These five women saved the life of the child who eventually would become the leader who delivered Israel from their oppressive situation in Egypt. J. Cheryl Exum, discussing the role of these women in preserving the life of Moses,

1. Jopie Siebert-Hommes, "The Female Saviors of Israel's Liberator: Twelve 'Daughters' in Exodus 1 and 2," in *Torah*, vol. 1.1 of *The Bible and Women: An Encyclopedia of Exegesis and Cultural History*, ed. Irmtraud Fischer and Mercedes Navarro Puerto (Atlanta: Society of Biblical Literature, 2011), 298.

writes, "Without Moses there would be no story, but without the initiative of these women, there would be no Moses."[2]

Shiphrah and Puah, the Midwives

The two midwives who provided midwifery to the Hebrew women were named Shiphrah and Puah (Exod 1:15). According to Brevard S. Childs, the Masoretic Text identifies the midwives as Hebrew through two key textual elements: the direct designation "Hebrew midwives" (Exod 1:15) and the statement that "God gave them families" (Exod 1:21). Childs interprets the latter as indicating that God provided them "a posterity within the people of Israel," which would only be meaningful if the women were themselves Hebrew.[3] This textual evidence supports the interpretation that Shiphrah and Puah were not Egyptian women serving the Hebrew community but rather Hebrew women courageously defying Pharaoh's genocidal decree from within their own community. Pharoah summoned these two women, then ordered them to kill every Hebrew male child (Exod 1:16). Since the midwives feared God, they did not obey the orders of Pharaoh (Exod 1:17). These women defied Pharaoh and preserved the male children's lives. They rescued hundreds, if not thousands, of baby boys, including Moses himself.

Miriam, Moses's Sister

According to Exodus 7:7, Moses was three years younger than his brother Aaron, who was possibly born before Pharaoh issued the decree that all Hebrew boys should die. The name of Moses's sister does not appear in the story of Moses's birth. We only learn her name, Miriam, in Exodus 15 when she sings a song commemorating Israel's exodus from Egypt (Exod 15:20).

After the birth of Moses, "his sister" assisted her mother in preserving her brother's life by negotiating with Pharaoh's daughter on behalf of his mother. After the servants of Pharaoh's daughter found the basket with the boy inside, Miriam approached Pharaoh's daughter and asked her, "Shall I go and get you a nurse from the Hebrew women to nurse

2. J. Cheryl Exum, "'You Shall Let Every Daughter Live': A Study of Exodus 1:8–2:10," in *A Feminist Companion to Exodus to Deuteronomy*, ed. Athalya Brenner, Feminist Companion to the Bible (Sheffield: Sheffield Academic Press, 1994), 52.
3. Brevard S. Childs, *The Book of Exodus*, OTL (Louisville: Westminster John Knox, 2004), 16.

the child for you?" (Exod 2:7). Miriam's suggestion that she could find a nurse "for you" intimates that Pharaoh's daughter should become the child's legal guardian.

Jochebed, Moses's Birth Mother

When the birth of Moses was announced, the biblical writer did not give the name of his mother: "Now a man from the house of Levi went and married a Levite woman. The woman conceived and bore a son; and when she saw that he was a fine baby, she hid him three months" (Exod 2:1–2).

Jochebed's name appears only twice in the genealogies associated with her husband, Amram. Exodus 6:20 reads, "Amram married Jochebed his father's sister and she bore him Aaron and Moses, and the length of Amram's life was one hundred thirty-seven years." And in Numbers 26:59: "The name of Amram's wife was Jochebed, daughter of Levi, who was born to Levi in Egypt; and she bore to Amram: Aaron, Moses, and their sister Miriam." We learn several things about Jochebed from these two genealogical notices. First, Jochebed was the daughter of Levi. Second, she was born in Egypt. Third, Jochebed was the aunt of her husband, Amram. Later, Levitical laws declared that a marriage between an aunt and her nephew was incestuous: "You shall not uncover the nakedness of your father's sister; she is your father's flesh" (Lev 18:12).

After the baby was born, Jochebed saw that her child was beautiful (Exod 2:2 TNK). She hid him for three months; this action, however, placed the child in jeopardy of being found and killed. As the boy grew up, she realized that she would be unable to hide him any longer. Out of love for her newborn son, Jochebed decided to defy the king's order and save her son.

So Jochebed devised a plan. "When she could hide him no longer she got a papyrus basket for him, and plastered it with bitumen and pitch; she put the child in it and placed it among the reeds on the bank of the river" (Exod 2:3). These actions were the work of a mother who loved her child. She took the basket and placed it on the Nile River, not to kill him but to give him life. Did Jochebed know that Pharaoh's daughter would be bathing on that section of the Nile? The text does not tell us. Jochebed and her daughter Miriam used deception to save the life of her newborn son. Further, Jochebed was able not only to save his life but also to spend several years nursing him and providing early instruction on the traditions of the Hebrews and the faith of her people.

No record of Moses's Hebrew name has survived. His adoptive mother, Pharaoh's daughter, gave him the name Moses. It is inconceivable, however, that after spending three years nursing and nurturing her son that Jochebed would not have given him a Hebrew name.

Pharaoh's Daughter, Moses's Adoptive Mother

One day when Pharaoh's daughter came to the Nile to bathe, she saw a basket among the papyrus plants and sent her slave girl to get it. Pharaoh's daughter opened the basket, looked inside, and saw a baby. It was a boy, and he was crying. She felt compassion for him because she realized that he was a Hebrew child, one of the many babies her father had condemned to death.

The daughter of Pharaoh faced a dilemma. If she decided to save the life of this Hebrew boy, then she would go against her father's will and jeopardize her own life. Despite this danger, she decided to save the baby from her father's decree. When a young Hebrew girl approached her and offered to find "one of the Hebrew women to nurse the baby" (Exod 2:7 NIV), she readily agreed, perhaps because she feared that an Egyptian nurse would tell the Egyptian authorities about the boy and the baby would be killed. Childs writes, "In the Ancient Near East infants were usually suckled by their own mothers. However, in certain instances among aristocratic families a wet nurse was hired. This practice was also common where the mother was unable to nourish her child or where the mother was unknown. The nurse assumed responsibility of raising the child as well as suckling it during the stipulated period."[4]

Pharaoh's daughter accepted the suggestion of the young girl and hired a Hebrew woman to take care of the child. The text does not tell us, however, if she suspected she was delivering the child into the care of his birth mother who "took the child and nursed him" (Exod 2:9 NIV). Jochebed took her son to her home where she nursed him until he was weaned. According to Ziesel, a mother would nurse her child for a minimum of two years "with an awareness that nursing longer

---

4. Brevard S. Childs, "The Birth of Moses," *JBL* 84 (1965): 112.

was probably the norm."[5] In Hebrew society, a mother would wean her child generally around year three.[6] During the persecution of the Jews by Antiochus Epiphanes, seven sons of a Jewish mother were put to death for their refusal to deny their faith. When her last son was about to be killed, his mother, "leaning close to him, . . . spoke in their native language as follows, deriding the cruel tyrant: 'My son, have pity on me. I carried you nine months in my womb, and nursed you for three years, and have reared you and brought you up to this point in your life, and have taken care of you'" (2 Macc. 7:27).

Ziesel writes that a "quality of both maternal nursing and wet nursing was that children were thought to take on the mental and emotional characteristics of the women whose milk they drank."[7] Thus, Moses's personality grew under the influence of a mother whose devotion to God was strong.

"When the child grew up, she brought him to Pharaoh's daughter, and she took him as her son" (Exod 2:10). These words indicate that Pharaoh's daughter adopted the child as her own son. Thus, the Pharaoh who intended to have the child killed at birth became the adoptive grandfather of Moses.

Pharaoh's daughter, taking on the role of mother, named her son Moses.[8] Moses is an Egyptian name that means "son of," as in Rameses ("Son of the God Ra"), Thutmose, and Ahmose. Hebrew tradition gave the Egyptian name a Hebrew meaning by associating its pronunciation with the similar-sounding Hebrew term that means "to draw out." Though Moses is an Egyptian name, the author of Exodus gives it a Hebrew meaning so that it could be understood from a Hebrew perspective (Exod 2:10).

Moses was a fortunate and blessed man. He had two mothers who loved him, two mothers who did all they could to save him from a certain death. Jochebed, his biological mother, loved her son and kept him as long as she could after he was born. When she could no longer keep him, she gave him away to save his life. By giving him away and

5. Laura Rogers Ziesel, "'Like a Weaned Child': Breastfeeding Practices in the Biblical Period," *Wesleyan Theological Journal* 52 (2017): 145.
6. Mayer I. Gruber, "Breast-Feeding Practices in Biblical Israel and in Old Babylonian Mesopotamia," *JNES* 19 (1989): 63.
7. Ziesel, "'Like a Weaned Child,'" 146.
8. J. Gwyn Griffiths, "The Egyptian Derivation of the Name Moses." *JNES* 12 (1953): 225–31.

by depriving herself of the blessing of seeing him grow into adulthood, Jochebed saved her son's life and the lives of thousands of people who were delivered from their servitude through the son she loved.

The Bible never reveals the name of Pharaoh's daughter. According to Jewish tradition, her name was Bithiah, the daughter of the pharaoh mentioned in 1 Chronicles 4:17, although this identification is doubtful.[9] As an adopted child, Moses was blessed to know he had two mothers who loved him. Jochebed, his birth mother, did not abandon him but gave him away so that he might live. Pharaoh's daughter could have allowed him to die, and yet she chose life for him.

9. Sara Japhet, *I & II Chronicles*, OTL (Louisville: Westminster John Knox, 1993), 115.

CHAPTER 18

Samson's Mother: A Mother's Disappointment

Plenty of ink has been spilled on both Samson and his father Manoah. This chapter will take a closer look at Samson's mother, the focus of Samson's birth narrative that appears in Judges 13.

A Woman from Zorah

Samson's mother played a significant role in Samson's early life. She hailed from Zorah, a village in the tribe of Dan. Like Jephthah's daughter in Judges 11 and the Levite's concubine in Judges 19, Samson's mother remains unnamed. The biblical writer identifies her as the wife of Manoah (Judg 13:2), the mother of Samson (Judg 14:2), and "the woman" (Judg 13:6). Even nameless, Samson's mother is the primary protagonist in the narrative announcing the birth of the one who would begin to deliver Israel from Philistine oppression.

The narrative begins by announcing that the woman who would become Samson's mother was barren. God opened the wombs of five other barren women in the Old Testament, Manoah's wife and the Shunammite woman are the only ones whose name are never mentioned.[1] Because Manoah is not the main character of the birth narrative and because the woman does not become Samson's mother until after the birth of her son, this study follows the biblical writer (Judg 13:3, 6) and the angel (Judg 13:13) by referring to Samson's mother as "the woman." The biblical text says little about Samson's mother. We do not know whether she was young or old or whether she prayed for a son. We do know that God takes the initiative to give

1. Sarah (Gen 11:30), Rebekah (Gen 25:21), Rachel (Gen 29:31), Hannah (1 Sam 1:1–2), and the Shunammite woman (2 Kgs 4:14–15).

the woman a son as part of his purpose to liberate the Israelites from oppression.

The Announcement of the Birth of a Son

A divine messenger appeared to the woman announcing that her barrenness had ended. He told her, "Although you are barren, having borne no children, you shall conceive and bear a son" (Judg 13:3). The identification of this heavenly messenger is ambiguous. He is called variously "the angel of the LORD " (Judg 13:3), "the angel of God" (Judg 13:9), "the man of God" (Judg 13:8), "a man of God having the appearance of an angel" (Judg 13:6), or simply "the man" (Judg 13:10). This ambiguity signal that this episode is another instance of the embodiment of God in the Old Testament, when the invisible God revealed himself to people in Israel as the angel of the Lord. Although the divine messenger appeared as a man, in the end Manoah realized that he and his wife had seen God himself.

When the angel of the Lord told the woman that she would become the mother of a son, he also instructed her on what she must do during her pregnancy and what her son would do in his life. He said to her, "Now be careful not to drink wine or strong drink, or to eat anything unclean, for you shall conceive and bear a son. No razor is to come on his head, for the boy shall be a nazirite to God from birth. It is he who shall begin to deliver Israel from the hand of the Philistines" (Judg 13:4–5). Although the NRSV says that the boy would "be a nazirite to God from birth," the Hebrew text says that the boy would be a Nazirite "from the womb."

We find the law regulating the vow of the Nazirite in Numbers 6:1–8. The Nazirite vow was a voluntary and temporary vow that individuals, men and women, took for a limited period to consecrate themselves to the service of God. Benjamin Johnson points out that "Samson's vow is unique in three ways: (1) it is divinely imposed; (2) it is from birth to death; and (3) it imposes his mother to keep the sanctions during her pregnancy."[2]

Samson was to be a Nazirite for life. According to Numbers 6, the Nazirites had to observe three rules: (1) they must abstain from wine and

2. Benjamin J. M. Johnson, "What Type of Son Is Samson? Reading Judges 13 as a Biblical Type-Scene," *JETS* 53 (2010): 277.

all other products of the wine, (2) they must not allow the hair of their head to be cut by a razor, and (3) they must not come near a dead body. Because the boy was to be a Nazirite "from the womb," the mother of the boy must also—as long as she carried her son in her womb—observe the Nazirite vow. Therefore, she must "be careful not to drink wine or strong drink, or to eat anything unclean." The mother's observation of the Nazirite vow ensured that her son would be consecrated to God from the very moment of conception—"from the womb." Samson's mother was committed to her son's vocation as a Nazirite because of the special mission God had assigned to him and was therefore willing to abstain from foods and drinks forbidden to a Nazirite.

After her conversation with the angel, the woman met her husband and relayed what the divine messenger had said, though slightly edited: "You shall conceive and bear a son. So then drink no wine or strong drink, and eat nothing unclean, for the boy shall be a nazirite to God from birth to the day of his death" (Judg 13:7). By adding the phrase "from birth to the day of his death," she probably meant that her son would be a Nazirite for life, but she unintentionally and prophetically announced his death for breaking his vow of a Nazirite: "When Samson breaks his vow and finally ceases to be a Nazirite in any sense of the word, his death quickly follows. Thus, it turns out to be true that Samson was a Nazirite 'until the day of his death.'"[3]

The Birth of the Son

The birth of the child is shrouded in mystery. When the angel first appeared to the woman, he said, "Although you are barren, having borne no children, you shall conceive and bear a son" (Judg 13:3). In the second announcement, however, the woman seems to be already pregnant, "For you are with child and will give birth to a son" (Judg 13:5 BBE). Although most English translations say that the pregnancy is yet to come—"you will conceive and give birth to a son" (Judg 13:5 NIV)—the Hebrew text's use of the perfect tense of the verb implies that the woman is already pregnant. The text never says that Manoah knew his wife sexually, and there is no mention of a conception. It only states that "the woman bore a son" (Judg 13:24).

3. Johnson, "What Type of Son Is Samson?," 276.

After the child was born, his mother named him Samson. Samson's mother is one of the few women in the Old Testament who named their sons at birth. The woman does not give a reason for naming her son Samson, which is derived from the Hebrew word *šmš* and means "Little Sun." The reference to the sun may be related to a village in the tribe of Dan called Ir-shemesh ("City of the Sun," Josh 19:41) or the city of Beth-shemesh ("House/temple of the sun [god]"), a city in the tribe of Issachar (Josh 19:17, 22). The reason for the solar implication in Samson's name, however, is unknown.

A Mother's Disappointment

When the angel announced the birth of Samson, the angel said to the woman that her son "shall begin to deliver Israel from the hand of the Philistines" (Judg 13:5). From his birth, Samson was set apart and given a special status by God to be a savior in Israel. The angel's words imply that Samson would do the same work that previous judges had done in delivering Israel from the hands of their enemies. Though Samson failed to deliver Israel from their Philistine oppression, he did indeed "begin" to do so. More significantly, he failed to keep his Nazirite vow.

Against his mother's will, Samson married a Philistine woman. Samson told his parents, "I saw a Philistine woman at Timnah; now get her for me as my wife" (Judg 14:2). Both parents objected, pleading, "Isn't there even one woman in our tribe or among all the Israelites you could marry? . . . Why must you go to the pagan Philistines to find a wife?" (Judg 14:3 NLT). In addition to marrying a Philistine woman, Samson "went to the Philistine town of Gaza and spent the night with a prostitute" (Judg 16:1 NLT). Further, Samson fell in love with another Philistine woman, Delilah. who betrayed him and sold him to her countrymen.

Samson's mother had kept the Nazirite vow during her pregnancy and while she nursed him, a total of three or four years. Samson, for his part, dishonored his mother's sacrifice by breaking his Nazirite vow for selfish motives. Samson likely drank wine at his wedding (Judg 14:10); he also touched the carcass of the lion (Judg 14:8), the bodies of dead Philistines (Judg 14:19), and allowed his hair to be cut (Judg 16:19). Samson failed as a Nazirite, failed as a judge, and failed to deliver Israel from the Philistines. He married a Philistine woman against his mother's wishes and violated his Nazirite vow at a Philistine woman's urging.

Conclusion

Samson is numbered among the judges of Israel, but his many failures make clear that he was not a good judge. Only his mother was faithful and righteous of all the four women in Samson's life. As McCann writes, "If there's a faithful hero in the story, besides Samson's mother, it is the God who proves persistently faithful to Samson (see 16:28–31), who proves himself persistently unfaithful to God."[4]

In addition to the love and commitment of a faithful mother, we can glean another lesson from Samson's story: "The significance of Samson's story is as an expression of YHWH's willingness to work wonders in Israel in spite of the vessels he chooses to use."[5]

4. J. Clinton McCann, *Judges*, Int (Louisville: John Knox, 2002), 101.
5. Johnson, "What Type of Son Is Samson?," 285.

CHAPTER 19

Hannah: "The Barren Has Borne Seven"

Whenever one thinks of mothers in the Old Testament, Hannah, the mother of Samuel, likely comes to mind. In 1 Samuel 1 we read of her utter despair at being barren. As noted previously, barrenness was a disgrace in the ancient Near East, considered by many Israelites as the harshest punishment with which Yahweh could visit a female.[1] Just as Sarah attributed her barrenness to God (Gen 16:2), the author of Samuel states that Hannah was barren "because the LORD had closed her womb" (1 Sam 1:6). This view of Yahweh's power over the womb is consistent with God's promise in Exodus 23:26; if the Israelites would remain faithful to Yahweh, then "none will miscarry or be barren in your land," (Exod 23:25–26) a promise repeated in Deuteronomy: "You will be blessed the most blessed of peoples, with neither sterility nor barrenness among you or your livestock" (Deut 7:14).

Hannah Prays for a Child

In her desperation for a child, Hannah prayed. Her prayer reveals several important things about her. First, it shows that she was a woman of faith. She believed that God could perform a miracle and give her a son. Hannah's faith is a good example to mothers—and fathers—everywhere because it offers us all a picture of trust amid painful circumstances.

Second, Hannah's prayer shows that she was a woman of prayer. Hannah prayed for her child before he was born, revealing a commitment to pray for her son as long as she lived. Her faithful devotion laid a

1. Joel S. Baden, "The Nature of Barrenness in the Hebrew Bible," in *Disability Studies and Biblical Literature*, ed. Candida R. Moss and Jeremy Schipper (New York: Palgrave Macmillan, 2011), 13–27.

spiritual foundation for Samuel who grew into one of the greatest men in Israel: a faithful judge, priest, and prophet.

Third, Hannah recognized that she was a steward of a precious gift from God. She prayed, "O Lord of hosts, if you will only look on the misery of your servant, and remember me, and not forget your servant, but will give to your servant a male child, then I will set him before you as a nazirite until the day of his death" (1 Sam 1:11). Hannah asked God for a son, but she promised to give her son back to God. Hannah's son was a special gift of grace; it was God who formed that child in her womb, who gave life and health to Hannah's baby. Hannah was the mother, but that child belonged to God.

Hannah kept her vow. After Samuel was weaned, probably at the age of two or three (1 Sam 1:22), Hannah returned to the house of the Lord at Shiloh and she spoke to Eli the priest: "As you live, my lord, I am the woman who was standing here in your presence, praying to the Lord. For this child I prayed; and the Lord has granted me the petition that I made of him. Therefore I have lent him to the Lord; as long as he lives, he is given to the Lord" (1 Sam 1:26–28).

Three Statements About Hannah

Three statements in Hannah's story stand out: (1) Elkanah's statement about Hannah's situation, (2) Hannah's statement about her condition, and (3) the writer's statement about Hannah's blessing.

Elkanah's Statement

When Elkanah, Hannah's husband, saw how unhappy she was, he said to her, "Hannah, why are you weeping? Why don't you eat? Why are you downhearted? Don't I mean more to you than ten sons?" (1 Sam 1:8 NIV). The answer to Elkanah's question was never given, but the reader can almost guess the answer. Elkanah's well-meaning attempt to comfort his wife was in vain. He was not "better than ten sons" because the joy of motherhood is different from joy of marriage—especially to a woman in ancient Israel who hoped to be delivered from barrenness. After all, one could always find a husband, but only the Lord could give a son.

Hannah's Statement

After the Lord answered Hannah's prayer through the birth of Samuel, she sang a song of thanksgiving: "My heart exults in the Lord" (1 Sam

2:1). Hannah's outburst of joy resulted from the divine favor she received in answer to her prayer. Exulting in God's power and provision, Hannah said, "She who was barren has borne seven children" (1 Sam 2:5 NIV). "The barren has borne seven" points to the generosity of God when he chooses to bless his people, since seven represents completeness and perfection. We see a similar reference in Ruth 4, when the women of Bethlehem expressed Naomi's joy in terms of seven sons: "He shall be to you a restorer of life and a nourisher of your old age; for your daughter-in-law who loves you, who is more to you than seven sons, has borne him" (Ruth 4:15).

The Writer's Statement

Now that "the barren has borne seven," Hannah understood that God had performed a miracle and that he could give her more children. Although Hannah had only one son and that son was given back to God, she hoped for more children, and her hope did not disappoint

The writer of the book of Samuel declared that Hannah was blessed by the Lord: "And the Lord was gracious to Hannah; she gave birth to three sons and two daughters" (1 Sam 2:21 NIV). The story of Hannah is the story of a woman who was bowed down and afflicted by her situation, who earnestly prayed to God with the longings of a mother's heart. Her experience inspires mothers everywhere.

CHAPTER 20

Rizpah: Reflections on a Mother's Love

Then Rizpah the daughter of Aiah took sackcloth, and spread it on a rock for herself, from the beginning of harvest until rain fell on them from the heavens; she did not allow the birds of the air to come on the bodies by day, or the wild animals by night" (2 Sam 21:10).

The stories of many Old Testament mothers show their love for their children and the important contributions they have made in their children's lives. Sermons on women such as Hannah abound, but we hear very few sermons about Rizpah and her love for her children preached in churches today. In fact, most Bible readers have likely never read about the extreme demonstration of love Rizpah displayed on behalf of her sons.

During David's reign over the kingdom of Israel, the land suffered a severe, three-year famine. Not knowing the reason for the famine, David inquired of Yahweh to ascertain the famine's cause and understand the reason Yahweh was punishing Israel. Yahweh told David that Saul and his house were guilty because of the massacre Saul had inflicted upon the Gibeonites. The Gibeonites were part of the original inhabitants of the land. They had deceived Joshua and the people of Israel into making a covenant with them against the command of the Lord (Josh 9:1–15). The biblical text makes no mention of the alleged massacre referenced in this context, nor does it provide any indication of what precipitated the event. We only know that Saul, because of his zeal for the honor of Israel and Judah, persecuted the Gibeonites and planned to exterminate them so that they would be completely removed from all the territory of Israel (2 Sam 21:5).

When David learned that Saul's bloodshed had caused the famine, he called the Gibeonites together to decide how to repair the wrong done to them. "What shall I do for you?" David asked. "And how shall I make expiation, that you may bless the heritage of the LORD?" (2 Sam 21:3 RSV).

The Gibeonites refused to take any money from David or from his family. When David asked again what he could do to make amends for the crime committed against them, the Gibeonites answered, "The man who consumed us and planned to destroy us, so that we should have no place in all the territory of Israel—let seven of his sons be handed over to us, and we will impale them before the LORD at Gibeon on the mountain of the LORD" (2 Sam 21:5–6). David agreed to their request. David selected Armoni and Mephibosheth, the two sons of Saul's concubine Rizpah, in addition to the five sons of Merab, Saul's daughter. In making his selection, David spared Mephibosheth, the son of Jonathan, because of his promise to Jonathan (2 Sam 9:6–7). The Gibeonites impaled these seven descendants of Saul on the mountain before the Lord at the beginning of the barley harvest. There, at the foot of the impaling pole, "Rizpah the daughter of Aiah took sackcloth, and spread it on a rock for herself, from the beginning of harvest until rain fell on them from the heavens; she did not allow the birds of the air to come on the bodies by day, or the wild animals by night" (2 Sam 21:10). Sackcloth was a type of clothing worn when mourning for the dead. Out of love for her dead sons, Rizpah kept a watch over them "from the beginning of harvest until rain fell on them from the heavens" (2 Sam 21:10), that is, from March until October—six months.

Israelite law demanded that when a person was impaled, the body should be removed at the end of the day. "When someone is convicted of a crime punishable by death and is executed, and you hang him on a tree, his corpse must not remain all night upon the tree; you shall bury him that same day" (Deut 21:22–23). The sons of Rizpah remained on the stake for six months, with Rizpah next to them. The bodies were left on the pole to make atonement for Saul's sin, and they had to remain there until the end of the drought. The coming of the rain indicated that God's judgment had ceased and that the sins of the nation had been forgiven.

Day and night, week after week, Rizpah kept a dreary watch over her dead sons, scaring away scavenger birds from feeding on their bodies during the day and not allowing wild animals to eat their bodies at night. This demonstration of maternal affection is deeply moving.

This mother was moved by grief, deeply affected by the agony her sons suffered on that cruel tree. Her attempt at protecting the integrity of the exposed bodies of her sons reveals the fire of love that burned intensively in Rizpah's heart. Rizpah's agony has been captured in the poem by Felicia Hemans:

The Vigil of Rizpah

Who watches on the mountain with the dead,
Alone before the awfulness of night?
A seer awaiting the deep spirit's might?
A warrior guarding some dark pass of dread?
No, a lorn woman!—On her drooping head,
Once proudly graceful, heavy beats the rain;
She reeks not—living for the unburied slain,
Only to scare the vulture from their bed.
So, night by night, her vigil hath she kept
With the pale stars, and with the dews hath wept.
Oh! surely some bright Presence from above
On those wild rocks the lonely one must aid!
Even so; a strengthener through all storm and shade,
The unconquerable Angel: mightiest Love!
May the memory of this loving mother be a blessing to all.

CHAPTER 21

Bathsheba: A Mother with Determination

Most people think of Israelite women in the context of taking care of their family, grinding grain and baking bread, and being occupied with the affairs of their household. Such a view reflects the patriarchal society that existed in ancient Israel. The Old Testament, however, also mentions many mothers who played significant roles in Israelite society. One such mother is Bathsheba, Solomon's mother.

Bathsheba and David

Bathsheba became David's wife as a result of his villainous act against her, the wife of one of his warriors. When she became pregnant with David's child, he ordered the death of her husband, Uriah (2 Sam 11:15). Bathsheba then moved into David's house as a pregnant widow, joining his other wives. Though the child Bathsheba carried died shortly after his birth, she and David later had other children, including Solomon (2 Chr 3:5).

The extent of Bathsheba's influence in making Solomon the king of Israel goes mostly unrecognized. This "queen mother" (1 Kgs 2:19) played a key role in the struggle for David's throne between her son Solomon and Adonijah, Solomon's brother and the son of Haggith, another of David's wives (2 Sam 3:4).

Adonijah Becomes King

Typically, in the ancient world, the king's oldest son stood first in line to inherit the throne. In David's case this was Amnon, whom David loved because he was his firstborn (2 Sam 13:21). But Amnon's younger brother Absalom killed him in defense of their sister, whom Amnon had raped (2 Sam 13). David's second son, Chileab, from his wife Abigail

(2 Sam 3:3), possibly died in infancy—Scripture says nothing more about him after mentioning his birth. Absalom later rebelled against David and was killed by Joab. That left Adonijah, David's fourth son with his wife Haggith (2 Sam 3:4), as the oldest surviving son of David and the first in line for David's throne. When he saw that David was too old to be a king, Adonijah said: "I will be king" (1 Kgs 1:5).

Since David had not named his successor, and because he was now the heir apparent to his father's throne, Adonijah took matters into his own hands. He prepared a contingent of chariots and horsemen and fifty men to serve as his bodyguards. He also invited two of David's most faithful supporters—Joab, the commander of the army, and Abiathar, the high priest.

Adonijah also welcomed his brothers, the king's sons, all the royal officials of Judah, and those who served in David's government. Because Adonijah had the support of most of the people in David's kingdom and because he was the oldest living son of David, he believed that he had the right to claim David's throne. He was also right that "all Israel expected [him] to reign" (1 Kgs 2:15).

However, Adonijah did not invite Zadok, a high priest who served under David, and he did not invite Benaiah, the commander of the Cherethites and the Pelethites, the elite group of soldiers who served as David's personal bodyguards. Neither did he invite the prophet Nathan nor Shimei and Rei, two of David's elite warriors (1 Kgs 1:5–10). Finally, Adonijah did not invite Solomon. Adonijah and his party made a public sacrifice (1 Kgs 1:9) and proclaimed: "Long live King Adonijah!" (1 Kgs 1:25). When Nathan heard what Adonijah had done, he told Bathsheba that Adonijah had proclaimed himself king (1 Kgs 1:11). Nathan then told Bathsheba how to acquire the throne for her son. Nathan's motive in this plot is unknown, but he certainly wanted to save her and Solomon's lives (1 Kgs 1:12).

Bathsheba approached David and reminded him that he had promised to make Solomon king: "My lord, you swore to your servant by the Lord your God, saying: Your son Solomon shall succeed me as king, and he shall sit on my throne. But now suddenly Adonijah has become king, though you, my lord the king, do not know it" (1 Kgs 1:17–18). Scripture does not tell us when or in what context David made such a promise, but Adonijah's belief that he would be king indicates that David's statement about Solomon had not been made public, as do Nathan's words to David, "The eyes of all Israel are on you to tell them who shall sit on the throne of my lord the king after him" (1 Kgs 1:20).

Nathan tells Bathsheba to remind David of his promise to make Solomon king. Then, while she was still talking to the king, he would come before David and confirm her words. When Bathsheba approached the king, Abishag was at his side. Bathsheba did as Nathan said, and David swore to her that Solomon would reign after him (1 Kgs 1:28). David called together the government leaders and ordered them to anoint Solomon as the next king. Without Bathsheba's active involvement in the process, Adonijah would have become king, and she and her son would have certainly been killed.

Bathsheba and Adonijah

Though Solomon became king, Adonijah remained a threat because he was still David's oldest living son. Soon after Solomon took the throne, Adonijah approached Bathsheba with a personal request. He opened the conversation by reminding her that the kingdom had been his and that all Israel had expected him to be the next king, but now it was his brother's "from the Lord" (1 Kgs 2:15).The reminder called into question Solomon's kingship and implied that granting his request would be recompense for the kingdom he lost. Recognizing Bathsheba's maternal influence over the king, Adonijah enlisted her as an intermediary to approach Solomon with his petition. He calculated that Solomon would not deny his mother's request, and through her, Adonijah asked that Abishag be given to him as a wife.

Much more is at stake in Adonijah's request for Abishag than is readily apparent to modern readers. By asking Abishag to be his wife, Adonijah was staking another claim to David's throne, just as Absalom had done when he had sex with David's concubines during his revolt (2 Sam 16:20–21). Adonijah thought Bathsheba would make the offensive request more palatable to Solomon and that the king would be unable to disappoint his mother. In a very real sense, Adonijah wanted Bathsheba to betray her son and help him to obtain the throne he believed belonged to him, but his scheme backfired.

Since Adonijah's request was an indirect claim to Solomon's throne, Keil questions whether Bathsheba understood its meaning. In his commentary on 2 Kings, Keil writes that "Bathsheba did not detect" the malice in Adonijah's words.[11] Bathsheba knew that Adonijah threatened Solomon's kingship, and she had to act to save her son.

Bathsheba took Adonijah's request to Solomon, but the request gave the king an opportunity to eliminate his rival to the throne. Solomon—seeing through Adonijah's deception—responded to his mother, "And why do you ask Abishag the Shunammite for Adonijah? Ask for him the kingdom as well! For he is my elder brother; ask not only for him but also for the priest Abiathar and for Joab son of Zeruiah!" (1 Kgs 2:22). Solomon then took an oath to kill Adonijah: "So may God do to me, and more also, for Adonijah has devised this scheme at the risk of his life." Then Solomon sent Benaiah, the commander of his army, to kill Adonijah (1 Kgs 2:23–25).

Solomon's action may seem to contradict his portrayal as a wise and merciful king, but Adonijah's threat to the throne justified Solomon's action. Further, Bathsheba's role in preserving her son's throne demonstrates that she was a wise and skilled strategist who did what was necessary to preserve her son's life and throne. Although she had to marry the man who murdered her husband, although she had to grieve the loss of a child, and although she lived as one of many wives put aside in her old age for a younger woman, Bathsheba persevered and overcame these tragedies to achieve a position in life that enabled her to wield power and help her son.

---

1. C. F. Keil, *The Book of Kings*, Biblical Commentary on the Old Testament (Grand Rapids: Eerdmans, 1950), 31.

CHAPTER 22

Solomon and the Two Mothers

After Solomon became king of Israel, the Lord appeared to him in a dream and said, "Ask what I should give you" (1 Kgs 3:5). In response to God's offer, Solomon asked God for "an understanding mind to govern your people" (1 Kgs 3:9). The first recorded ruling he would make demonstrated that God had indeed given him wisdom and discernment. Two mothers appeared before the king.

> Later, two women who were prostitutes came to the king and stood before him. The one woman said, "Please, my lord, this woman and I live in the same house; and I gave birth while she was in the house. Then on the third day after I gave birth, this woman also gave birth. We were together; there was no one else with us in the house, only the two of us were in the house. Then this woman's son died in the night, because she lay on him. She got up in the middle of the night and took my son from beside me while your servant slept. She laid him at her breast, and laid her dead son at my breast. When I rose in the morning to nurse my son, I saw that he was dead; but when I looked at him closely in the morning, clearly it was not the son I had borne." But the other woman said, "No, the living son is mine, and the dead son is yours." The first said, "No, the dead son is yours, and the living son is mine." So they argued before the king.
>
> Then the king said, "The one says, 'This is my son that is alive, and your son is dead'; while the other says, 'Not so! Your son is dead, and my son is the living one.'" So the king said, "Bring me a sword," and they brought a sword before

> the king. The king said, "Divide the living boy in two; then give half to the one, and half to the other." But the woman whose son was alive said to the king—because compassion for her son burned within her—"Please, my lord, give her the living boy; certainly do not kill him!" The other said, "It shall be neither mine nor yours; divide it." Then the king responded: "Give the first woman the living boy; do not kill him. She is his mother." All Israel heard of the judgment that the king had rendered; and they stood in awe of the king, because they perceived that the wisdom of God was in him, to execute justice. (1 Kgs 3:16–28)

The story is a legal dispute between two mothers who both claimed to be the mother of the living baby rather than the mother of the baby who had died. The events that led to this legal dispute happened at night while both women slept.

According to the woman telling the story (Woman A), the other woman's (Woman B) baby died at night because she had laid on him. She then took the dead baby and exchanged him for the other baby, the one who was alive. When Woman A woke up to nurse her son, she noticed that the child was dead. When she looked at the dead child, she realized that he was not her son. According to Woman A, the dead baby belonged to Woman B. When Woman B did not return the living child to Woman A, the two women came before Solomon to argue their case before him.

The mothers in the story are said to be "prostitutes," which is borne out by the fact that the women were living alone in the same residence, without a husband, and both were pregnant at the same time.[1] Because of their social status, the women lacked community support and thus appealed directly to the king, who was ultimately responsible for maintaining justice. The story displays the strong love of a mother for her son, a love so strong that the real mother of the child preferred to give her son away rather than see him killed.

Verse 18 stresses that no one could corroborate either woman's story: "We were together; there was no one else with us in the house, only the two of us were in the house." The obvious difficulty with the

---

1. Marvin Sweeney, *I & II Kings*, OTL (Louisville: Westminster John Knox, 2007), 82.

stories is that they were different and contradictory, which posed an urgent problem for Solomon because the living baby was in danger of being placed in the custody of the wrong mother.

A primary duty of the Israelite king was to judge the people fairly. Isaiah said of the ideal king: "He shall not judge by what his eyes see, or decide by what his ears hear; but with righteousness he shall judge the poor, and decide with equity for the meek of the earth" (Isa 11:3–4). Solomon could not decide "by what his ears hear"; he could only rely on the gift God had given him: "a wise and discerning mind" (1 Kgs 3:12).

One critical issue for Solomon was that he was listening to the words of one mother against those of another. The king, in making his decision, repeated the argument made by the two women (1 Kgs 3:23). Then Solomon ordered his servants to cut the child in two and give each woman a half of the child. Solomon's decision obviously placed the life of the child in jeopardy, but the threat to the child's life revealed the identity of the child's actual mother. One of the women, moved by compassion, asked the king not to kill the child but to give him to the other woman. "Please, my lord, give her the living boy; certainly do not kill him!" The woman's love for her son caused her to advocate for the child's life even though he would be raised by the other woman.

The Hebrew word translated "compassion" is *raḥamîm*, "tender mercy," and refers to the deep love of a mother for her child. The intensity of this love is reflected by the connection of this word with the word *rāḥam*, "womb." So deep was the woman's love for her child that some translations say that "compassion for her son burned within her" (NRSV) and "her heart yearned for her son" (ESV). This deep love revealed who the true mother of the child was.

The other woman, the one who was not the child's mother, interrupted the woman's speech by saying that neither of them should have the baby and that the king should cut him in two. The woman's heartless response made Solomon's decision much easier, and Solomon gave the baby to the right mother. But who was the child's mother? Was the real mother Woman A, the first woman who said that the dead baby was not hers, or was she Woman B, the woman who refused to give the living baby to Woman A? As Lasine, notes, "The story also becomes a riddle for the reader, who is challenged to identify the mothers solely on the basis of their quoted words."[2] Ellen van Wolde has taken a similar approach. She writes, "The readers do not yet know whether the first or the second woman is [his] mother, and they will never will."[3]

Some Bible translations inaccurately render the original Hebrew in identifying the rightful mother of the living child. For example, the NRSV states, "Then the king responded: 'Give the first woman the living boy; do not kill him. She is his mother'" (1 Kings 3:27), Similarly, the ESV, NIV, and several other versions use the phrase "first woman." However, this wording does not appear in the original Hebrew, which simply says "give to her" (Hebrew: *tenû-lâ*). Translations such as the KJV maintain closer fidelity to the source text: "Then the king answered and said, 'Give her the living child, and in no wise slay it: she is the mother thereof.'" The Jewish Publication Society's version (TNK) aligns with this reading as well: "Then the king spoke up. 'Give the live child to her,' he said, and do not put it to death; she is its mother."

There are a few reasons for not believing the story of Woman A. Mordechai Coogan sums up the matter well: "How could she be believed, when she has slept so soundly through the claimed switch of infants?"[4] Van Wolde makes a similar observation: "The king and the readers learn about this event only through the eyes and the mouth of this woman, and they may ask themselves how it is possible that the one woman is so sure that the other woman lay on her son in the night, while she herself was firmly asleep. So firmly asleep that she did not even perceive that her son was taken from her side."[5]

Hayyim Angel has presented another reason to doubt the story of the first woman. Woman A mentioned the dead child first, while Woman B mentioned the living child first, which what the true mother of the living child would do. Angel concludes, "A mother attempting to demonstrate that her child was alive would mention him first since that is foremost on her mind."[6] Van Wolde argues that "The second

2. S. Lasine, "The Riddle of Solomon's Judgment and the Riddle of Human Nature in the Hebrew Bible," *JSOT* 45 (1989): 61.
3. Ellen van Wolde, "Who Guides Whom? Embeddedness as Perspective in Biblical Hebrew and in 1 Kings 3:16–28," *JBL* 114 (1995): 638.
4. Mordechai Coogan, *I Kings*, AB (New York: Doubleday, 2001), 195.
5. Van Wolde, "Who Guides Whom?," 629–30.
6. Hayyim Angel, "Cut the Baby in Half: Understanding Solomon's Divinely-Inspired Wisdom," JBQ 39 (2011): 191.

woman is considerably briefer than the first; she does not give her view of the events in the form of a story but confines herself to stating that her son is the living one. Because she is so brief, or because the narrator represents her words so briefly, it is not so easy for the readers to sympathize with her. Therefore, most readers are inclined to follow the view of the first woman: readers have been able to share her arguments and her language, and particularly her observation and awareness."[7]

Van Wolde notes that the first woman initially states that only the two women were present in the house (1 Kgs 3:18). She emphasizes that readers never definitively learn which woman, first or second, is the biological mother.[8] According to van Wolde, the true mother eventually stops defending herself against her rival (whom she refers to as "that woman") and instead allows her maternal instinct to prevail, breaking the previously unresolvable deadlock.

The rival woman responds unexpectedly by declaring: "The child shall belong to neither of us; cut it." Van Wolde says this reaction is perplexing since the first woman had just conceded the child to her. Her desire to have the child divided suggests she wants the living child to share the fate of her own deceased infant. Her command to "cut" the child, despite having just been granted custody, reveals she cannot be the true mother.

Van Wolde references George E. Mendenhall's alternative interpretation that the second woman's reaction could also be consistent with maternal love, suggesting that a true mother might prefer to see her child killed rather than surrendered to someone she views as untrustworthy.[9] Thus, van Wolde clearly believes the first woman is the real mother of the child.[10] This is made clear by her statement that the real mother breaks the deadlock by allowing her heart to speak and stopping fighting against "that woman." Van Wolde's presentation consistently aligns the first woman with the child's real mother, even by mentioning Mendenhall's contrary interpretation.

---

7. Van Wolde, "Who Guides Whom?," 630.
8. Van Wolde, "Who Guides Whom?," 638.
9. George E. Mendenhall, "The Shady Side of Wisdom: The Date and Purpose of Genesis 3," in *A Light unto My Path: Old Testament Studies in Honor of Jacob M. Myers*, ed. H. N. Breamet et al. (Philadelphia: Temple University Press, 1974), 324.
10. Van Wolde, "Who Guides Whom?," 639.

When the narrative is divided according to the speakers, one notices that the women alternate their words in presenting their case, making it clear that Woman B is the mother of the living child.[11] In addition to the alternative reading of the speakers, Gary Rendsburg has shown the way the narrator introduces the speech of the two women also provides a clue for their identity. According to Rendsburg, the narrator is consistent in introducing the two women. Woman B is introduced as "this one says" and Women A is introduced as "and this one says." In presenting the words of the women below, I will follow the Hebrew text and introduce the speech of the women as they appear in the Hebrew text.

Narrator: Later, two women who were prostitutes came to the king and stood before him. The one woman said,

Woman A: Please, my lord, this woman and I live in the same house; and I gave birth while she was in the house. Then on the third day after I gave birth, this woman also gave birth. We were together; there was no one else with us in the house, only the two of us were in the house. Then this woman's son died in the night, because she lay on him. She got up in the middle of the night and took my son from beside me while your servant slept. She laid him at her breast and laid her dead son at my breast. When I rose in the morning to nurse my son, I saw that he was dead; but when I looked at him closely in the morning, clearly it was not the son I had borne.

Narrator: But the other woman said,

Woman B: No, the living son is mine, and the dead son is yours.

Narrator: And this one says,

Woman A: No, the dead son is yours, and the living son is mine.

Narrator: So they argued before the king.

11. Gary A. Rendsburg, "The Guilty Party in 1 Kings III 16–28," *VT* 48 (1998): 536–37.

The King: Then the king said,

(*Quoting Woman B*): This one says this is my son that is alive, and your son is dead

The King: and this one says,

(*Quoting Woman A*): Not so! Your son is dead, and my son is the living one.

Narrator: So the king said,

The King: "Bring me a sword," and they brought a sword before the king. The king said, "Divide the living boy in two; then give half to the one, and half to the other."

Narrator: But the woman whose son was alive said to the king—because compassion for her son burned within her—

Woman B: Please, my lord, give her the living boy; certainly, do not kill him!

Narrator: And this one says,

Woman A: It shall be neither mine nor yours; divide it.

The King: Then the king responded: "Give to her the living boy; do not kill him. She is his mother."

The narrative before the king's decision is very revealing. When the narrator said, "And this one says, 'It shall be neither mine nor yours; divide it,'" he was introducing the speech of Woman A, the mother of the dead child. Although a superficial reading of the text may not reveal who the mother of the living child was, a careful analysis of the dialogue and a rhetorical study of the text reveals that the second woman, the one designated Woman B, was the real mother of the living child.

It was the tender love of a mother who allowed the king to decide who the true mother of the infant was. Were it not for her compassionate motherly love, the king would have a difficult time solving this unsolvable situation. Because of the "wise and discerning mind" God gave Solomon, he was able to solve a very difficult issue between two of his subjects. It was the true, compassionate love of a mother, however, who made Solomon's decision much easier saved the child's life.

CHAPTER 23

Jeroboam's Wife: A Mother's Agony

The story of Jeroboam's wife tells the tale of a mother's love for a sick son and the agony of her heart as she contemplated his imminent death. Her story is found in 1 Kings 14:1–18. A detailed analysis of the text helps us understand this mother's agony.

> At that time Abijah, son of Jeroboam, fell sick. Jeroboam said to his wife, "Go, disguise yourself, so that it will not be known that you are the wife of Jeroboam, and go to Shiloh; for the prophet Ahijah is there, who said of me that I should be king over this people. Take with you ten loaves, some cakes, and a jar of honey, and go to him; he will tell you what shall happen to the child."
>
> Jeroboam's wife did so; she set out and went to Shiloh and came to the house of Ahijah. Now Ahijah could not see, for his eyes were dim because of his age. But the Lord said to Ahijah, "The wife of Jeroboam is coming to inquire of you concerning her son; for he is sick. Thus and thus you shall say to her." When she comes, she will pretend to be another woman.
>
> When Ahijah heard the sound of her feet, as she came in at the door, he said, "Come in, wife of Jeroboam; why do you pretend to be another? For I am charged with heavy tidings for you. Go, tell Jeroboam, 'Thus says the Lord, the God of Israel: . . . I will bring evil upon the house of Jeroboam. I will cut off from Jeroboam every male, both bond and free in Israel, and will consume the house of Jeroboam, just as one burns up dung until it is all gone. Anyone belonging to Jeroboam who dies in the city, the dogs shall eat; and anyone who dies in the open country, the birds of the air shall eat; for the Lord has spoken.'

> "Therefore set out, go to your house. When your feet enter the city, the child shall die." . . . Then Jeroboam's wife got up and went away, and she came to Tirzah. As she came to the threshold of the house, the child died. (1 Kgs 14:1–7, 10–12, 17)

This mother's name is never mentioned in the text, and she never says a word throughout the whole ordeal. Jeroboam, Ahijah, and God speak, but the sick child and his mother never say a word. This mother and her sad story go into history in anonymity.

The story begins by recounting that the king's child was very sick and probably approaching death. In desperation, Jeroboam summons his wife and sends her to the prophet Ahijah. The woman, without saying a word, did what her husband told her to do. Given that the woman is nameless and voiceless, Robin G. Branch reads between the lines to argue that Jeroboam's wife was an abused woman.[1] Branch writes, "The wife of Jeroboam and her marriage indicates the classic signs of spousal abuse. Granted, the verses about her reveal no physical beating. But other textual evidence suggests that she is an abused wife and that Jeroboam is the abuser."[2]

Despite Jeroboam's evil, this passage tells the story of parents desperate because their son is dying. They loved their son and were willing to do whatever was necessary to save him—even consulting a prophet of Yahweh whom they believed could heal their son. Ahijah, in fact, was the prophet who announced that Jeroboam would become king of the northern tribes after Solomon's death. Upon becoming king, Jeroboam abandoned the Lord. He built temples at Bethel and Dan and established the worship of the golden calves in these sanctuaries. These pagan practices eventually caused the destruction of the northern kingdom (1 Kgs 12:25–33).

Jeroboam likely sent his wife because he was afraid of what the prophet would say about his apostasy. So he sent his wife disguised as a poor woman with a humble gift to gain a more favorable judgment from the prophet. Ahijah was blind, but the Lord revealed to him that

1. Robin G. Branch, *Jeroboam's Wife: The Enduring Contributions of the Old Testament's Least-Known Women* (Peabody, MA: Hendrickson, 2009).
2. Branch, *Jeroboam's Wife*, 96.

Jeroboam's wife was coming to visit: "When she came, she pretended to be another woman" (1 Kgs 14:5).

When she arrived, Ahijah invited the king's wife in and immediately exposed her ruse: "Come in, wife of Jeroboam. Why do you pretend to be another? For I am charged with heavy tidings for you" (1 Kgs 14:6). Instead of giving good news to the woman about her sick child, Ahijah pronounced a message from God of judgment upon her husband and his kingdom. Although the prophet was kind to the woman, he spoke a harsh truth. Ahijah spoke about what God had done for Jeroboam and how the Lord had promised him that he would reign over the northern tribes after Solomon's death. Because Jeroboam had departed from the Lord by promoting idolatry and pagan practices and leading Israel astray, the Lord was bringing judgment upon him, his house, and his kingdom. In addition, Ahijah delivered sad news about the woman's son. The woman approached Ahijah's house hoping the prophet would offer an encouraging message to heal her child. Instead, Ahijah declared that once she returned to her sick child in Tirzah, he would die.

Jeroboam's wife knew that as soon as she entered the city and reached her doorstep, her son would die. Ahijah's words revealed the imminent heartbreak awaiting this mother, illuminating the anguish that accompanies profound love. Fully aware that her return home would coincide with her son's death, she departed from the prophet's house bearing this devastating burden in her heart.

So she must now decide: "Do I run away from home so that my son may live, or do I go home knowing that each step I take is one more step toward my son's death?" She decided to return home. And although the text is silent, one can imagine the agony in that mother's heart, for each step she took brought her son closer to his tragic demise.

The first step she took to return home marks the beginning of an unimaginable ordeal, each step bringing her closer to her son's death. The agony this mother endured during her journey home transcends comprehension; every step shortened the remaining moments of her son's life. Ahijah had prophesied: "When your feet enter the city, the child shall die." Yet her suffering intensified because her son survived her entry into the city only to die upon her crossing her own threshold. What compelled this mother to return home, knowing her arrival would trigger her son's death? When she arrived home, like Mary in the New Testament (Luke 2:35), a sword pierced her soul: her son died.

The child's death was soon followed by a funeral and a burial. Because Abijah was only a child and had not participated in the sins of his father, he was the only member of the house of Jeroboam to receive a decent burial: "All Israel shall mourn for him and bury him; for he alone of Jeroboam's family shall come to the grave, because in him there is found something pleasing to the LORD, the God of Israel, in the house of Jeroboam" (1 Kgs 14:13).

No words can explain the untimely death of a young child. No one can understand the agony and the grief a mother experiences when she loses the fruit of her womb. Recognizing the brokenness of this mother's heart, the reader can only sympathize with Jeroboam's wife and salute her for her love and dedication to her son.

CHAPTER 24

Jesus's Great-Grandmothers

Genealogies in the Old Testament

The Old Testament contains two types of genealogies: linear and segmented. Linear genealogies present the names of individuals who belong to the same family. They list the name of a father and his son and then continue for successive generations. Matthew's genealogy is linear. Segmented genealogies name many family members within a specific generation. Thus, a segmented genealogy includes not only the name of the father but also the names of sons and daughters, brothers and sisters, as we see in Genesis 10:1–32.

Most genealogies in the Old Testament are patrilineal, tracing descent through the fathers.[1] Matthew's genealogy is patrilineal. Rarely do the writers include the names of females, making it difficult to construct a genealogy that includes mothers and daughters. In his genealogy of Jesus, Matthew makes this task a little easier for two reasons. First, since the book of Genesis presents the story of both the patriarchs and the matriarchs of Israel, we know the names of several of the wives whose husbands are included in Matthew's genealogy. Second, all the names of the mothers of the kings of Judah appear in the book of 1–2 Kings, with the exception of the mothers of Jehoram and Ahaz.

Matthew cites fourteen generations from the exile in Babylon to Joseph, the husband of Mary. The Old Testament does not give the names of the wives of the men listed in Matthew's genealogy who

1. In a few cases, traces of matrilineal genealogies are also found in the Old Testament; see Dorothy J. Gaston, "Matrilineal Background of Genealogies in Genesis," *Semiotics* (1981): 505–19.

lived in the postexilic period. The same problem is found for some of the men listed in Matthew's genealogy who lived between the time of the patriarchs and David. This chapter will begin with the named women in Jesus's genealogy, continuing with the women whose names we know from the Old Testament. We then discuss the women associated with kings omitted from the genealogy for theological reasons and conclude with a reconstructed genealogy of Jesus.

Jesus's Great-Grandmothers

Jesus's genealogy appears in two specific places in the New Testament: Matthew 1:1–17 and Luke 3:23–38. In Matthew, Jesus's genealogy is presented in a descending order from Abraham to Joseph. Luke constructs Jesus's genealogy in ascending order from Joseph to Adam. Both genealogies are given to emphasize that Jesus is the fulfillment of God's purpose of redemption, that Jesus is the Messiah descended from David and Abraham. This means that the focus of the genealogies is theological.

As a descendant of Abraham, Jesus fulfills God's covenantal promise to Abraham that he would be a blessing to the nations: "in you all the families of the earth shall be blessed" (Gen 12:3). As a descendant of David, Jesus fulfills God's covenantal promise to David that his throne would be established forever (2 Sam 7:16), with a Davidic king always sitting on Israel's throne (1 Kgs 2:4).

Matthew's genealogy makes reference to four women in Jesus's family tree: Tamar, Rahab, Ruth, and Bathsheba.[2] Bathsheba's name is only identified as Uriah's wife. Matthew also mentions a fifth woman, Mary, the mother of Jesus, who falls outside the purview of this chapter, which will explore the role of Jesus's great-grandmothers.

The Named Women in Matthew's Genealogy

Tamar

The first woman listed in Matthew's genealogy is Tamar: "Judah [was] the father of Perez and Zerah by Tamar" (Matt 1:3). We read Tamar's story—a story of love, betrayal, and righteousness—in Genesis 38.

2. Irene Nowell, "Jesus' Great-Grandmothers: Matthew's Four and More," *CBQ* 70 (2008): 1–15.

Judah had married a Canaanite woman and had three sons by her: Er, Onan, and Shelah. Tamar was the wife of Er, Judah's oldest son. Though the text does not specify whether Tamar was Hebrew or Canaanite, the context makes clear that she was Canaanite.

The Bible tells us that "Er, Judah's firstborn, was wicked in the sight of the LORD, and the LORD put him to death" (Gen 38:7). Judah then told Onan, his second-born son, to take Tamar and perform the duty of a levirate, in which a brother of a deceased man marries his brother's widow to raise up an offspring for the deceased brother. Onan, however, did not want to give Tamar a son. So whenever he had sexual relations with Tamar, he would spill his semen on the ground.[3] His action "was displeasing in the sight of the LORD, and he put him to death also" (Gen 38:10). Judah then told Tamar to remain a widow until Shelah, his youngest son, grew up. Judah, however, never intended to give Shelah to Tamar for fear that Shelah would also die.

Since Judah refused to fulfill his promise, Tamar disguised herself as a prostitute, came to the road leading to the city of Enaim, and sat at the entrance of the city. When Judah came, he solicited her for sex. Tamar became pregnant, and when Judah threatened to kill her, Tamar revealed that Judah had impregnated her. Judah acknowledged that he was the father and said, "She is more in the right than I, since I did not give her to my son Shelah" (Gen 38:26). Tamar became the mother of twin sons: Perez and Zerah.

Rahab

The second woman listed in Matthew's genealogy is Rahab: "Salmon [was] the father of Boaz by Rahab" (Matt 1:5). Rahab was a Canaanite woman who lived in Jericho; her story appears in Joshua 2. She was the prostitute who protected the two spies who secretly entered Jericho on the eve of Israel's conquest of Canaan. When the king of Jericho heard that the spies had come to her house, the king ordered Rahab to surrender the men to him.

However, Rahab had heard that Yahweh had delivered Israel from their oppression in Egypt and was planning to give them the land. Rahab declared her allegiance to Yahweh and promised to protect the two men if they promised to spare her and her family when they conquered the city.

3. Claude F. Mariottini, "Onan (Person)," *ABD* 5:21.

When Israel entered the land and conquered Jericho, Joshua and the army of Israel spared Rahab, her family, and all that belonged to her. Rahab later married Salmon, a Judahite, and she became the mother of Boaz.

Ruth

Ruth is the third woman listed in Matthew's genealogy: "Boaz [was] the father of Obed by Ruth" (Matt 1:5). Ruth was one of the hated Moabites; they were forbidden to enter "the assembly of the Lord" to the tenth generation (Deut 23:3). The story of Ruth occurred in the days of the judges. Because of a great famine in Israel, an Ephrathite man from Bethlehem named Elimelech and his wife Naomi left their land and went to find a better life in Moab. This couple had two sons, Mahlon and Chilion, who married Moabite women. Mahlon's wife was Ruth and Chilion's wife was named Orpah.

Eventually Elimelech and his two sons died in Moab, leaving Naomi widowed and childless. When she decided to return to Bethlehem, Ruth went with her. Upon their return, Ruth began gleaning in the fields of Boaz, a respected landowner and relative of Naomi's late husband. When Naomi realized Ruth was working in Boaz's fields, she set Ruth up to request Boaz's legal and ethical provision through marriage. He proved to be a righteous man. After Boaz exercised his right of redemption, they married, and in time Ruth gave birth to Obed, bringing great joy to Naomi in her old age.

The book of Ruth ends with the genealogy of David: "Now these are the descendants of Perez: Perez became the father of Hezron, Hezron of Ram, Ram of Amminadab, Amminadab of Nahshon, Nahshon of Salmon, Salmon of Boaz, Boaz of Obed, Obed of Jesse, and Jesse of David" (Ruth 4:18–22). Ruth's marriage to Boaz established her as King David's great-grandmother. According to this passage, Jesus is part Judean, part Canaanite, and part Moabite.[4]

Bathsheba

The fourth woman listed in Matthew's genealogy is Bathsheba: "David was the father of Solomon by [Bathsheba] the wife of Uriah" (Matt 1:6). Although Bathsheba appears in Matthew's genealogy as "the wife

4. Mark McEntire and Wongi Park, "Ethnic Fission and Fusion in Biblical Genealogies," *JBL* 140 (2021): 41.

of Uriah," she plays a significant role in David's life and in the genealogy of Jesus. Her story appears in 2 Samuel 11–12.

Bathsheba was married to Uriah, one of David's mighty warriors. While Uriah and the army of Israel were fighting a war against the Ammonites, David remained in Jerusalem. When David saw Bathsheba bathing, he lusted after her because she was "very beautiful" (2 Sam 11:2). David then took Bathsheba, and she became pregnant. When David heard that Bathsheba was with child, he devised a plan to convince Uriah to come home and sleep with his wife so that the pregnancy could be attributed to Uriah. When the plan failed, David schemed to put Uriah in the forefront of the battle so that he would die at the hands of the Ammonites.

After Uriah's death, David married Bathsheba, and she gave birth to their child, who died soon thereafter. David and Bathsheba had another child, Solomon, who reigned over Israel after David's death. After that, every king of Judah was also a descendant of Bathsheba.

Many have asked why Matthew included these four women in the genealogy of Jesus. One traditional answer is that these four women were sinners.[5] Jesus was born to save sinners, and the four women prove this truth. Another answer is that these four women serve as a contrast to Mary, who was "a paragon of virtue."[6] This view attempts to affirm that Mary was a virgin when Jesus was conceived and to address the view that Jesus was an illegitimate child. Finally, some argue that these women were included in Jesus's genealogy because they were Gentile women, thus emphasizing that Jesus came to save Jews and Gentiles.[7]

It is interesting that Matthew did not include the well-known matriarchs Sarah, Rebekah, Leah, and Rachel. Rather, he chose to highlight other great-grandmothers who carried on the covenant line during times of crisis so that God's chosen family, and the lineage of Christ, would continue. Jesus is the son of Abraham because Tamar kept Judah's line alive. Rahab and Ruth were grafted into the people of Israel, pointing to the universality of Jesus's kingdom. Jesus is the son of David through the woman David sinned against—what grace for her and other marginalized women. In including these particular women in

5. A. T. Hanson, "Rahab the Harlot in Early Christian Tradition," *JSNT* 1 (1978): 53–60.
6. Edwin D. Freed, "The Women in Matthew's Genealogy," *JSNT* 29 (1987): 6.
7. John C. Hutchison, "Women, Gentiles, and the Messianic Mission in Matthew's Genealogy," *BSac* 158 (2001): 152–64.

his genealogy, Matthew offered hints about both Jesus's rightful heritage and the nature of the kingdom he was bringing.

The Unnamed Women in Matthew's Genealogy

Matthew omitted the rest of the mothers who correspond to the fathers mentioned in the genealogy. But we know most of their names from the Old Testament record. The names of all mothers of the kings of Judah are named in the book of Kings except for the mothers of Jehoram (2 Kgs 8:16) the son of Jehoshaphat (Matt 1:8), and Ahaz (2 Kgs 16:1) the son of Jotham (Matt 1:9). Since the names of these two mothers are unknown, we will not include them in this modified list of Jesus's great-grandmothers.

Matthew includes a break in his listing of the kings of Judah. Matthew lists Jehoshaphat as the father of Joram (also known as Jehoram) and Joram as the father of Uzziah (Matt 1:8). Matthew omits the names of Ahaziah, Jehoash, and Amaziah, whom we will explore in the next section. Matthew lists Joram as the father of Uzziah, but in 2 Kings 15:1–2 the author lists Amaziah, whose wife was Jecoliah, as the father of Uzziah. These are some of the other great-grandmothers of Jesus that Matthew omitted in his genealogy of Jesus:

Sarah

"Abraham was the father of Isaac" (Matt 1:2). Sarah was Abraham's wife and Isaac's mother. Because Sarah was barren and unable to conceive a child, she gave Hagar to Abraham as a wife. The child born of this union, Ishmael, is not included in Matthew's genealogy because the child who would carry God's promise to Abraham's would be Isaac and not Ishmael.

Rebekah

"Isaac [was] the father of Jacob" (Matt 1:2). Rebekah was the daughter of Bethuel and sister of Laban. She was chosen to be Isaac's wife because she was a relative of Abraham. Rebekah was the mother of Jacob and Esau.

Leah

"Jacob [was] the father of Judah" (Matt 1:2). Leah was the elder daughter of Laban. Jacob was in love with Rachel, Leah's sister, and worked seven years for Rachel. On Jacob's wedding night, however, Laban gave Leah to him instead of Rachel. In addition to Judah, Leah's fourth son, she also bore Reuben, Simeon, Levi, Issachar, Zebulun, and Dinah, Leah's only daughter.

Naamah

"Solomon [was] the father of Rehoboam" (Matt 1:7). The mother of Rehoboam was Naamah, an Ammonite woman who married Solomon (1 Kgs 14:21). The Ammonites appear in Scripture as an enemy of Israel, and they were forbidden to enter "the assembly of the LORD" to the tenth generation (Deut 23:3). Solomon married Naamah to establish a treaty between the Israelites and the Ammonites.

Maacah

"Rehoboam [was] the father of Abijah" (Matt 1:7). Maacah was the favorite wife of Rehoboam. In 1 Kings 15:2 Maacah is listed as the mother of Abijah and the daughter of Abishalom, a man who is generally identified with Absalom, David's son.[8] Maacah is also called the mother of Asa, king of Judah (1 Kgs 15:10) whom Matthew calls Asaph (Matt 1:7). 1 Kings 15:10 also says, however, that Maacah was the daughter of Abishalom. This suggests that Maacah was Asa's grandmother, a view adopted by the NIV and the CSB.

Maacah is one of four women in the Old Testament who is called a *gebîrâ*, the official title of the queen mother.[9] Asa deposed his grandmother Maacah from her position as *gebîrâ* because she was a worshiper of Asherah, the Canaanite fertility goddess (1 Kgs 15:13).

Azubah

"Asaph [Asa was] the father of Jehoshaphat" (Matt 1:8). Azubah, the daughter of Shilhi, was the wife of Asa and the mother of Jehoshaphat (1 Kgs 22:42). Nothing is known about Azubah.

Jecoliah

[Amaziah was] the father of Uzziah (Matt 1:8). Jecoliah, a woman from Jerusalem (2 Kgs 15:2), was the wife of King Amaziah and the mother of Uzziah. Nothing is known about Jecoliah.

---

8. David M. Howard Jr., "Absalom (Person)," *ABD* 1:46.
9. Two of the other three women who are called a *gebîrâ* in the Hebrew Bible are Jezebel, the mother of Queen Athaliah (2 Kgs 10:13), and Nehushta, the mother of King Jehoiachin (Jer 29:2).

Jerusha

"Uzziah [was] the father of Jotham" (Matt 1:9). Jerusha, the daughter of Zadok, was the wife of Uzziah and the mother of King Jotham (2 Kgs 15:33). Nothing is known about Jerusha, though it is possible that Jerusha's father belonged to a priestly family and was a descendant of the high priest Zadok who served under David (2 Sam 8:17).

Abi

"Ahaz [was] the father of Hezekiah" (Matt 1:9). Abi, the daughter of Zechariah, was the wife of King Ahaz and the mother of Hezekiah. Her name is a shortened form of the name Abijah (2 Chr 29:1). Her place of origin is unknown.

Hephzibah

"Hezekiah [was] the father of Manasseh" (Matt 1:10). Hephzibah was the wife of King Hezekiah and the mother of King Manasseh (2 Kgs 21:1). Nothing is known about Hephzibah; she is the only queen mother whose father's and mother's names are omitted.

Meshullemeth

"Manasseh [was] the father of Amos [Amon]" (Matt 1:10). Meshullemeth, the daughter of Haruz of Jotbah, was the wife of Manasseh and the mother of Amon (2 Kgs 21:19). Nothing else is known about Meshullemeth.

Jedidah

"Amos [Amon was] the father of Josiah" (Matt 1:10). Jedidah, daughter of Adaiah of Bozkath, was the wife of Amon and the mother of Josiah (2 Kgs 22:1). The place of her birth, Bozkath, was located near Lachish and Eglon in the Shephelah of Judah (Josh 15:39).

Nehushta

"Josiah [was] the father of Jechoniah" (Matt 1:11). Nehushta, the daughter of Elnathan of Jerusalem, was the wife of Josiah and mother of Jechoniah (2 Kgs 24:8). Nehushta's name was related to Nehushtan, the bronze serpent destroyed by King Hezekiah (2 Kgs 18:4). Jechoniah is also known by his throne name Jehoiachin, the king of Judah who was deported to Babylon in 597 BC (2 Kgs 24:8). All that is known about Elnathan, Nehushta's father, is that he lived in Jerusalem. It is possible that Elnathan was an officer in King Jehoiakim's court. Jehoiakim was Jehoiachin's father (2 Kgs 24:6). According to 2 Kings 24:12 and 24:15, Nehushta was taken into exile together with her son Jehoiachin.

Matthew deliberately excluded these great-grandmothers from Jesus's genealogy because, unlike Tamar, Rahab, Ruth, and Bathsheba, they did not advance the distinctive theological narrative Matthew sought to construct through his selective genealogical account. Though their names have been forgotten and remain unmentioned by Matthew, however, they all belong to the family tree of Jesus. There are four other great-grandmothers of Jesus who were not mentioned in this list. One of them is the woman most Christians consider to be one of the most evil women of the Bible. Her name is Jezebel, the evil queen who was the wife of Ahab.

The Deliberately Unnamed Women in Matthew's Genealogy

Fourteen Generations

Matthew's genealogy concludes with the following statement: "So all the generations from Abraham to David are fourteen generations; and from David to the deportation to Babylon, fourteen generations; and from the deportation to Babylon to the Messiah, fourteen generations" (Matt 1:17). Matthew may have divided his genealogy this way to represent the 490 years of Israelite history or perhaps because the fourteen generations from Abraham to David provided symmetry that Matthew continued into the other two sections of the genealogy.[10]

The three sections in Matthew's genealogy are as follows:

> Section 1. Fourteen generations from Abraham to David: Abraham, Isaac, Jacob, Judah, Perez, Hezron, Ram (listed as Aram), Aminadab, Nahshon, Salmon, Boaz, Obed, Jesse, and David.
>
> Section 2. Fourteen Generations from David to the exile of Judah: Solomon, Rehoboam, Abijah, Asa (listed as Asaph),

10. George F. Moore, "Fourteen Generations: 490 Years: An Explanation of the Genealogy of Jesus," *HTR* 14 (1921): 97–103.

Jehoshaphat, Joram (also known as Jehoram), Uzziah, Jotham, Ahaz, Hezekiah, Manasseh, Amon (listed as Amos), Josiah, Jechoniah (also known as Jehoiachin).

Section 3. Fourteen generations from the exile to Jesus: Shealtiel (listed as Salathiel), Zerubbabel, Abiud, Eliakim, Azor, Zadok, Achim, Eliud, Eleazar, Matthan, Jacob, Joseph, and Jesus. Although Matthew mentions fourteen generations, only thirteen names are listed in section 3.

Matthew listed many important people in Jesus's genealogy, but his list is incomplete. For example, in section 2 Matthew writes that Asa was the father of Jehoshaphat, and Jehoshaphat was the father of Joram, and Joram was the father of Uzziah (Matt 1:8). 1 Chronicles, however records these names differently: "The descendants of Solomon: Rehoboam, Abijah his son, Asa his son, Jehoshaphat his son, Joram his son, Ahaziah his son, Joash his son, Amaziah his son, Azariah his son, Jotham his son" (1 Chr 3:10–12). Thus, Matthew omitted three names: Ahaziah, Joash, and Amaziah, all of them were kings of Judah and descendants of David. We will return to these kings in the next section. Matthew also omits the names of Jehoahaz, Jehoiakim, and Zedekiah, but he indirectly refers to them by mentioning "Jeconiah and his brothers" (Matt 1:11).

Something similar occurs in the third section of Matthew's genealogy. Matthew says that Jeconiah (Jehoiachin) was deported to Babylon and that after the deportation there are fourteen generations until Jesus. If, however, one counts Salathiel as the first generation after the deportation to Joseph, the adoptive father of Jesus, there are only twelve names. Jesus would be the thirteenth generation.[11]

The Purpose of Matthew's Genealogy

The purpose of Matthew's genealogy is theological; that is, it was designed to convey a message to its readers. It offers a theological interpretation of Israel's history from Abraham to Christ. It demon-

11. Luke's genealogy of Jesus lists eighteen names from Zerubbabel to Joseph (Luke 3:23–27). There are several ways of understanding why Matthew only lists eleven names in his recounting of the same group of names. The simplest response is that "father of" can refer either to one's immediate biological father or to one's ancestor.

strates that when the history of Israel is read in light of God's promises, the meaning of this history is Jesus, the son of David. Another theological purpose of Matthew's genealogy is to legitimize Jesus as a son of Abraham and a son of David. Through Abraham, Jesus was an heir of the promise that in Abraham "all the families of the earth shall be blessed" (Gen 12:3). As a legitimate descendent of David, Jesus was an heir to the royal throne of Israel and to God's promise that David's throne would be established forever (2 Sam 7:16).

Jesus was the fulfillment of the messianic expectations of Israel and God's promise through the prophet Ezekiel: "I will set up over them one shepherd, my servant David, and he shall feed them: he shall feed them and be their shepherd. And I, the LORD, will be their God, and my servant David shall be prince among them" (Ezek 34:23–24).

Matthew's genealogy excludes three Judean kings—Ahaziah, Joash, and Amaziah—whose place in the genealogy should appear between Jehoshaphat and Uzziah. The most probable reason these three kings were omitted is their association with Ahab, king of the northern kingdom, and their relationship with Jezebel, Ahab's wife. Jezebel promoted the worship of Baal and Asherah and persecuted and killed the prophets of Yahweh. Because of her evil acts, Elijah placed a curse on the house of Ahab: "I will bring disaster on you; I will consume you, and will cut off from Ahab every male, bond or free, in Israel" (1 Kgs 21:21).

Athaliah

"Jehoshaphat [was] the father of Joram" (Matt 1:8). Although 1 Kings 22:42 tells us that Azubah was the mother of Jehoshaphat, it does not name Jehoshaphat's wife. Jehoshaphat was the father of Joram, also known as Jehoram. Jehoshaphat made a military alliance with Ahab to fight against the Arameans. This alliance was sealed with the marriage between Joram, Jehoshaphat's son, and Athaliah, the daughter of Ahab and Jezebel (2 Kgs 8:18; 2 Chr 21:6). Joram and Athaliah had a son whose name was Ahaziah.

There is a scholarly debate on whether Jezebel was Athaliah's mother. 2 Kings 8:18 and 2 Chronicles 21:6 say that Athaliah was the daughter of Ahaz, while 2 Kings 8:26 and 2 Chronicles 22:2 say that Athaliah was the daughter of Omri. Because of the seemingly conflicting statements, some scholars believe that Athaliah was the daughter of Omri who was raised by Ahab or that she was the daughter of Ahab by a different wife. Irene Nowell argues that Athaliah was the biological daughter of Jezebel and Ahab (2 Kgs 8:18) and that "daughter of Omri" in 2 Kings 8:26 signifies that she belonged to the house of Omri.[12] Rabbinic tradition affirms that Athaliah was the daughter of Ahab and Jezebel.[13]

Jezebel

Since Athaliah was the wife of the king of Judah and mother of a king of Judah (Ahaziah), Jezebel can also claim the title of great-grandmother of Jesus.[14] Jezebel enters Jesus's family line because of her direct relationship with Athaliah. Jezebel was the grandmother of Ahaziah, Athaliah's son.

Zibiah

"Joram was the father of Ahaziah" (1 Chr 3:11). Ahaziah's wife was Zibiah, a woman from Beer-sheba. Ahaziah was killed by Jehu, but Zibiah's son Joash did not become king of Judah after the death of his father because Athaliah tried to kill Joash.

Jehoaddin

"Ahaziah was the father of Joash" (1 Chr 3:11). After Athaliah took the throne of Judah by force, she killed all the members of the royal family. One member of the royal family, however survived: "Jehosheba, King Joram's daughter, Ahaziah's sister, took Joash, son of Ahaziah, and stole him away from among the king's children who were about to be killed; she put him and his nurse in a bedroom. Thus she hid him from Athaliah, so that he was not killed" (2 Kgs 11:2).

When Joash came of age, he married Jehoaddin of Jerusalem (2 Kgs 14:2; "Jehoaddah" in 2 Chr 25:1). Jehoaddin's son was Amaziah. Nothing is known about Jehoaddin, but with the marriage of Amaziah to Jecoliah (see above), the story of David's family continues with Uzziah (Azariah).

---

12. Irene Nowell, "Jesus' Great-Grandmothers," *CBQ* 70 (2008): 8. See also Claudia V. Camp, "1 and 2 Kings," in *Women's Bible Commentary*, ed. Carol Ann Newsom and Sharon H. Ringe (Louisville: Westminster John Knox, 1992), 104.
13. For discussion, see Reuven C. Klein, "Queen Athaliah: The Daughter of Ahab or Omri?," *JBQ* 42 (2014): 11–20; and H. Jacob Katzenstein, "Who Were the Parents of Athaliah?," *IEJ* 5 (1955): 194–97.
14. Nowell, "Jesus's Great-Grandmothers," 9.

The Reconstructed Genealogy of Jesus According to His Great-Grandmothers

The family tree of Jesus contains many known and unknown people. All of them have something to contribute to the bloodline of the son of Mary. The women Matthew mentioned in his genealogies and the ones he failed to mention reveal the inclusive nature of God's plan for humanity. The indirect inclusion of Athaliah, whom the Chronicler calls "that wicked woman" (2 Chr 24:7), and Jezebel, whom Jehu called a whore and a witch (2 Kgs 9:22), also reveals that Jesus is the Messiah for all people. To reconstruct the genealogy of Jesus according to his great-grandmothers, I use Matthew's genealogy as the foundation for the present reconstruction.

It will be impossible to recover the names of the unknown women who were the wives of some of the men mentioned in Matthew's genealogy. Thus, to build a genealogy according to the women in Jesus's family tree, I have chosen to list these unknown women as the wife of whoever the man was. This way, the present genealogy is based entirely on Jesus's known and unknown great-grandmothers.

1. An account of the genealogy of Jesus the Messiah, the grandson of Bathsheba, the grandson of Sarah.
2. Sarah was the mother of Isaac, and Rebekah was the mother of Jacob, and Leah was the mother of Judah and his brothers,
3. and Tamar was the mother of Perez and Zerah, the wife of Perez was the mother of Hezron, and the wife of Hezron was the mother of Aram,
4. and wife of Aram was the mother of Aminadab, and the wife of Aminadab was the mother of Nahshon, and the wife of Nahshon was the mother of Salmon,
5. and Rahab was the mother of Boaz, and Ruth was the mother of Obed, the wife of Obed was the mother of Jesse,
6. and the wife of Jesse was the mother of King David. Bathsheba was the mother of Solomon,
7. and Naamah was the mother of Rehoboam, and Maacah was the mother of Abijah, and Maacah was also the grandmother of Asaph [Asa],
8. and Azubah was the mother of Jehoshaphat, and the wife Jehoshaphat the mother of Joram [Jehoram],

[and Athaliah, the daughter of Jezebel was the mother of Ahaziah, Zibiah was the mother of Joash, Jehoaddin was the mother of Amaziah, Jecoliah was the mother of Uzziah],

9. Jerusha was the mother of Jotham, the wife of Jotham was the mother of Ahaz, Abi was the mother of Hezekiah,
10. Hephzibah was the mother of Manasseh, Meshullemeth was the mother of Amos [Amon], Jedidah was the mother of Josiah, [Zebidiah was the mother of Jehoiakim], Nehushta was the mother of Jechoniah [Jehoiachin] and his brothers, at the time of the deportation to Babylon.
11. And after the deportation to Babylon: the wife of Jechoniah was the mother of Salathiel, and the wife of Salathiel was the mother of Zerubbabel,
12. and the wife of Zerubbabel was the mother of Abiud, and the wife of Abiud was the mother of Eliakim, and the wife of Eliakim was the mother of Azor,
13. and the wife of Azor was the mother of Zadok, and the wife of Zadok was the mother of Achim, and the wife of Achim was the mother of Eliud,
14. and the wife of Eliud was the mother of Eleazar, and the wife of Eleazar was the mother of Matthan, and the wife of Matthan was the mother of Jacob,
15. and the wife of Jacob was the mother of Joseph, and Mary was the mother of Jesus.
16. So all the generations from Sarah to Bathsheba are fourteen generations; and from Bathsheba to Nehushta, fourteen generations; and from the wife of Jechoniah to Mary, the mother of the Messiah, fourteen generations.

PART 4

ABUSED WOMEN

CHAPTER 25

Dinah, the Daughter of Jacob

The story of Dinah (Gen 34:1–31) is a tale of love and rape, honor killing and violence, intermarriage and family dynamics. It is the story of a young woman who was raped and was subsequently denied a voice in determining her future relations with her assailant.

Dinah Leaves Her Family

Dinah was Jacob's only daughter. She was born to Leah, his first wife. The Old Testament mentions her three times: her birth (Gen 30:21), her rape (Gen 34:1–31), and in the genealogy of Jacob (Gen 46:15).

After Jacob returned from Paddan-aram, he came to the city of Shechem and bought a plot of land from Hamor (Gen 33:18–19). While Jacob was living in Shechem with his family, Dinah went to visit the women who lived in the city of Shechem (Gen 34:1). Why Dinah left the family encampment is unknown.

Shechem and Dinah

While Dinah was out, Shechem, the son of the ruler of the city, saw Dinah and "seized her and lay with her by force" (Gen 34:2). The text clearly says that Shechem took Dinah and had sex with her by force. Although biblical Hebrew has no word for rape, the text uses three words that indicate that Shechem's violation of Dinah, by modern definition, was rape.

First, Shechem "seized her." The Hebrew word *lāqah* means "to take, to capture." The word carries the idea of taking by force. The second word is *šākab*, which means "to lie down." When the word is used in the context of a man lying down with a woman, it carries the idea of copulation. The third word is *ʿānâ*. This Hebrew word carries various meanings: "to afflict," or "to humble." English translations use different words to express what Shechem did to Dinah: "defiled her" (KJV), "humbled her" (RSV), and "raped her" (NIV, CSB).

Some scholars, such Lyn Bechtel, argue that Dinah was not raped. Bechtel believes that the act of "humiliation" came after the act of copulation and related to Dinah's no longer being a virgin. In addition, Bechtel points out that there is no evidence that Dinah called for help as she was being raped (Deut 22:24). Since there was no cry for help, Bechtel argues, Dinah did not resist the advances of Shechem.[1] Despite this questionable interpretation, the word *ʿānâ* clearly indicates that Dinah was raped, as many translations recognize.

The rape of Dinah was an act of defilement to Jacob and his family. Defilement is the act of making something unclean, the violation of something considered sacred. The word "defile" appears three times in the story of Dinah. The first time is when Jacob heard what Shechem had done to his daughter: "Jacob heard that Shechem had *defiled* his daughter Dinah" (Gen 34:5, emphasis added). Second, Dinah's brothers spoke deceitfully to Shechem and his father: "The sons of Jacob answered Shechem and his father Hamor deceitfully, because he had *defiled* their sister Dinah" (Gen 34:13, emphasis added). Third, we hear the word describing how the brothers justified their massacre of the Shechemites: "The other sons of Jacob came upon the slain, and plundered the city, because their sister had been *defiled*" (Gen 34:27, emphasis added).

After Shechem raped Dinah, "he fell in love with her, and he tried to win her affection with tender words" (Gen 34:3 NLT). Shechem was attracted to Dinah; he wanted to marry her. The rapist becomes a suitor due to the transforming power of love. Because of his love for Dinah—twisted though it was—Shechem said to his father, Hamor, "Get me this girl for my wife" (Gen 34:4). Hamor recognized that the marriage of his son to Jacob's daughter was a great business opportunity because Dinah belonged to an Israelite family that owned much of the surrounding land.

1. Lyn Bechtel, "What if Dinah Is Not Raped?" *JSOT* 62 (1994): 27.

Honor Killing

Dinah's brothers Simeon and Levi were outraged at what Shechem had done to their sister (Gen 34:7). When Shechem came to Jacob to ask permission to marry Dinah, Jacob was speechless. His sons spoke for him and agreed with the proposal: "The sons of Jacob answered Shechem and his father Hamor deceitfully, because he had defiled their sister Dinah" (Gen 34:13). They laid down one condition for the marriage: the men of Shechem must be circumcised.

The men of Shechem agreed, but three days after they were circumcised, the sons of Jacob descended on them and killed all the men. To avenge the dishonor Shechem had brought to their family, Jacob's sons stripped the dead bodies and ransacked the city. Jacob's sons seized the flocks, herds, donkeys, and everything within the city and in the fields, including their children, their wives, and everything in the houses of the Shechemites (Gen 34:27–29).

Neither Jacob nor his sons questioned the killing of the men of Shechem, nor the plunder of the city, nor the violation of the Shechemite women as a proper compensation for the violation of Dinah. But, what about Dinah? How about her feelings? Did her brothers ask her if she wanted to marry Shechem? They simply "took Dinah out of Shechem's house, and went away" (Gen 34:26).

In his book *Reclaiming Her Story: The Witness of Women in the Old Testament*, Jon Berquist writes about Dinah as a victim of rape:

> As a rape victim, she became damaged property. She could have married her rapist, Shechem, but now her only possible mate was dead at the hands of her ever-loving brothers (cf. Deut 22:25–29). They consigned her to a life of solitude. Throughout all of the brothers' actions, they never asked her about what she wanted, and they never thought about how to help her. Instead, they only considered what would help their finances and their reputation.
>
> Violence begat violence, and many people died, but Dinah's own problems as a victim were ignored. Because she was property to be bought and sold, she never spoke and never acted throughout the story, even though the tale began when she journeyed to speak with other women. She began an innocent person with vivacious curiosity and hopes for a magnificent

> future, but she ended the story thoroughly crushed with no hopes at all, even though her brothers had made themselves rich through the situation.[2]

That is the tragedy of honor killing: the women remain silent throughout the process. Their fate is not the concern of the men in their lives, and the men protect their own honor by condemning the women into oblivion.

Violence Against Women

The story of Dinah and Shechem raises several issues that deserve consideration. Most significantly, it portrays an act of violence against a woman. Shechem "committed an outrage in Israel by lying with Jacob's daughter, for such a thing ought not to be done" (Gen 34:7). The Hebrew word *nebālâ* ("outrage") describes a vile act against an individual, including rape (e.g., 2 Sam 13:12). Simeon and Levi aim to vindicate their sister's honor: "Should our sister be treated like a whore?" (Gen 34:31). Ronald Clark argues that the murder of Shechem was an act of "social justice."[3]

Another issue in the story is Jacob's silence. According to Clark, "Jacob was silent and failed to act on behalf of Dinah, his violated daughter. . . . Dinah was called the daughter of Leah (34:1). Since Jacob loved Rachel more than Leah, is it possible that Jacob's failure to act was due to his dislike for Dinah? Is it possible that Jacob felt a prejudice against Dinah due to her mother or her 'improper actions?' "[4]

During this critical trauma in his daughter's life, Jacob's response was passive and inadequate, failing to provide the protection and support his daughter deserved. Rather than immediately taking action to help Dinah, a more caring and protective father would be concerned with his daughter's well-being and wishes rather than allowing her to become a pawn in negotiations. His silence regarding her rape suggests failure to fulfill his protective role as a father. Furthermore, Jacob's silence during this crisis allowed his sons to take extreme,

---

2. Jon Berquist, *Reclaiming Her Story: The Witness of Women in the Old Testament* (St. Louis: Chalice, 1992), 64.
3. Ronald R. Clark Jr., "The Silence in Dinah's Cry," *RQ* 49 (2007): 153.
4. Clark, "The Silence in Dinah's Cry," 156.

violent action, indicating his inability to guide his family or maintain appropriate authority as their father.

Dinah herself also remains silent. The reader does not know Dinah's perspective on the events that changed her life. After she was raped, Dinah remained in Shechem's house, which raises questions of its own. We must take care, however, not to judge people trapped in the horrors of domestic violence and abuse. As Clark points out, "Condemning women caught in sexual or domestic violence for their location or powerlessness is an example of ideological abuse. The victims should not be further victimized. Dinah should not be victimized or further humiliated. Her movement, location, dress, motives, or attitudes should not be used to condone her oppression."[5] Why did Dinah stay with Shechem until her brothers freed her? The text does not tell us, but we must take care not to further victimize Dinah—or other survivors of violence—by blaming her.

5. Clark, "The Silence in Dinah's Cry," 155.

CHAPTER 26

The Levite's Concubine

The story of the Levite and his concubine in Judges 19:1–30 is one of the most misunderstood stories in the Bible. Many Christians have never read the story and are unfamiliar with its gruesome details. Why write a chapter on a story of violence against a woman who did not deserve the horror inflicted on her? Phyllis Trible explains why we must study this story.

> The betrayal, rape, torture, murder and dismemberment of an unnamed woman is a story we want to forget but are commanded to speak. It depicts the horrors of male power, brutality, and triumphalism, of female helplessness, abuse, and annihilation. To hear this story is to inhabit a world of unrelenting terror that refuses to let us pass by on the other side.[1]

A Story of Violence

The story of the Levite's concubine is horrific. Many who read this story, both men and women, blame the woman for being unfaithful to her husband. Some people even believe that just by leaving her husband, the woman was being unfaithful to him.

There are two main characters in this story of brutality and violence. Levites were religious functionaries who served God as temple personnel. Because of their position in the religious life of Israel, Levites were honored and respected by the people of Israel and served in many important positions in the temple, court, and palace. This particular Levite was somewhat wealthy, since he could buy a concubine and had a servant and two donkeys.

1. Phyllis Trible, *Texts of Terror*, OBT (Philadelphia: Fortress, 1984), 65.

A concubine was a secondary wife. In some poor families, a father would sell his daughter to be a secondary wife, a maid, or a servant in the household of a man of means. The woman in this story was likely sold by her father to be a secondary wife of the Levite.

The Woman and the Text

The woman in this narrative is often blamed for what was done to her due to the unfortunate mistranslation of Judges 19:2 by the KJV, NIV, and other versions.[2] The KJV reads, "And his concubine played the whore against him, and went away from him unto her father's house." According to this reading, the woman betrayed her husband by becoming a prostitute. However, this translation finds no contextual support. As Boling writes, "It is strange that the woman would become a prostitute and then run home."[3] The NIV reads, "But she was unfaithful to him. She left him and went back to her parents' home" (Judg 19:2). According to this translation, the woman betrayed her husband by having sex with another man, an offense that carried the death penalty (Deut 22:22) and legally prevented the reunification of husband and wife (Deut 24:4).

Both of these translations obscure the real reason the concubine left her husband. It was not what *she* had done that prompted her to leave; it was what the husband *did to her*. The NRSV translates Judges 19:2 correctly: "But his concubine became angry with him, and she went away from him to her father's house" (see also NET, NJB, and NLT, among others).

Translations of this verse differ because there are different textual traditions about what happened between the Levite and his concubine. Some textual traditions say the woman was unfaithful to her husband. Others say the woman was angry at her husband for something that he did to her. G. R. Driver explains the issue:

> In the story of the outrage at Gibeah the Hebrew text, in speaking of the estrangement between the Levite and his concubine, says *wattizneh ʿalayw* (Jud. XIX 2), which cannot mean "and

2. Claude F. Mariottini, *Rereading the Biblical Text: Searching for Meaning and Understanding* (Eugene, OR: Wipf and Stock, 2013), 43–46.
3. Robert G. Boling, *Judges*, AB (New York: Doubleday, 1975), 273.

> she played the harlot against him" (R.V.) because this verb is never followed by this preposition and especially because the cause of the estrangement was obviously a passing disagreement and not an act of unfaithfulness. The LXX makes admirable sense and may be accepted as correct; for the [Akkadian] *zinû* "to be angry" supports it and suggests a Hebrew *zānâ* "was angry," totally different from the Hebrew *zānâ* "committed adultery, fornication." Two homonymous verbs have here been confused by all interpreters except the LXX who, as so often, have preserved the true sense.[4]

That is, several translations, including the Vulgate, Septuagint, and Targum, do not understand the Hebrew word *zānâ* to imply any act of conjugal infidelity on the woman's part. The word *zānâ* has two meanings. The first is "to be unfaithful" or "to commit adultery." The second is "to be angry." In light of how the Septuagint and the Targum translate the word, Soggin—following Driver—writes, "In no way can this be the *zānāh*, 'practice prostitution,' in the sense of 'betrayed him.'" Because *zānâ* in Judges 19:2 means "to be angry," Soggin concludes that "the responsibility for the matrimonial crisis, on which the text gives us no information, must have lain with the husband, at least in view of his later behaviour."[5]

This is the same view of Josephus, the Jewish historian who wrote a few years after Paul's death. In his *Antiquities of the Jews*, Josephus writes,

> There was a Levite, a man of a vulgar family, that belonged to the tribe of Ephraim, and dwelt therein; this man married a wife from Bethlehem, which is a place belonging to the tribe of Judah. Now he was very fond of his wife and overcome with her beauty; but he was unhappy in this, that he did not meet with the like return of affection from her, for she was averse to him, which did more inflame his passion for her, so that they quarreled one with another perpetually; and at last the woman

4. G. R. Driver, "Mistranslations in the Old Testament," *WO* 1 (1947): 29–30.
5. J. Alberto Soggin, *Judges*, OTL (Philadelphia: Westminster, 1981), 284.

> was so disgusted at these quarrels, that she left her husband, and went to her parents in the fourth month.[6]

The biblical text presents multiple reasons that compelled the concubine to part ways with her husband.

The Woman's Reason for Leaving Her Husband

In light of the textual evidence presented above, why was the woman not guilty of the accusations of infidelity lodged against her? The text presents several clues to indicate that the separation should be blamed on the husband.

First, the woman's husband made her angry, so she left. The Bible does not provide any information on why she became angry, though it was clearly severe enough that she had to leave. Second, it is important to notice that the woman takes the initiative to leave her husband. This is the only time in the Old Testament where a woman takes such initiative to leave her husband. This fact may also explain another textual problem in the story. When the Levite came to Bethlehem to bring his wife back, translations differ on what happened next.

The NRSV says, "When he reached her father's house, the girl's father saw him and came with joy to meet him" (Judg 19:3; cf. NLT, NJB). The NIV reads, "She took him into her parents' home, and when her father saw him, he gladly welcomed him" (Judg 19:3; cf. KJV, ESV, CSB). The NIV and similar translations follow the Masoretic Text in saying that the women brought the man into her father's house. The Septuagint and the Syriac versions, on the other hand, say that the man came to her father's house. The Masoretic text indicates that the woman met her husband and brought him into the house based on the scribes' understanding of the meaning of *zānâ* discussed above. That is, since they viewed *zānâ* as indicated that the wife betrayed her husband, then she should take the initiative to welcome him back.

The third reason to see the man as culpable is the wife's apparent reluctance to return with her husband. The text never explicitly mentions whether the woman desired to return with her husband, but clues in the narrative point readers in that direction. First, it took four months for him to come after her (Judg 19:2), and it took five days of

6. Josephus, *Ant.* 5:2, 8.

dealing between the woman's father and the Levite before he was able to leave with his wife. Second, the text says that the Levite came "to speak tenderly to her" (Judg 19:3). The Hebrew says "to speak to her heart." This expression is used six times in the Hebrew Bible, and in a few places (Gen 34:3; Judg 19:3; 2 Sam 19:7; Hos 2:14) it carries the idea of convincing someone.[7] The Levite's effort to go from the hills of Ephraim to Bethlehem of Judah to reconcile with his concubine and convince her to return with him implies that she was the one in the right, not him.

The Abusive Husband

Although the text does not give the reason the woman left, even before the tragedy the passage hints that the Levite was an abusive husband. We see this, first, in the Levite making his wife angry enough to leave him and, second, in his coming after her to "speak to her heart," that is, to convince her to come home with him.

When the Levite and his concubine left her father's house, they came to Gibeah, where he planned to spend the night. In Gibeah, the Levite met an old man who offered him hospitality. When the Levite met the old man of the city, not wanting to be a burden to him, the Levite said: "We have both straw and feed for our donkeys, with bread and wine for me and your female servant and the young man with your servants" (Judg 19:19 ESV). With these words, the Levite demeans his concubine by saying that she was "your female servant;" that is, inferring that the woman was the man's property. After he came to the man's house, the men of the city threatened his life. To save his own life, the Levite sacrificed the concubine's life: "So the [Levite] seized his concubine, and put her out to them. They wantonly raped her, and abused her all through the night until the morning" (Judg 19:25).

The action of the Levite shows the tragedy of this story. The Hebrew word translated "seized" comes from a word that means "to be strong." In this story, the word carries the idea of taking hold or grabbing the woman by force. He brought his wife back from her father's house only to deliver her into the hands of evil men who raped her and abused her mercilessly all night.

7. Gen 34:3; Judg 19:3; Ruth 2:13; 2 Sam 19:7; Isa 40:2; Hos 2:14.

When morning came, the Levite "opened the doors of the house, and went out to leave on his journey" (Judg 19:27 CSB)—without his wife. As he exited, he found the woman lying on the doorstep, whether alive or dead the text does not say. The text's silence may indicate that she was still alive; however, to mitigate the brutality of what happens next, the Septuagint says, "for she was dead" (Judg 19:28 LXX).

When the Levite arrived home, he took a knife, took hold of the battered body of his concubine, and cut her into twelve pieces, sending them throughout the land. When the men of Israel gathered and asked what had happened, the Levite lied to justify what he did: "I came to Gibeah that belongs to Benjamin, I and my concubine, to spend the night. The lords of Gibeah rose up against me, and surrounded the house at night. They intended to kill me, and they raped my concubine until she died" (Judg 20:3–5). The men of Gibeah did not try to kill him; they wanted to rape him, and they only raped his concubine because he gave her to them in his place.

The Truth of the Story

Judges 19:2 provides evidence that the woman had reasons to leave her husband. Later in the narrative, it becomes clear that he was an abusive husband, a selfish man who treated his wife as an object to be disposed of, who did not value her as a woman and as a wife. Although some versions seem to justify the Levite by saying that the woman departed from her husband to have sexual relations with another man, a proper reading of the Hebrew and its translation history shows that she was faithful to her husband. To blame the woman for what happened is to ignore the fact that the Levite's actions clearly show that the woman had a reason to fear him, and her rape, abuse, death, and dismemberment proved that she was right all along. May she rest in peace.

CHAPTER 27

Bathsheba, the Wife of Uriah

When looking at David's sin against Bathsheba (2 Sam 11:1–17), two things must be said of David. First, David was a man after God's own heart (1 Sam 13:14). God chose him to take the place of Saul as the king of Israel. God made a covenant with David and told him that he would "establish the throne of his kingdom forever" (2 Sam 7:13). Second, one must remember that David was a man, and some men covet their "neighbor's wife" (Exod 20:17), as David did—though most stop short of rape and murder to get what they want.

David coveted Uriah's wife. He saw Bathsheba bathing (2 Sam 11:2), and sent his men to get her. David's servants took Bathsheba and brought her to him. While some argue that what happened that night was an "affair," there is irrefutable textual evidence that Bathsheba did not consent to David.

The attempt at defending David from the charge of rape is not new, likely because the Bible does not explicitly say that Bathsheba attempted to escape or to persuade David to stop. Caspi and Cohen trace the defense of David to rabbinic literature, stating that "rabbinic literature attempts to explain and solve some of David's issues and his relationship with Bathsheba and Abishag, since in their minds he was the rightful and chosen founder of the royal house. There is no way for them to portray him, the King, the Psalmist and the source of the future Messiah as evil, human and weak."[1]

Others attempt to justify David's sin by saying that his affair was a part of a divine plan. "According to R. Simeon bar Yohai, . . . God predestined the incident in order to teach the people of Israel the power

1. Michael M. Caspi and Sascha B. Cohen, *Still Waters Run Deep: Five Women of the Bible Speak* (New York: University Press of America, 1999), 54.

of repentance."[2] Thus, the rabbis justify the violation of Bathsheba by claiming that it was predestined by God to teach repentance. David's repentance is found in Psalm 51.

Some defenders of David say that David was "a man after [God's] own heart" (1 Sam 13:14) and, as such, would not rape a woman. The same argument was presented centuries ago by the rabbis. Another way of defending David is to say that Bathsheba enticed David to have sex with her by bathing nude on the rooftop of her house (2 Sam 11:2).[3]

The common assumption is that Bathsheba was bathing after her menstrual period.[4] This view is based on the translation of the Hebrew words *miṭṭum'ātāh* in 1 Samuel 11:4. The words are translated as "after her period" by NRSV, as "her menstrual uncleanness" by the NET Bible, as "her menstrual period" by the NLT, and as "her uncleanness" by the KJV. As Chankin-Gould shows, however, this expression does not address menstruation.[5]

Tikva Frymer-Kensky writes that the bathing in 1 Samuel 11:2 and the purification in 1 Samuel 11:4 are two separate events, and they are not related to Bathsheba's menstrual period. According to Frymer-Kensky, the view that a woman in ancient Israel bathed after menstruation is anachronistic since it is based on later rabbinic law, which was unknown in David's time.[6] Auld writes that the Hebrew Bible does not contain one example of washing after menstruation, a Jewish practice initiated after the biblical period.[7]

R. C. Bailey argues that Bathsheba was a coconspirator in a political scheme to marry David[8] and therefore "is no longer an innocent victim but a willing partner in the affair who wishes her own son to

---

2. Caspi and Cohen, *Still Waters Run Deep*, 54.
3. George G. Nicol, "The Alleged Rape of Bathsheba: Some Observations on Ambiguity in Biblical Narrative," *JSOT* 73 (1997): 44.
4. For a detailed study of Bathsheba's bathing and her ritual purification, see Claude F. Mariottini, "Bathsheba and Her Menstrual Period," July 23, 2019, https://claudemariottini.com/2019/07/23/bathsheba-and-her-menstrual-period/.
5. J. D'ror Chankin-Gould et al., "The Sanctified 'Adulteress' and Her Circumstantial Clause: Bathsheba's Bath and Self-Consecration in 2 Samuel 11," *JSOT* 32 (2008): 348.
6. Tikva Frymer-Kensky, *Reading the Women of the Bible: A New Interpretation of Their Stories* (New York: Schocken, 2002), 147.
7. A. Graeme Auld, *I & II Samuel*, OTL (Louisville: Westminster John Knox, 2011), 456.
8. Randall C. Bailey, *David in Love and War: The Pursuit of Power in 2 Samuel 10–12*, JSOTSup 75 (Sheffield: JSOT Press, 1990), 87–88.

become king. David is able to convince her to marry him by promising that her son would be his heir to the throne."[9]

The accusations lobbed at Bathsheba and defenses of David are without merit. David forced himself on Bathsheba even though the word for "rape" does not appear in the text. In fact, the Hebrew Bible does not have a word for "rape." The truth is that an innocent man does not make plans to kill the husband of the woman he slept with.

Brueggemann says that the illicit relationship between David with Bathsheba came at a time of "abrupt transition from a life under blessing to a life under curse."[10] To understand that David's affair with Bathsheba was rape, we must look at the facts in the story and see what the text says about David, the sin, and Bathsheba.

First, when David took Bathsheba, he already had many wives. Before David conquered Jerusalem, he already had seven wives. After he conquered Jerusalem, David "took more concubines and wives; and more sons and daughters were born to David" (2 Sam 5:13). This was about David's lust—for power over others and for the women he wanted. As Brueggemann puts it, "There is no hint of caring, of affection, of love—only lust."[11]

David took another man's wife, against which Israel had severe laws. Leviticus states that the penalty for adultery is death: "If a man commits adultery with the wife of his neighbor . . . the adulterer . . . shall be put to death" (Lev 20:10). "The wording is significant; the man is not killed because he is married but because the woman, his partner, is married. The male adulterer is polluting another man's seed."[12] Deuteronomy says that "If a man is discovered having sexual relations with another man's wife, both the man who had sex with the woman and the woman must die. You must purge the evil from Israel" (Deut 22:22 CSB). Though David was guilty of violating adultery laws, it is doubtful that the legal system in Israel would put the king to death for committing adultery.

9. Gale A. Yee, "Bathsheba (Person)," *ABD* 1:627.

10. Walter Brueggemann, *First and Second Samuel*, Int (Louisville: Westminster John Knox, 1990), 272.

11. Brueggemann, *First and Second Samuel*, 273.

12. Susan Niditch, "The Wronged Woman Righted: An Analysis of Genesis 38," *HTR* 72 (1979): 146.

After David saw Bathsheba bathing, he sent messengers to find out who she was. David was told that she was a married woman named Bathsheba and that she was the wife of Uriah, one of the members of his elite group of soldiers known as "the Thirty" (2 Sam 23:24). Even knowing this, David took her to have sex with her.

David sent "messengers"—plural—to bring Bathsheba to the palace (2 Sam 11:4). The messengers "took her" to David. Most English translations translate the Hebrew verb *lāqaḥ* as "get": "David sent messengers to get her" (2 Sam 11:4). The Hebrew verb *lāqaḥ*, however, means "to take," and in some contexts it means to take by force, even "to steal." The use of *lāqaḥ*, and the fact that David had to send several men to "take" Bathsheba, indicates that she was compelled to come to David. David's action, as Brueggemann describes it, was a demonstration of "human desire and human power."[13]

Samuel had already warned the people of Israel about kings' proclivity to do exactly what David did: "He will take your sons. . . . he will take your daughters" (1 Sam 8:11, 13). In 1 Samuel 8:10–18, Samuel tells the Israelites that the king would take everything the people had as his own. The king was often able to do as he pleased, seek what he desired, and receive justification after all his actions. The king had much authority over the people and the nation, and he took whatever he desired. Samuel's warning came true with David. The king saw Bathsheba bathing, desired her, and took what he desired. Bathsheba, like all the king's subjects, had no power to refuse the king's sexual demands.

Bathsheba was the daughter of Eliam (2 Sam 11:3), and her grandfather was Ahithophel (2 Sam 23:34). Ahithophel was a trusted advisor of David. When Absalom rebelled against David, Ahithophel took the side of Absalom against David. The motive for Ahithophel's defection from David was because he was angry and unhappy at David for what he had done to Bathsheba and the murder by proxy of her husband, Uriah the Hittite. Ahitophel blamed David for what he did to Bathsheba.[14] Yahweh likewise blames David for what he did: "But the thing David had done displeased the LORD" (2 Sam 11:27 NIV). But Yahweh was more than just displeased with David. The Hebrew

13. Brueggemann, *First and Second Samuel*, 272.
14. D. G. Schley, "Ahithophel (Person)," *ABD* 1:121.

text says, "But the thing David had done was evil and displeased the Lord." David did the evil, not Bathsheba.

In his rebuke of David, Nathan portrays Bathsheba as a lamb (2 Sam 12:1–3). The lamb in Nathan's parable represents a position of vulnerability and powerlessness. Like the "little ewe lamb," Bathsheba lived in a profound power imbalance with King David. As king, David commanded absolute authority, while Bathsheba, particularly as a woman in ancient Israel whose husband was away at war, had virtually no capacity to refuse the king's summons. Bathsheba was taken by force and was an unwilling participant in the sordid affair. Nathan's parable portrays Bathsheba as a victim of David's abuse of royal authority.

The Lord was not happy with what David had done. The prophet Nathan told David that the Lord had passed judgment on him. Nathan rebuked David for committing adultery with Bathsheba, but David was not put to death as the Levitical laws demanded. In his rebuke of David for what he had done to Bathsheba, Nathan told David, "Why have you despised the word of the Lord, to do what is evil in his sight? . . . You . . . have taken his wife to be your wife . . . you have despised me. . . . Thus says the Lord: I will raise up trouble against you from within your own house; and I will take your wives before your eyes, and give them to your neighbor, and he shall lie with your wives in the sight of this very sun. For you did it secretly; but I will do this thing before all Israel, and before the sun" (2 Sam 12:9–12). Amnon, David's son, later took his sister Tamar, David's daughter, and "raped her" (2 Sam 13:14 NIV). When Absalom, David's son, revolted against David, to show the people that he was the new king instead of his father, "Absalom had sex with his father's concubines in the sight of all Israel" (2 Sam 16:22 NET). Absalom raped David's wives in public.

The story of David and Bathsheba is a tale of lust, self-gratification, rape, lies, power, deceit, and murder. Some people say that it was not rape because Bathsheba never protested and did not resist, but we have shown that such a reading is faulty. The narrator clearly states what David did: He sent, he took, she came, and he had sex with her. The writer does not say anything about Bathsheba's reactions. According to Israelite laws, however, Bathsheba had no right to consent to having sex with David, and she is never once pronounced guilty in the narrative. In fact, Nathan portrays Bathsheba as an innocent lamb while placing all the blame squarely on David. There was no "affair" between David and Bathsheba. David raped Bathsheba, murdered her husband, and destroyed her honor.

Unfortunately, we will never know what Bathsheba said or how she felt. Israel's patriarchal society did not provide an adequate voice for Bathsheba or other females to express their feelings. A patriarchal society allowed certain freedoms for men that were not allowed to women. A patriarchal society empowered the king to do as he pleased, which in certain situations could mean the violation of the rights of another person. In light of what the text says about David, it is wrong to defend David and blame Bathsheba for his actions against her. Bathsheba experienced shame and dishonor at David's hands. She was used and abused and yet, in the mind of some people, she should be blamed for what happened. The text shows, however, that David is to blame and that readers should sympathize with Bathsheba, not David.

CHAPTER 28

Tamar, the Daughter of David

Tamar was the daughter of David and Maacah, David's fourth wife. Maacah was also the mother of Absalom, which made him Tamar's full brother. Maacah was a princess, the daughter of Talmai, king of Geshur. David married her to facilitate a diplomatic alliance between Israel and the kingdom of Geshur.

Amnon was David's firstborn son by his third wife Ahinoam. Amnon raped his half-sister Tamar and was killed by Absalom. The story of Tamar's rape is not only a story of lust but also of political ambition. As the first and second sons of David, both Amnon and Absalom were in the line of succession for the throne. But this story reveals Tamar's powerlessness, a reflection of the vulnerable estate of all women who lived in a patriarchal society.

In his introduction to the story of Tamar, the writer of the biblical text introduces the four protagonists who will play the key roles in the tragic story of the virgin daughter of David. "David's son Absalom had a beautiful sister whose name was Tamar; and David's son Amnon fell in love with her" (2 Sam 13:1).

This introduction clearly reflects the society in which Tamar lived. Both Absalom and Amnon are introduced as sons of David. Yet Tamar is introduced only as the beautiful sister of Absalom and is not identified as David's daughter. This pattern of giving prominence to sons reflects an attitude in which only David's sons, but not his daughter, have the right to succeed to the king's throne. Frymer-Kensky says that "Tamar, the center of the story, is presented as an object."[1]

---

1. Tikva Frymer-Kensky, *Reading the Women of the Bible: A New Interpretation of Their Stories* (New York: Schocken, 2002), 157.

The biblical text says that Amnon fell in love with Tamar (2 Sam 13:1). As Wilda Gafney writes, however, the word "love" in the text "is a challenging word here because of its incompatibility with rape."[2] Amnon was unable to touch Tamar because she was a virgin (2 Sam 13:2). Virgin daughters were to be protected by the head of the household because their virginity was a prized asset in Israelite society. Fathers were compensated by prospective bridegrooms when they gave their daughters in marriage. Virgin daughters required a large *mōhar*—the money a prospective husband gave to the father of the bride as compensation to the family.

Amnon was so obsessed with Tamar that he made himself sick. In his desire to have sex with his half-sister, Amnon followed the advice of his friend Jonadab to lure Tamar to his house so that he could seduce her. According to Jonadab's advice, Amnon would pretend to be sick and then ask his father to allow Tamar to come and prepare a meal and feed him (2 Sam 13:5).

Frymer-Kensky suggests that David was led to believe that Amnon wanted Tamar to perform some form of a healing ceremony. The Hebrew word for food is *biryâ*. Frymer-Kensky says that "the word comes from the root meaning 'fat' or 'healthy' and may mean a healing substance. The *biryâ* is not simply a food, and making it is not simply an act of cooking; it is the preparation of a medicinal concoction. Perhaps, we could speculate, the princesses of the realm were instructed in the creation of healing foods."[3] The text, however, indicates that Tamar was coming to Amnon's house to feed him.

David consented to Amnon's request. He told Tamar, "Go to your brother Amnon's house, and prepare food for him" (2 Sam 13:7). With her father's consent, Tamar went to Amnon's house and prepared the special food for Amnon to eat, but Amnon "refused to eat" (2 Sam 13:9). To be alone with Tamar, Amnon sent his servants out of the room.

Amnon invited Tamar to bring the food to his bedroom so that she could feed him. Not knowing her brother's intentions, Tamar took him the food she had prepared. When Tamar approached Amnon, he grabbed her and said, "Come, lie with me, my sister" (2 Sam 13:11).

---

2. Wilda C. Gafney, *Womanist Midrash : A Reintroduction to the Women of the Torah and the Throne* (Louisville: Westminster John Knox, 2017), 227.
3. Frymer-Kensky, *Reading the Women of the Bible*, 158.

Amnon overpowered Tamar and humiliated her by raping her. The Hebrew word *ḥāzaq* means "to be strong" and can be translated as "overpower" (2 Sam 13:14 TNK) and "to force" (2 Sam 13:14 NRSV). When the word is used to describe the action of an individual against another, the word carries the idea of violence. The use of *ḥāzaq* in this context implies that Tamar struggled valiantly with Amnon in her attempt to resist her attacker.

Amnon "is brusque, blunt, and brutal. He is coarse, calloused, and cruel. He is devious, demonic, and destructive."[4] Second Samuel 13:14 reads that "he forced her and lay with her." The Hebrew word behind the expression "he lay with her" (2 Sam 13:14) is much more graphic than the English translation reveals. As Kyle McCarter points out, Hebrew scribes substituted the form of a Hebrew verb for another because they deemed the original form of the verb to be too obscene.[5]

This graphic language appears in Deuteronomy 28:30: "You shall become engaged to a woman, but another man shall *šāgal* her." In biblical Hebrew, *šāgal* refers to forced sexual intercourse or rape. The term denotes violent or coercive sexual activity rather than consensual relations. The word carries such strong connotations that in Jewish tradition, when the biblical text was read aloud in synagogues, the Masoretes (Jewish scribes) provided a *qere* (reading instruction) to substitute the less explicit term *šākab* ("to lie with") in place of *šāgal* to avoid pronouncing the harsher term.

Tamar immediately rebuked her brother. She said, "No, . . . don't rape me! That shouldn't be done in Israel. Don't do this godless act" (2 Sam 13:12 GW). But Amnon refused to listen to Tamar. Trible describes Amnon's refusal in this way: "Passionately, Amnon has desired to see and touch her, for with these senses he has made of her what he wills. But to hear her voice is another matter; it disturbs the fantasies that eyes and hands have fashioned. To hear might mean repentance. So Amnon chooses to close out her voice, even leaving his refusal for the narrator to report. Amnon cares not at all for his sister. He acts against her will to pursue his lust."[6]

---

4. J. Alfred Smith Sr., "Break the Silence: Justice Is Waiting for You to Speak," *RevExp* 110 (2013): 15–16.
5. P. Kyle McCarter Jr., *II Samuel*, AB (New York: Doubleday, 1984), 317.
6. Phyllis Trible, *Texts of Terror*, OBT (Philadelphia: Fortress, 1984), 46.

Tamar told Amnon to appeal to the king, and he would allow her to marry him. Without the benefit of marriage, Tamar would become an outcast. She told Amnon, "where could I carry my shame?" (2 Sam 13:13). Tamar's honor was crucial for the society in which she lived. Amnon, however, refused to listen to his sister.

After raping Tamar, "Amnon's love turned to hate, and he hated her even more than he had loved her" (2 Sam 13:15 NLT). Tamar once again protested and made an impassionate appeal to Amnon, "No, brother! To send me away would be worse than the other wrong you have done me" (2 Sam 13:16 NJB). But Amnon refused to listen to his sister's appeal and sent her away. Amnon "called his personal attendant and said to him, 'Take this woman out of my sight and lock the door behind her!'" (2 Sam 13:17 NET). In describing Ammon's act of casting Tamar out of his house, Diane Jacobson writes, "We watch as Amnon casts Tamar aside, calling her a thing, and commanding his servant to bar the door—his cruelty compounded, stripping the other not only of her clothes and her honor, but even of her humanity. We watch Amnon, because through this true portrayal of sin we viscerally learn the destructive power of self-centered love. Never has a rapist been painted more pointedly. Amnon is the very picture of a self-serving, lust-crazed miscreant, willing to violate both this woman and this home, to violate both the object of his purported love and the sacred trust of his people."[7]

Amnon's raping and sending Tamar away had a lifelong, devastating consequence for Tamar. After Tamar left Amnon's house, "Tamar put ashes on her head, and tore the long robe that she was wearing; she put her hand on her head, and went away, crying aloud as she went" (2 Sam 13:19). This act of deep grief and public humiliation was designed to make known her violation and desolation to her father David and to the people of Jerusalem.

Absalom, Tamar's brother, tried to console her. He said to her, "Be quiet for now, my sister; he is your brother; do not take this to heart" (2 Sam 13:20). But Tamar took what had happened to her "to heart." She lived as a desolate woman, uncomforted and grief-stricken, in the house of her brother Absalom (2 Sam 13:20). When King David heard what Amnon had done, he became very angry, but did not punish his firstborn son.

7. Diane Jacobson, "Remembering Tamar," *WW* 24 (2004): 355.

Many troubling circumstances in Tamar's rape are consistent with the plight of most violated and raped women. Frymer-Kensky says that Tamar was sexually assaulted and raped, not by a stranger but her brother, and not in a dark and remote place but in the house of her brother.[8] Amnon took advantage of Tamar's willingness to help him in his time of distress and used her kindness to perpetrate the vile act of violating his sister. Amnon ignored her pleas, raped her, and abandoned her to live a desolate life as a widow in the house of her brother.

Tamar lived in Absalom's house for the rest of her life. But though she was abandoned, she was not forgotten. When Absalom's daughter was born, Absalom named her Tamar because "she was a beautiful woman" (2 Sam 14:27), just like her aunt Tamar. In Absalom's daughter, Tamar is remembered, "and in this acknowledgment is heard the promise that violence will not have the last word."[9]

Jacobson urges each one of us to remember Tamar, her plight, and her humiliation. Jacobson writes,

> to remember is to give honor, to give voice, to give substance. To remember is to claim that this woman's story belongs at the heart of the story of God, whose compassion is never ending. To lament with Tamar and to remember is to say that God lives within the lives of the downtrodden and shamed. To remember and to tell this story is to say that we know, we understand, we see, and we name the truth. To remember is to receive her story as a gift offered to us in the tenderly cupped, yet bleeding hands of the Almighty, given into our care that we might practice the divine task of remembering.[10]

Raped and rejected, Tamar finds refuge in the house of her brother Absalom, where she remained as if in a state of widowhood. In her desolate condition, Long writes, "We watch not a beautiful young woman, but a woman become old in her desolation, wearing the shredded tokens of a bereaved widow without ever having been a wife."[11]

---

8. Frymer-Kensky, *Reading the Women of the Bible*, 159.
9. Jacobson, "Remembering Tamar," 357.
10. Jacobson, "Remembering Tamar," 357.
11. Burke O. Long, *Images of God and Man: Old Testament Short Stories in Literary Focus*, BLS 1 (Sheffield: Almond, 1981), 29.

PART 5

WOMEN OF DISTINCTION

CHAPTER 29

Deborah: A Judge in Israel

Deborah was a woman from Ephraim who served as a tribal leader and as a prophet (see ch. 7 above). The book of Judges presents Deborah as one of the heroes "who act on Yhwh's behalf and lead Israel against Canaan's mighty forces."[1] Judges 4:4–5 speaks of Deborah's dual role in Israel: "At that time Deborah, a prophetess, wife of Lappidoth, was judging Israel at that time. She used to sit under the palm of Deborah between Ramah and Bethel in the hill country of Ephraim; and the Israelites came up to her for judgment."

Deborah was called a *šôpēṭ*, a "judge." The verb *špṭ* can be translated as "deliver," "rule," "govern," or "decide." The plural word (Hebrew *šôpəṭîm*) can be translated as "saviors." None of the individuals in the book of Judges are called a "judge" in the sense that we use the word today. The word "judge" was used by the writer of Judges to describe the work of the main characters of the book.

> Then the Lord raised up judges, who delivered them out of the power of those who plundered them. Yet they did not listen even to their judges; for they lusted after other gods and bowed down to them. They soon turned aside from the way in which their ancestors had walked, who had obeyed the commandments of the Lord; they did not follow their example. Whenever the Lord raised up judges for them, the Lord was with the judge, and he delivered them from the hand of their enemies all the days of the judge. (Judg 2:16–18)

1. Jacob L. Wright, *Why the Bible Began: An Alternative History of Scripture and Its Origins* (Cambridge: Cambridge University Press, 2023), 43.

The book of Judges shows that the judges directed military campaigns (Judg 2:16; 3:10), led the community (Judg 10:3; 12:7), and also administered justice (Judg 4:4). In the Old Testament, a judge functioned in a judicial and institutional context. Most of Israel's judicial functions were performed by the elders who served as judges at its city gates. These elders convened to render verdicts on disputes brought before them. Their judicial authority encompassed family conflicts, property disagreements, inheritance cases, and matters of local criminal justice. No textual evidence supports the view that Deborah and the other judges in the book of Judges administered judicial proceedings similar to those conducted by the elders.

In Israelite society the *šôpēṭ* described an arbitrator of local disputes without any institutional authority. Due to the tribal structure of Israel, the judges had little influence outside their own tribes. A better interpretation of the role of the *šôpəṭîm* was that these individuals served as civil or military leaders in their communities. The only exception was Deborah. Even in her case, however, it is possible to credit Deborah with military leadership, for she assumed the authority to summon Barak to serve as her military commander and to fight against the Canaanites. Barak declined the leadership of the army unless Deborah joined him in battle.

In addition to her role in the military campaign against the Canaanites, Deborah counseled the people and settled disputes in the community. The biblical text states that Deborah held court under the palm of Deborah between Ramah and Bethel in the hill country of Ephraim. It was there that the people of Israel came to her to have their disputes settled (Judg 4:4–5).

Deborah was not a judge or a deliverer in the same way that the other deliverers mentioned in the book of Judges were. The reason for distinguishing Deborah from the other judges is because Deborah's story omits several important elements present in the accounts of the other judges. These elements include the absence of the statement that Yahweh raised up a deliverer, the fact that Deborah was not involved in direct military action as the other judges were, and the lack of a reference to Deborah as being empowered by the Spirit of Yahweh.

In ancient Israel it is possible that most villages would have wise persons to whom the people would come to seek resolution for their problems. These wise persons would be sought by the community because of their wisdom and the soundness of their advice. These persons did not assume the function of counselors or advisors by having received some official sanction or appointment but by having the confidence of the people or by being recognized as individuals who were endowed by God with special gifts.

In Israel, the administration of justice was dispensed at the city gates. Job said that before his illness he dispensed justice at the city gate: "Those were the days when I went to the city gate and took my place among the honored leaders" (Job 29:7 NLT). In particular, Job dispensed justice for people in need: "For I assisted the poor in their need and the orphans who required help. I helped those without hope, and they blessed me. And I caused the widows' hearts to sing for joy" (Job 29:12–13 NLT).

In a patriarchal society, however, where the elders of the city would decide questions of justice, would Deborah have been welcomed at the city gates? Deborah demonstrated her leadership as a judge by establishing her judicial authority outside patriarchal structures. Rather than attempting to integrate into elder councils at the city gates, Deborah met the people under the palm of Deborah (Judg 4:5), free of the traditional constraints of a male-oriented society. Deborah's influence as a judge is reflected in those Israelites who came to her seeking judgment. Her palm tree court represents accessibility to those who require prophetic affirmation. Her leadership as a judge drew its legitimacy directly from her prophetic connection to Yahweh.

How difficult was it for Deborah to fulfill her role as a judge? It is possible that in ancient Israel women sought advice from other women, but nothing in the biblical text indicates that Deborah's work as a judge was limited to advising women. Because she functioned as God's spokesperson, the people of Israel would evaluate Deborah's wisdom and the conviction of her call as a validation of her work as a judge. Because of her God-given abilities, the people would accept her work and follow her leadership. This is clearly expressed in the poetic section of the story of Deborah: "Warriors were scarce, they were scarce in Israel, until you arose, Deborah, until you arose as a motherly protector in Israel" (Judg 5:7 NET).

The declaration that Deborah was a motherly protector of Israel indicates that the people of Israel considered Deborah to be "a real-life leader in her people's history."[2] Wright calls Deborah, "a paragon of national leadership"[3] and says, "As a woman . . . Deborah governs Israel and commissions an officer to lead the people into battle."[4]

Advice and counsel given by women was not unknown to men in Israel. The Bible mentions other women who were wise and served as counselors. One of these wise women was the woman from Tekoa whose counsel to David led to his reconciliation with his son Absalom (2 Sam 14:1–20). Another wise woman was the woman from Abel who saved her city by persuading Joab not to destroy it and who counseled the city elders "with her wise plan" to deliver Sheba to Joab (2 Sam 20:22).

The Song of Deborah

The Song of Deborah (Judg 5:1–31) is a masterpiece of Old Testament poetry, with vivid imagery portraying Israel's victory against the Canaanite army. Through this song of triumph, Deborah and the people of Israel celebrated their liberation from the oppression they suffered for twenty years (Judg 4:3).

The narrative section of the story of Deborah (Judg 4:1–24) presents her as a prophetess and a judge; the Song of Deborah introduces her as "a mother in Israel" (Judg 5:7). Although Judges mentioned that Deborah was married to a man named Lappidoth (Judg 4:4), there is no mention, neither in the narrative nor in the song, that Deborah had any children.

The translation of Judges 5:7 is difficult because the meaning of the Hebrew word *perēzôn* (Judg 5:7, 11) is difficult to establish. The word is translated as "peasantry" (NRSV), "villages" (CSB), and "villagers" (ESV, NIV). The Septuagint translates the word as "mighty men." This uncertainty about the word's true meaning creates different readings of the text. The verse, however, clearly indicates that because of the oppression under Jabin, the people of Israel suffered under the Canaanite yoke until Deborah arose as a leader in Israel. Under her leadership, the oppression was broken, and the people

2. Wright, *Why the Bible Began*, 43.
3. Wright, *Why the Bible Began*, 371.
4. Wright, *Why the Bible Began*, 44.

were set free from Canaanite oppression: "The villages in Israel were no more, they were no more until you arose, O Deborah, until you arose, mother of Israel!" (Judg 5:7 NJB). This verse indicates that the people of Israel were suffering greatly until Deborah arose to lead the forces of Israel against Sisera's army. Thus, the deliverance of Israel happened when Deborah arose as "a mother in Israel." Barak is not even mentioned in this act of deliverance.

In Judges 5, Deborah appears as the commander of Israel's military force. Barak, on the other hand, appears as someone who is under Deborah's command. The superiority of Deborah over Barak is seen in the way she is portrayed in the song. In the Song of Deborah, Deborah is mentioned four times (Judg 5:1, 7, 12, 15), while Barak is mentioned only three times (Judg 5:1, 12, 15). Further, Barak always appears associated with Deborah, never by himself, and always as a secondary character.

The title "a mother of Israel," then, seems to indicate that Deborah had the primary leadership in the fight against the army of Sisera. It was to Deborah to whom the leaders of Issachar came (Judg 5:15), it was Deborah who sent Barak into battle (Judg 5:12), it was because of Deborah that the oppression in Israel ceased (Judg 5:7), and it was Deborah who celebrated with song the victory against the enemies (Judg 5:1).

The Song of Deborah begins by declaring that the leaders of the tribes and the people answered the call to fight against the Canaanites (Judg 5:2, 9). In view of the dedication of the people to fight against the army of Sisera, Deborah said: "My heart goes out to the commanders of Israel who offered themselves willingly among the people. Bless the Lord" (Judg 5:9). Deborah's poignant declaration that her heart went out to those who gave themselves to save their nation shows how much Deborah was personally involved in this war of liberation.

The declaration that Deborah was "a mother of Israel" (Judg 5:7 NJB) is related to the statement in 5:5 where Yahweh is called "the God of Israel." The poetic structure of the two verses, the repetition of the phrases "before the Lord" in verse 5 and "until you arose" in verse 7, and the identification of Yahweh as the God of Israel and Deborah as a mother in Israel emphasize that Deborah was God's representative in Israel. In Israel's war ideology, Yahweh the Divine Warrior led Israel into battle, and Deborah was Yahweh's representative who led the nation into war.

Deborah became known as "a mother in Israel" because the people of Israel regarded her as a woman of exceptional character who used her skills to help the people and to defend her nation, who identified with the people in their suffering, whose strong leadership aroused the leaders of the tribes of Israel to resist their oppressors, and whose enthusiasm inspired the people to rise up to fight for their nation.[5] Indeed, Deborah was a revered and successful *šôpēṭ* in Israel.

5. Susan Ackerman, *Warrior, Dancer, Seductress, Queen: Women in Judges and Biblical Israel*, ABRL (New York: Doubleday, 1998), 27–88.

CHAPTER 30

Ahinoam: The Mother of Amnon

There are two women named Ahinoam in the Old Testament. The first woman was Saul's wife (1 Sam 14:50). The second woman, and the subject of this chapter, was David's third wife and the mother of Amnon, David's firstborn son. The Bible does not provide much information about her. As one of the many women mentioned in David's stories, Ahinoam is silent; her voice is never heard, and her story is indirectly implied in the texts where her name is mentioned.

Ahinoam and David

By the time David married Ahinoam, he already had two wives. David's first wife was Michal, the daughter of Saul (1 Sam 18:27–28). Because of the animosity between Saul and David, Saul gave Michal to another man (1 Sam 25:44). Because Saul had given Michal to another man, David married two other women, Abigail and Ahinoam (1 Sam 25:42–43).

Diana Edelman suggests that, because David's marriage to Ahinoam was announced immediately after his marriage to Abigail, the biblical writer intended his readers to know that Ahinoam was one of the five female servants (1 Sam 25:42) who came with Abigail when she married David; that is, Ahinoam was "Abigail's attendant-turned-fellow-wife." According to Edelman, the biblical writer intended his readers to know that David married Ahinoam "for the common reason of physical attraction, Abigail was married primarily for her influence, insight, and wealth as the widow of Nabal, and secondarily for her beauty."[1] Edelman's view is possible, but it finds no support in the biblical text.

1. Diana V. Edelman, *King Saul in the Historiography of Judah*, JSOTSup 121 (Sheffield: JSOT Press, 1991), 221.

Although David married Abigail first, Ahinoam's name is always mentioned ahead of Abigail, except in one context. Linda Schearing writes, "Of the five contexts in which Ahinoam appears, only in her marriage notice (1 Sam 25:43) does she come after Abigail."[2] Ahinoam holds priority over Abigail because she was the mother of David's firstborn son.

Ahinoam was from Jezreel. During her marriage to David, she endured "the rigors of an irregular life on the fringe of the desert."[3] She married him during the seven years David lived as a fugitive evading Saul's pursuit. During this time, David did not have a permanent home. Throughout this ordeal Ahinoam remained by David's side, not knowing if he would be restored to his previous position or would perish in battle.

When David left Saul's service he found refuge with Achish, a king of the Philistines: "David stayed with Achish at Gath, he and his troops, every man with his household, and David with his two wives, Ahinoam of Jezreel, and Abigail of Carmel, Nabal's widow" (1 Sam 27:3). While David was away from Ziklag, together with the Philistine army at Aphek in preparation to fight against Saul and the army of Israel (1 Sam 29:1–3), the Amalekites attacked and conquered Ziklag. Ahinoam was taken as a spoil of war.

> Now when David and his men came to Ziklag on the third day, the Amalekites had made a raid on the Negeb and on Ziklag. They had attacked Ziklag, burned it down, and taken captive the women and all who were in it, both small and great; they killed none of them, but carried them off, and went their way. When David and his men came to the city, they found it burned down, and their wives and sons and daughters taken captive. Then David and the people who were with him raised their voices and wept, until they had no more strength to weep. David's two wives also had been taken captive, Ahinoam of Jezreel, and Abigail the widow of Nabal of Carmel. (1 Sam 30:1–5)

2. Linda Schearing, "Ahinoam 2," in *Women in Scripture*, ed. Carol Meyers, Toni Craven, and Ross Shepard Kramer (Boston: Houghton Mifflin, 2000), 48.
3. David Jobling, *1 Samuel*, Berit Olam (Collegeville, MN: Liturgical Press, 1998), 186.

David and his men wept bitterly because of the devastation caused by the Amalekites. In her analysis of David's tears, Gafney writes, "Although David's tears could signify his care and concern for his two wives, they could also be tears of rage."[4] David and his men attacked the Ammonites and brought Ahinoam back: "David recovered all that the Amalekites had taken; and David rescued his two wives" (1 Sam 30:18).

After Saul's death, David and his family moved to Hebron where David became king over Judah. Ahinoam accompanied him: "So David went up there, along with his two wives, Ahinoam of Jezreel, and Abigail the widow of Nabal of Carmel" (2 Sam 2:2). David ruled over Judah seven years and six months (2 Sam 5:5). While he was at Hebron, several sons were born to David. His firstborn was Amnon, (2 Sam 3:2). His second son was Chileab, the son of Abigail (2 Sam 3:3). Chileab is called Daniel in 1 Chronicles 3:1, but nothing else is said about him in the Old Testament; he possibly died as an infant.

Although David married Abigail before Ahinoam, it was Ahinoam who gave David his firstborn son, Amnon. It is possible that Ahinoam had more children, but only Amnon, the firstborn, is listed. Daughters were often not mentioned in the genealogies of their fathers. Gafney said that David wanted to make sure Abigail was not pregnant with Nabal's child before he slept with her. She writes, "Abigail does not give birth until after Ahinoam, suggesting that David did not sleep with her until he was sure she was not pregnant with Nabal's child."[5] This view, however, is untenable because Ahinoam and Abigail had already lived with David about two years before they moved to Hebron.

Jon D. Levenson suggests that on the basis of Nathan's words to David (2 Sam 12:8) that Ahinoam was Saul's wife and that David married her before Saul's death. He writes, "Could it be that David swaggered into Hebron with the wife of a Calebite chieftain on one arm and that of the Israelite king on the other? A remark of Nathan's to David suggests that there was but one Ahinoam, wife of Saul, then of David, 'I gave you the household of your lord and the wives of your lord in your bosom, and I gave you the Houses of Israel and Judah. A little longer, and I would have given you more like these' (2 Sam 12:8).

---

4. Wilda C. Gafney, *Womanist Midrash: A Reintroduction to the Women of the Torah and the Throne* (Louisville: Westminster John Knox, 2017), 209.
5. Gafney, *Womanist Midrash*, 207.

Nathan alludes to David's marriage to Saul's wives, as if it were well-known."[6]

Levenson supposes that David had married Ahinoam while Saul was still alive. This view means that David took Ahinoam, Saul's wife, before Saul died. This view, however, should be rejected. Diana Edelman rightly responds to Levenson's proposal: "Such a presumption would require David to have run off with the queen mother while Saul was still on the throne, which seems unlikely. In view of the possession of the royal harem as a claim to royal legitimacy, Nathan's comment can be related to David's eventual possession of Saul's wives after he ascended the throne in the wake of Eshbaal's death. Nathan refers to David's possession of more than a single wife of Saul's in verse 23, which precludes the application of the phrase to Ahinoam alone."[7] If Ahinoam was Saul's wife, then David married his mother-in-law since Ahinoam was the mother of Michal, David's first wife, and also the mother of Jonathan, David's friend.

Ahinoam and Amnon

After the birth of Amnon in Hebron, the biblical text says nothing further of Ahinoam, but her story does not end with the birth of her son. Since Amnon was born in Hebron during David's reign there (2 Sam 3:2), and the tragic incident involving Tamar occurred later in Jerusalem (2 Sam 13), it is reasonable to assume that Ahinoam was still alive at the time Amnon raped his sister. As a mother, she will experience the tragedy of knowing that her son raped his half-sister Tamar, and she will mourn the death of her son who was murdered by his half-brother Absalom in revenge for the rape of his sister.

Ahinoam is known for two important things: for being David's third wife and for being the crown prince's mother. In the list of David's children by his many wives, only the firstborn sons of his wives are mentioned. This is one of the reasons the author of 2 Samuel emphasizes that Amnon was David's firstborn son.

Amnon, Ahinoam's son, is well-known for raping his half-sister, Tamar (see discussion above in ch. 28). When David heard what Amnon had done, he became angry but refused to punish him "because

6. Jon D. Levenson, "I Samuel 25 as Literature and as History," *CBQ* 40 (1978): 27.
7. Diana V. Edelman, "Ahinoam (Person)," *ABD* 1:118.

he loved him, for he was his firstborn" (2 Sam 13:21). Absalom made plans to kill Amnon, and two years later, he fulfilled his vow to kill his brother. Ahinoam was probably still alive when Amnon was killed by Absalom, since Amnon was about twenty to twenty-five years old when he raped Tamar, a *betûlâ*, "virgin," which designates a young woman of marriageable age.

Ahinoam was likely devastated by what Amnon had done to Tamar. Amnon's death deprived Ahinoam the right to become queen mother if Amnon succeeded his father. He brought shame to her and to her family. Amnon's act was repulsive, but Ahinoam grieved for the son whom she nursed and whom she loved. Although she was horrified by his action, as a mother, Ahinoam shed tears for her dead son.

CHAPTER 31

Abishag, the Shunammite

Abishag's story takes place during David's last days of his life, at a time when he was unable to get himself warm and retain his body heat. David's old age and his illness would present several challenges to his ability to lead Israel as king.

The Young Woman from Shunem

Abishag was a young woman from the village of Shunem, a village located near Jezreel in the tribe of Issachar (Josh 19:17–18). Abishag is introduced as a *naʿarâ*, a young woman of marriageable age. This indicates that when Abishag was taken to David's palace she was a teenager. She is also called a *betûlâ*, an unmarried young virgin. Abishag was beautiful. The Hebrew word refers to Abishag's outward appearance; she was beautiful in appearance. During her early days in the palace, Abishag ministered to David as his nurse and as his concubine. After David's death, Abishag is indirectly involved in the struggle between Adonijah and Solomon for the throne of David.

Abishag and David

David was thirty years old when he became king, and he ruled over Israel for forty years (2 Sam 5:4). Thus, the story of David and Abishag occurred when David was almost seventy years old. During his many years as a soldier in Saul's army and then as a king over Israel, David was active in fighting against Israel's enemies and enlarging his empire. As David grew old, however, his abilities as a fighter began to diminish.

In his old age, David suffered from an unknown ailment such that "he could not get warm" (1 Kgs 1:1). His servants tried to cover him, but his body could not retain heat. Worried about the health of the king, his servants decided that the king needed a nurse to attend to his needs. They said to David, "A young virgin must be found for our master, the king, to take care of the king's needs and serve as his nurse. She can also sleep with you and keep our master, the king, warm" (1 Kgs 1:2 NET). When the text says that David "did not know her sexually" (1 Kgs 1:4), it is possible that this statement means that Abishag was not David's concubine and that there was no implication that David was impotent or that Abishag was brought to the palace to have sexual relations with David. The expression "she can also sleep with you" (1 Kgs 1:2 NET), however, clearly indicates that David would have sex with Abishag.

Russell Meek proposes that the selection of Abishag to be David's nurse is not related to David's "sexual prowess but rather with his ability to judge his kingdom effectively."[1] The expression "the king did not know her sexually" (1 Kgs 1:4), however, implies that David was unable to have sex with Abishag. The Hebrew verb *yāda*ʿ is a common euphemism for sexual intercourse in the Hebrew Bible (Gen 4:1). Thus, this statement refers to David's physical decline and impotence.

Gray writes that David's authority as king corresponded to his virility. David's impotence as a man was a reflection on his impotence as a king.[2] Thus, Abishag's presence in the palace was a test to see whether David could continue as a king. Schearing writes, "His failure to 'know' Abishag (1 Kings 1:4) indicates his failure as king and precipitates the fight for succession which follows. If Abishag's function was to test David's virility, then it is possible she was admitted into David's harem either as concubine or wife."[3] Nelson points out that "Abishag became both a nurse for David's failing health and the prescribed medicine for his impotence. David remains impotent, however, and this failure precipitates a political crisis to which first Adonijah and then Nathan respond."[4]

Brueggemann says Abishag's role in David's bedroom "is to arouse the king sexually." He writes, "Because of the last phrase of v. 4, 'did not know her sexually,' it is probable that 'not get warm' means not to have an erection. Thus, the point of the opening paragraph is to

---

1. Russell L. Meek, "The Abishag Episode: Reexamining the Role of Virility in 1 Kings 1:1–4 in Light of the Kirta Epic and the Sumerian Tale 'The Old Man and the Young Woman,'" *BBR* 24 (2014): 1.
2. John Gray, *I & II Kings: A Commentary*, OTL (Louisville: Westminster John Knox, 1970), 77.
3. Linda S. Schearing, "Abishag (Person)," *ABD* 1:24.
4. Richard D. Nelson, *First and Second Kings*, Int (Louisville: Westminster John Knox, 1987), 16.

report the king's sexual impotence, his loss of virility, and therefore his disqualification as king."[5]

Abishag and Adonijah

The introduction of David as an old and sick man also serves to introduce the struggle between Solomon and his half-brother Adonijah to become the next king of Israel after David's death. Adonijah's ambition to become the new king after David began before the death of David. Adonijah began to display his ambition to be king when he gathered chariots and horsemen and a group of people and declared, "I will be king" (1 Kgs 1:5). He proclaimed himself king because David was old and sick, and apparently because he believed that David was near death. Before David died, he named Solomon to succeed him on the throne. Once Solomon ascended to the throne and became king of Israel, Adonijah went to Bathsheba, the queen mother to ask for Abishag as his wife. He wanted to marry Abishag to gain the throne through her (see discussion above in ch. 21).

The story of Abishag reflects the problems women faced in a patriarchal setting. As a teenager living in her father's house, Abishag was taken to David's palace to live with him. Whether she went willingly or was forced to go, the text does not say. She was in the prime of her life, taken from her home to marry an old man who was near death.

Abishag became a sex object to a man who could not have sex with her. Throughout her story, Abishag is silent; she never speaks about her feelings or about her situation. Abishag was brought to David to help him maintain control of his kingship, but it did not work because of David's impotence. Abishag then becomes the focus of a power play for David's throne when Adonijah attempts to marry her. The power play for the throne did not work because another woman, Bathsheba, intervened to save the life and the throne of her son Solomon. In the end, we know little about Abishag herself. From a teenager living in a small town in Israel to a woman who lived with a king in a palace in Jerusalem, her life became the focal point in the struggle between two men for the throne of her husband.

5. Walter Brueggemann, *1 & 2 Kings*, Smyth & Helwys Bible Commentary (Macon, GA: Smyth & Helwys, 2000), 12.

CHAPTER 32

Esther, the Queen of Persia

Queen Esther may be one of the best-known women in the Old Testament. Christian women relate to Esther's story because of her character, her endurance, and her faithfulness to her God. Esther lived in a situation challenging for her as a person, for her oppressed people, and for her religious views.

Esther and Her Struggle for Survival

Esther is recognized and praised for what she did to save her people from extermination by a wicked man. When Esther became queen, the Jewish people were living in exile in Persia. The Babylonians conquered Jerusalem in 587 BC, and the Jewish people were exiled and dispersed throughout the Babylonian Empire. After Cyrus, the king of Persia, conquered the Babylonians, the Jewish people became subjects of the Persian Empire for many years.

During their time in exile, the Jewish people had to learn how to live without a king, temple, or priesthood. Although some people prospered, most of the Jews experienced great distress because of their oppressive situation.

Esther's story occurred in the days of Ahasuerus, also known as Xerxes, the king of Persia who ruled from 485–465 BC. Ahasuerus's palace was in the fortress of Susa, a city at the foot of the Zagros Mountains in modern-day Iran. Ahasuerus ruled over a large empire divided into 127 provinces that extended from India to Sudan.

The royal city of Susa, one of the world's oldest cities, was one of the four capital cities of the Persian Empire and served as the winter residence of the kings of Persia (Neh 1:1; Esth 1:2). The city was in the ancient Elamite territory near the Ulai Canal (Dan 8:2), in what is now the modern Iranian city of Shush.

Esther's story began when King Ahasuerus deposed his queen, Vashti. Ahasuerus sought a woman out of all the virgins in the Persian Empire to be his new queen. Esther, a beautiful Jewish woman, was chosen to be the new queen.

Esther's story, however, is not a beautiful romance. Esther's story reflects a woman of character and wisdom who learned how to survive under difficult circumstances. Esther, whose Hebrew name was Hadassah (Esth 2:7), was a young Jewish woman living in exile in a pagan world. She worshiped Yahweh, the God of Israel. Against her will, she was taken from her Jewish home to live in the palace of the king of Persia. Esther was taken to the palace not because of her character or wisdom, but because she "was fair and beautiful" (Esth 2:7).

Because Esther's parents were dead, her father's nephew Mordecai had adopted Esther as his own daughter (Esth 2:7, 15; 9:29). Mordecai remained a loyal ally to Esther even after she was named queen. When the king's associate Haman devised a plan to kill all the Jews in the empire—simply because he felt disrespected by Mordecai—Esther realized her position would not save her.

Haman approached Ahasuerus and said to him, "Your Majesty, there is a certain nationality scattered among—but separate from—the nationalities in all the provinces of your kingdom. Their laws differ from those of all other nationalities. They do not obey your decrees. So it is not in your interest to tolerate them, Your Majesty. If you approve, have the orders for their destruction be written" (Esth 3:8–9 GW). Deceived by Haman's speech, the king ordered his officials to kill all the Jews—young and old, women and children—on a single day and to seize their possessions (Esth 3:13).

When Mordecai heard about Haman's plan, he asked Esther to go before the king and intercede for her people. But Esther's situation was not easy. She told Mordecai, "All the king's servants and the people of the king's provinces know that if any man or woman goes to the king inside the inner court without being called, there is but one law—all alike are to be put to death. Only if the king holds out the golden scepter to someone, may that person live. I myself have not been called to come in to the king for thirty days" (Esth 4:11).

Esther was quite concerned about the fate of her people; however, she was also aware of what would happen to her if she came before the king without being summoned. Mordecai told Esther, "Do not think that in the king's palace you will escape any more than all the other Jews. For if you keep silence at such a time as this, relief and deliverance will rise for the Jews from another quarter, but you and your father's family will perish. Who knows? Perhaps you have come to royal dignity for such a time as this" (Esth 4:13–14).

Queen Vashti

The story of Esther is not like the stories of the princesses in a Disney movie. In a movie, the princess meets the prince, they find romance and love, and they live happily ever after. Although the story of Esther has a happy ending, her story is a nightmare. The only reason Esther survived her nightmare was because of faith in her God, even though God is never mentioned in her story.

The story of how Esther became the queen of Persia begins after Ahasuerus removed Vashti as the queen of Persia. The king ordered Vashti to wear the royal crown and come to the garden of the king's palace (Esth 1:5). Ahasuerus wanted to show the people and the officials Vashti's beauty because she was very attractive (Esth 1:11). Vashti, who at the time was hosting a party for women only (Esth 1:9), refused to come before the king and his drunken friends.

There is much debate about whether Ahasuerus wanted Vashti to parade naked before his officials. The biblical author seems to indicate that the king intended to show Vashti in full royal attire, including the crown. Ahasuerus had displayed the great wealth of his kingdom to the nobles of his kingdom and to the governors of the provinces (Esth 1:4), and now he wanted to show them his most precious possession, Queen Vashti.

Queen Vashti took offense at the king's request and refused to appear, a decision demonstrating her strong character. But the refusal also indicates that the king's request was an affront to her status as the queen of Persia.

Insulted by Vashti's dignified response to Ahasuerus, his men predicted that the queen's denial would affect their authority at home: "Not only has Queen Vashti done wrong to the king, but also to all the officials and all the peoples who are in all the provinces of King Ahasuerus. For this deed of the queen will be made known to all women, causing them to look with contempt on their husbands, since they will say, 'King Ahasuerus commanded Queen Vashti to be brought before him, and she did not come'" (Esth 1:16–17). In a patriarchal society, the queen's behavior was unacceptable. As the king's official told the king, "This very day the noble ladies of Persia and Media who have heard of the queen's behavior will rebel against the king's officials, and there will be no end of contempt and wrath" (Esth 1:18).

Convinced by his officials' argument, the king deposed Vashti and ordered that a search be made for attractive young women in the empire. These women would be brought to the king's harem so that he could select one woman to take the place of Vashti as queen of Persia.

The Search for a New Queen

Ahasuerus's decision to select the new queen is quite unusual. A queen typically would be selected based on her nobility. Instead, the new queen was to be selected for her appearance: "Let a search be made for beautiful young virgins for the king" (Esth 2:2 NIV). The Hebrew word for virgin means a young woman of marriageable age. Since most young women of marriageable age in the ancient Near East would have no sexual experience, the translation of the NIV reflects this cultural fact.

As Ahasuerus's edict was carried out, many young women were taken from their homes to Susa where the king's palace was located. Among them was Esther. Esther was very attractive and had a beautiful figure (Esth 2:7). She did not go voluntarily—she was abducted from her house to have sex with the king. These women could never return to their families. If they were not selected to be queen, they would remain in the king's harem.

Esther was facing a nightmare. Jewish women were supposed to marry Jewish men. Her marriage to Ahasuerus was not a dream come true. She had to depend on God to give her strength to face this ordeal.

Esther and the Absence of God

In Persia, Esther was an outsider, the "other." The "other" is the person who is socially and culturally different from those native to the society. Esther lived in a community of Jews who were strangers in a foreign land. Jewish culture and religion were fundamentally different from the culture and religion of Persia.

Though physically separated from her family and community, Esther's faith matured through divine presence working subtly beneath the surface of the events in Ahasuerus's court. Within the palace confines, she understood that God's providence operates through human agency rather than overt manifestation. The seclusion of the harem became the place where Esther discerned the quiet movements of divine guidance in her difficult situation. The mystery of God's hidden, yet active, presence may explain the literary decision to omit explicit divine references in the book. It should not be understood as absence, but rather as a profound illustration of how faith operates in complex situations where God works through human decisions rather than supernatural intervention.

The Septuagint translators were so baffled by the absence of God in the book that they inserted a preface to the book in which Mordecai cries to God for help. In addition, some scribes believed that a Hebrew sentence in Esther 5:4 contains the initial letters of the four Hebrew letters YHWH, the name of God.[11]

It is possible that Esther assumed that God was absent, unaware of her plight. But God was at work in the events that brought her to the palace. In fact, God's providence is the main message of the book. God was working in Esther's life the entire time. God was close to Esther, working behind the scenes to prepare her to become an agent of salvation for her people.

God shows his providence by working through other people. People are the avenue by which God works to bring his presence and his love to other people. The person whom God chose to help Esther in her time of need was Mordecai, her adoptive father.

Esther Becomes the Queen of Persia

When Esther and the other women arrived at the palace, she was placed in the in custody of Hegai, the eunuch who oversaw the women (Esth 2:8). In God's providence, Esther "pleased him and won his favor, and he quickly provided her with her cosmetic treatments and her portion of food, and with seven chosen maids from the king's palace, and advanced her and her maids to the best place in the harem" (Esth 2:9). Since these maids came from "the king's palace," it shows that Esther was receiving special attention from Hegai.

The preparation to spend a night with the king took twelve months—six months in cosmetic treatment with oil of myrrh and six months with

1. Jonathan Magonet, "The God Who Hides: Some Jewish Responses to the Book of Esther," *European Judaism* 47 (2014): 110.

perfumes and other cosmetics (Esth 2:12). When a young woman went before the king, she had one chance to please him. So anything the woman wanted to take with her from the women's quarter to the king's chamber was given to her (Esth 2:13). If she did not please the king, she would return to the harem and become the king's concubine.

What happened if a woman, when it was her turn in the king's chamber, did not sexually please him? In the morning, she returned to the second harem and was placed in the custody of Shaashgaz, the king's eunuch, who oversaw the concubines (Esth 2:14). The king's harem was divided into two areas: the first held the women preparing to spend the night with the king, while the second area housed the women who did not sexually please the king and were relegated to the status of concubines.

Esther's journey from her home to the throne of Persia unfolded in several stages. She was first taken from her family, then to the king's palace, and now Esther is taken into the king's chamber. Her nightmare continues as she prepares to meet the king. When the time came for Esther to present herself before the king, she did not request anything except what Hegai recommended. She knew that Hegai knew what the king wanted, and she trusted him in this matter.

We are not told what Esther took with her, but her decision shows the strength of her character. She accepted the advice of Hegai, but she was confident enough to go before the king with nothing else except the strength of her character. The text says that "Esther was admired by all who saw her" (Esth 2:15). The Hebrew word *ḥēn* means "favor, grace" and it is used to indicate "to find favor in the eyes of someone."

When Esther came to the king's chamber, Ahasuerus "loved Esther more than all the other women, and she met with his loving approval more than all the other young women" (Esth 2:17 NET). Four years after Vashti was deposed as queen, Ahasuerus placed the royal crown upon Esther's head, and Esther became the queen of Persia.

In God's providence, the king chose Esther. She eventually became queen, the one position of influence that would allow her to save her people. In this way her story is like that of Joseph in Egypt. Joseph was taken by force to Egypt, but he became an important official in the court of Pharaoh and used his position to save his people. What Joseph said to his brothers also applies to Esther: "Even though you intended to do harm to me, God intended it for good, in order to preserve a numerous people, as he is doing today" (Gen 50:20).

PART 6

NON-ISRAELITE WOMEN

CHAPTER 33

God's Sovereignty and the Inclusion of Non-Israelite Women

The Old Testament consistently affirms Yahweh's sovereignty over all nations, not just Israel. This divine sovereignty establishes the foundation for understanding how non-Israelite women interact with God's covenant people. The prophet Amos declares, "Are you not like the Ethiopians to me, O people of Israel? says the Lord. Did I not bring Israel up from the land of Egypt, and the Philistines from Caphtor and the Arameans from Kir?" (Amos 9:7). This rhetorical question highlights God's active role in the affairs of all nations, not only Israel.

In the ancient Near Eastern world, ethnic identity was paramount. Israel was commanded to remain separate from surrounding nations to preserve their covenant relationship with God. Yet paradoxically, God repeatedly incorporated non-Israelite women into his redemptive plan, demonstrating that salvation was never meant to be exclusively for one ethnic group.[1]

Israel's story unfolds not in isolation but within a broader cultural and historical landscape shaped by political alliances and familial connections that frequently crossed ethnic and religious boundaries. While the faithful women of Israel played significant roles in the unfolding narrative of God's chosen people, faith and influence were never confined to the boundaries of Israel alone.

While this project's focus remains on Israelite women such as Miriam, Deborah, Sarah, and Hannah, the inclusion of non-Israelite women such as Hagar, Ruth, Tamar, Jezebel, Jael, and Sisera's mother

1. Jiri Moskala, "The Mission of God's People in the Old Testament," *Perspective Digest* 16 (2011): 18.

provides a broader, richer perspective on the complex tapestry of biblical history. Their stories enhance our understanding by emphasizing God's sovereignty in working through those outside Israel for his divine purposes and by illustrating the broader implications of faith and divine justice.

God's sovereignty is evident throughout the biblical narrative as he orchestrates events and people to fulfill his divine plan.[2] One striking example is his use of non-Israelite women in Jesus's lineage and the broader history of redemption. These women play crucial roles in advancing God's plan, illustrating his grace, inclusivity, and ability to redeem and use individuals regardless of their background.

Including non-Israelite women in a study of Israel's women of faith allows for a clearer understanding of moral and spiritual contrasts in the biblical narrative. Faith, as represented in the Old Testament, is rarely simple. It weaves through stories of triumph and failure, unexpected alliances, and divine purposes that transcend the boundaries of nationality, ethnicity, or morality.

The inclusion of non-Israelite women alongside faithful Israelite women is not only justifiable but profoundly enriching. While these women were not born into the covenant community of Israel, their stories resonate with themes of redemption, justice, and divine providence. By examining their lives alongside those of Israelite women, we gain a richer understanding of the complexity of faith and the workings of God in human history.

From the perspective of divine sovereignty, non-Israelite women who advance, challenge, or illuminate God's purposes for Israel provide essential contrasts to the Israelite women of faith. Their inclusion demonstrates that God's redemptive narrative encompasses all peoples, sometimes working through outsiders to accomplish divine purposes for the covenant people. Therefore, a study of Israel's faithful women is incomplete without acknowledging the contributions of non-Israelite women who, in various ways, impacted or contrasted with the covenant people's history. These women's stories highlight themes of faith, divine judgment, and divine sovereignty, and includ-

2. Robin Routledge, *Old Testament Theology: A Thematic Approach* (Downers Grove, IL: IVP Academic, 2008), 315.

ing their accounts enriches our understanding of Israel's history while also showcasing how God's purposes transcend national boundaries.

God's sovereignty is displayed in his inclusion of non-Israelite women in his redemptive plan. Their lives testify to his unwavering intention to bring salvation to all nations, an intention that was ultimately fulfilled in the life and ministry of Jesus. These stories serve as a reminder that no one lies beyond the reach of God's grace and that he works through individuals of all backgrounds to accomplish his redemptive purposes for the world. As D. G. Firth points out, "Israel is continually being reformed, redefined as a community which includes all who share its faith in Yahweh. Foreigners, even those who would most obviously appear to be candidates for destruction, are included."[3]

These women's narratives reveal a God who consistently uplifts those people society often dismisses as insignificant. Their inclusion in the divine story was not despite their marginalized status but because of it, allowing God's grace to be displayed against the backdrop of human prejudice and limitation.

Through the lives of women born outside the covenant community, God demonstrated that true faith transcends ethnic boundaries, ritual practices, and cultural traditions. Their inclusion in the biblical narrative challenged Israel's tendency toward ethnic exclusivism, paving the way for the New Testament's declaration that in Christ, "there is no longer Jew or Greek, there is no longer slave or free" (Gal 3:28).

3. D. G. Firth, "Joshua 24 and the Welcome of Foreigners," *Acta Theologica* 38 (2018): 81.

CHAPTER 34

Hagar, the Surrogate Mother

In the story of Hagar we learn about a woman who gave birth to a son who was destined not to be her son. As we saw in the chapter about Sarah (ch. 15), Sarah gave her slave Hagar to Abraham so that Hagar could conceive a son who then would be adopted by Sarah. Phyllis Trible calls Hagar "the slave used, abused and rejected."[1]

Hagar, the Servant of Sarah

After realizing he had been tricked into thinking Sarah was only Abraham's sister, Pharaoh gave Abraham a *mōhar*, the bride price, as the guardian of his "sister." The *mōhar* included "sheep, oxen, male donkeys, male and female slaves, female donkeys, and camels" (Gen 12:16). Perhaps Hagar was among the female slaves given to Abraham. All we know for sure is that after their journey to Egypt, Hagar served Sarah as her personal attendant in the same way Deborah served Rebekah (Gen 35:8). Hagar, as a slave, was the property of Sarah; she was Hagar's *gebîrâ*, "her mistress" (Gen 16:4). A *gebîrâ* had authority and power over people.[2] In the Judean court, the *gebîrâ* was the queen mother who exercised some sort of political power during the reign of her son, the king. The word *gebîrâ* is generally translated as "Great Lady."

1. Phyllis Trible, *Texts of Terror*, OBT (Philadelphia: Fortress, 1984), 1.
2. Four royal women are named *gebîrâ* in the Old Testament: Queen Tahpenes, Pharaoh's wife (1 Kgs 11:19); Maacah, the mother of King Asa of Judah (1 Kgs 15:13); Nehushta, the mother of King Jehoiachin of Judah (Jer 29:2); and Jezebel, the mother of King Joram (Jehoram) of Israel (2 Kgs 10:13).

Sarah's Barrenness

Sarah was included in the promise and the covenant that God made with Abraham. Yet Sarah was barren. In the ancient Near East barrenness was a source of embarrassment and humiliation to a woman and brought disappointment to her husband, particularly since barrenness implied a curse from God.[3] Sarah determined to build her family through her slave, a practice attested to by documents found in the ancient Mesopotamian city of Nuzi.[4] As Sarah's slave, Hagar had no voice in the matter. As Fretheim writes, "She may have accepted the customs of surrogate motherhood current in that culture, but her vulnerability should not be downplayed. She has no legal rights in this situation, and when Abraham, having voicelessly accepted Sarah's proposal, shows up at her tent door to fulfil the 'obligation,' she has no choice but to acquiesce."[5]

A son by Hagar meant that Abraham would have an heir to receive the blessing and inherit the land Yahweh had promised. Thus, Abraham had sex with Hagar, and she became pregnant. Hagar was a slave. She belonged to Sarah, who exercised power over her. Not even Hagar's own body belonged to her; she was "a piece of property that can be bought, given away, or treated inhumanely; she is even given over to the head of the household by her mistress to have children for her."[6]

After Hagar became pregnant, she "looked with contempt on her mistress" (Gen 16:4) because, while she was fertile, Sarah remained barren. Hagar's actions unsurprisingly offended Sarah, who complained to Abraham, but he refused to intervene in the quarrel. He stated simply, "'Here, your slave is in your power; do whatever you want with her.' Then Sarai mistreated her so much that she ran away from her" (Gen 16:6 CSB).

Hagar and Abraham

When Sarah asked Abraham to have sex with Hagar, Abraham agreed to her request without a word. When problems arose between the two

---

3. Joel S. Baden, "The Nature of Barrenness in the Hebrew Bible," in *Disability Studies and Biblical Literature*, ed. Candida R. Moss and Jeremy Schipper (New York: Palgrave Macmillan, 2011), 13–27.
4. John Van Seters, "The Problem of Childlessness in Near Eastern Law and the Patriarchs of Israel," JBL 87 (1968): 401–8.
5. Terence E. Fretheim, *Abraham: Trials of Family and Faith* (Columbia: The University of South Carolina Press, 2007), 104.
6. Megan McKenna, *Not Counting Women and Children: Neglected Stories from the Bible* (Maryknoll, NY: Orbis Books, 1995), 174.

women, Sarah accused Abraham of causing this situation: "You are responsible for the wrong I am suffering" (Gen 16:5 NIV). Abraham could have acted and solved the problem between his two wives, but he chose not to intervene, doing nothing to relieve the tension between Sarah and Hagar. With Abraham's permission, Sarah tormented Hagar. The Hebrew word *ʿānâ*, translated "dealt harshly" (Gen 16:6), means "to oppress," "to inflict pain;" it implies that Sarah used violence to oppress Hagar. Despite his future son being in Hagar's womb, Abraham remained passive and disinterested.

Hagar fled to the wilderness after Sarah's harsh mistreatment. The angel of the Lord appeared to Hagar by a spring of water and said to her, "'Hagar, slave-girl of Sarai, where have you come from and where are you going?' She said, 'I am running away from my mistress Sarai.' The angel of the Lord said to her, 'Return to your mistress, and submit to her'" (Gen 16:8–9).

God wanted Hagar to return and continue living under Sarah's authority: "Go back to your mistress and submit to her authority" (Gen 16:9 CSB). In her book *Texts of Terror*, Phyllis Trible explains the severity of God's command to Hagar. She writes that God's two commands to "return and submit to suffering, bring a divine word of terror to an abused, yet courageous, woman. . . . Inexplicably, the God who later, seeing the suffering of a slave people, comes down to deliver them out of the hands of the Egyptians, here identifies with the oppressor and orders a servant to return not only to bondage but also to affliction."[7]

After Hagar's son was born, the conflict between Sarah and Hagar continued. Rather than ensuring that Hagar and Ishmael were properly cared for, Abraham left their fate up to Sarah, whose jealousy caused her to deal cruelly with Hagar. The turning point in their relationship came one day when Sarah saw Isaac and Ishmael together: "Sarah saw the son of Hagar the Egyptian, whom she had borne to Abraham, playing with her son Isaac" (Gen 21:9). English translations differ on what was happening between Ishmael and Isaac. The NIV says that Ishmael was "mocking" Isaac. The NLT says that Ishmael was "making fun of Isaac." In Genesis 26:8, the same Hebrew word is used to describe Isaac "fondling his wife Rebekah." The Hebrew word *ṣāḥaq* literally

7. Trible, *Texts of Terror*, 16.

means "laughter," and it seems to be a play on the name Isaac, which also means "laughter." Sarah's reaction may indicate that Ishmael was sexually abusing Isaac. The text, however, is silent regarding the details of what happened. Whatever happened between the two boys, Sarah saw Ishmael—Abraham's firstborn, although by his secondary wife—as a threat to Isaac. Sarah commanded Abraham, "Cast out this slave woman with her son; for the son of this slave woman shall not inherit along with my son Isaac" (Gen 21:10). Sarah's ultimatum "displeased Abraham greatly because Ishmael was his son" (Gen 21:11 NET).

Abraham was concerned for Hagar and Ishmael because the boy was his firstborn son whom he loved dearly.[8] God, however, calmed Abraham's fear by telling him that he would provide for them, "Do not be distressed because of the boy and because of your slave woman. . . . As for the son of the slave woman, I will make a nation of him also, because he is your offspring" (Gen 21:12–13). At the request of Sarah, and with the encouragement of Yahweh, Abraham sent Hagar away to an uncertain fate. "So Abraham rose early in the morning, and took bread and a skin of water, and gave it to Hagar, putting it on her shoulder, along with the child, and sent her away. And she departed, and wandered about in the wilderness of Beer-sheba" (Gen 21:14).

Hagar and God

Hagar must have felt that no one cared for her when she was banished into the unforgiving desert. And yet she was more concerned for her young son than for her own life.[9] God appeared a second time to Hagar while she and her son were in great distress. When their water was gone, she feared that she and Ishmael would die in the wilderness. Hagar put her son under one of the bushes, left him there alone, and went away: "'I refuse to watch the child die.' So she sat across from him and wept uncontrollably" (Gen 21:16 NET). While Hagar was weeping, the angel of the Lord appeared to her and said, "Do not be afraid; for God has heard the voice of the boy where he is. Come, lift up the boy and hold him fast

8. Moshe Reiss, "Ishmael, Son of Abraham," *JBQ* 30 (2002): 254.
9. In Gen 21:14 Ishmael is called a "child." The Hebrew word used in this text is *yeled*, meaning child, boy, or young person. The word can refer to a range of ages, and it does not always imply a small child. A closer look at the events in Abraham's life shows that Ishmael would have been around sixteen or seventeen years old at the time Hagar was sent into the wilderness.

with your hand, for I will make a great nation of him" (Gen 21:17–18). Hagar and her son lived because of divine intervention. Because Ishmael was Abraham's firstborn son, God also made a promise to Hagar that her son would become a great nation.

Hagar, a Caring Mother

Hagar had a very difficult life. First, she was taken away from her family and trafficked as a slave. She then suffered as a servant to Sarah. Without her consent, Hagar was forced to become a surrogate mother for Sarah, thus losing the son she had carried and then delivered. Sarah was so cruel that Hagar ran away to escape the brutal treatment. While in the wilderness, God told Hagar to return and submit to the harsh treatment imposed by Sarah. During the many years of conflict between Sarah and Hagar, Abraham, her husband, refused to protect her. Finally, at Sarah's urging, Abraham banished Hagar to the wilderness.

What distinguishes Hagar is the love and concern for her son in the midst of her suffering. Although the text says little about Hagar's relationship with Ishmael, the scene in the wilderness shows the broken heart of a mother who was contemplating a painful death for her son. Alone and afraid for the fate of her son, Hagar wept the tears of a loving and caring mother who was about to lose the son she loved. But Hagar's attitude was not one of hopeless resignation in the face of Ishmael's certain death; rather, it was a request to God for help. As Janzen and Noble write, "Hagar's words, together with her weeping, constitute a prayer that Ishmael's life may be spared."[10] Hagar's tears elicited a response from God: "Hagar, do not be afraid; for God has heard the voice of the boy where he is" (Gen 21:17).

Hagar's story reflects the oppressed conditions in many women's lives in today's society: the story of surrogate mothers, abandoned pregnant women, divorced mothers, abused wives. May these suffering mothers find comfort in the God who helped Hagar, who, alone in the wilderness, afraid for her life and without anyone to help, met God whom she called El-roi: "You Are the God Who Watches Over Me" (Gen 16:13 GW). In the midst of her loneliness, Hagar discovered that she was not alone.

10. J. Gerald Janzen and John T. Noble, "Did Hagar Give Ishmael Up for Dead?: Gen 21.14–21 Re-Visited," *JSOT* 44 (2020): 519.

CHAPTER 35

Tamar, the Wife of Er

Tamar was abused by her two husbands and wronged by her father-in-law, but she was a strong woman whom God used in his ultimate plan to reconcile the world unto himself. Because of her cunning, Tamar became one of the ancestors of David and Jesus.

The story of Tamar is found in Genesis 38:1–30. Tamar placed her own life in jeopardy to overcome the patriarchal structure and cultural oppression that many women faced in her society. Tamar lived in a male-dominated society in addition to being a Canaanite woman married to an Israelite man. As a wife, one of her many responsibilities was to give a son to her husband to ensure the survival of her husband's name. With the death of her husband Er and her father-in-law's dishonesty, Tamar initiated a plan to ensure that her husband's name would remain alive in Israel.

The Plight of Tamar

Tamar enters the narrative of Israel's history when Judah, Jacob's fourth son, separated himself from his brothers to live among the Canaanites. Judah came to Adullam, a city south of Jerusalem that later became one of the cities in the tribe of Judah (2 Chr 11:5, 7). While living among the Canaanites, Judah married a Canaanite woman whom the Chronicler tells us was named Bath-shua, "the daughter of Shua" (1 Chr 2:3). The woman gave birth to three sons: Er, Onan, and Shelah. Although the woman remains nameless, her voice is heard because she is the one who names her second and third sons. Judah was not present when his youngest son, Shelah, was born (Gen 38:5).

When Er came of age, Judah took a wife for him—Tamar. Since it was an arranged marriage, Tamar was not given the choice of whether she would marry Er. In a patriarchal society, a woman would marry whomever her father chose for her, whether the woman loved the man chosen to be her husband or not. Nothing is known about Tamar before she became a member of Judah's family. She left her father's house to live under the authority of another man. Marriage for Tamar meant security and acceptance into Judah's family, and providing a son would secure her position in the family.

Tamar and Her Two Husbands

Er was a wicked man who provoked Yahweh's anger. The nature of Er's wickedness is unknown, but it was so abominable that Yahweh took his life (Gen 38:7). We can imagine that living with such a wicked man was not easy, even though Scripture is silent on the issue. We can know that Er's death destabilized Tamar's life, for now she was widowed and childless in a society in which a woman's financial stability depended upon the men in her life.

After Er died, Judah commanded Onan (the secondborn son) to "go in to your brother's wife and perform the duty of a brother-in-law to her; raise up offspring for your brother" (Gen 38:8). Judah is here referring to the duties of the levir (Deut 25:5–10). The Levirate law specifies that "when brothers reside together, and one of them dies and has no son, the wife of the deceased shall not be married outside the family to a stranger. Her husband's brother shall go in to her, taking her in marriage, and performing the duty of a husband's brother to her, and the firstborn whom she bears shall succeed to the name of the deceased brother" (Deut 25:5–6). The Levirate law was designed to protect a widow's inheritance rights within her father-in-law's family.

Levirate marriage would ensure a widow's financial security with the birth of an heir to her dead husband. That is, the son through a Levirate marriage was a male heir who both enabled the deceased husband's name to live on and would inherit a portion of the family's property. As a widow, Tamar knew that her future depended on her ability to produce an heir for her dead husband. Judah also was concerned about the legacy of his dead son, for in ancient Israel it was considered a tragedy if a man died without leaving behind a male heir to continue the legacy of his name (2 Sam 18:18).

Onan was assigned to perform the Levirate duties so that Er's name would not be blotted out of Israel. Onan, however, was not willing to fulfill his Levirate duty "since Onan knew that the offspring would not be his, he spilled his semen on the ground whenever he went in to his brother's wife, so that he would not give offspring to his brother" (Gen 38:9).[1] As the oldest living son of Judah, now that Er had died, Onan was next in line for the family inheritance. Onan, therefore, did not want to give Tamar a son because that son would be Er's heir and thus would inherit Er's portion of the inheritance, significantly reducing the inheritance Onan now stood to gain.

For the second time, Tamar was subjected to the wickedness of a member of Judah's family. By refusing to impregnate Tamar and give an heir to his brother, Onan took advantage of Tamar's body, imposed upon her the pain of enforced barrenness, and treated her like an object to be used. Onan's action displeased God, and God vindicated Tamar by taking Onan's life. The death of a second husband likely had a profound effect on Tamar's sense of worth. As Juliana Claassens writes, "The death of the male providers has a marked effect on the worth of women in a society where a woman's honor is intrinsically linked to her male relatives."[2]

Tamar and Judah

With the death of Onan, it was Judah's responsibility to give his youngest son Shelah to Tamar to perform the Levirate duties. Tamar believed that through Shelah she would be able to obtain an heir for her dead husband. Judah, however, was reluctant to give Shelah to Tamar because of the deaths of his two sons. Judah said to Tamar, "'Remain a widow in your father's house until my son Shelah grows up'—for he feared that he too would die, like his brothers" (Gen 38:11). Frymer-Kensky highlights the implications of Judah's request: "By leaving her to be a 'widow in her father's house,' Judah binds her perpetually to his family without intending to provide her a secure future."[3]

Judah did not know his sons had died because of their own wickedness. Rather, he believed that Tamar was "a lethal woman, . . . a woman whose sexual partners are all doomed to die."[4] Tamar lived as a widow and mourned the death of her husband for many years, only

1. Claude F. Mariottini, "Onan (Person)," ABD 5:21.
2. L. Juliana M. Claassens, "Resisting Dehumanization: Ruth, Tamar, and the Quest for Human Dignity," *CBQ* 74 (2012): 662.
3. Tikva Frymer-Kensky, *Reading the Women of the Bible: A New Interpretation of Their Stories* (New York: Schocken Books, 2002), 268.
4. Tikva Frymer-Kensky, "Tamar 1," in *Women in Scripture*, ed. Carol Meyers, Toni Craven, and Ross Shepard Kramer (Boston: Houghton Mifflin, 2000), 161.

putting "off her widow's garments" years later when she decided to confront Judah (Gen 38:14). In addition to living in mourning, Tamar was forced to endure shame as she returned to her father's house to live as a childless widow. Emil Buhrer writes, "The shame that she brought on her father's house as a widow caused much despair. Legally and socially, the situation of a childless and therefore useless widow sent back to her original owner, her father, is the very worst imaginable for a woman."[5]

Judah feared that if Shelah died, his family lineage would die with him. But by sending Tamar away, Judah deprived Tamar of her right to become a mother and neglected his own responsibility to care for Tamar as a member of his household. Even though Tamar was sent back to live with her father, she was no longer part of her father's household. Legally, Tamar was still a member of Judah's family. In her father's house, Tamar lived a precarious life. She was neither an unmarried virgin nor a disgraced wife; rather, she was a childless widow whose sexuality was hostage to Judah's decision for an unspecified amount of time.

Tamar knew that Judah was not going to honor his word and give Shelah to her to fulfill his obligation as the levir. Tamar waited several years until Shelah had grown up, but Judah never contacted her. Judah was the only one who could set her free from her childless widowhood, but he deprived Tamar of her rights by his silence. So Tamar decided to claim her rights. She set her plan in motion when she received word that Judah's wife had died.

Tamar Deceives Judah

After Judah finished the grieving period for his wife, he and his friend Hirah, the Adullamite, went to Timnah where Judah's men were shearing his sheep. Tamar went to Timnah as well, dressed like a prostitute, and enticed Judah to sleep with her. On his approach to Timnah, Judah saw a woman sitting by the road and mistook her for a prostitute.

He approached the woman and said plainly, "I want to have sex with you" (Gen 38:16 NET). The woman asked Judah, "What will you give me in exchange for having sex with you?" (Gen 38:16 NET). Judah promised that he would send her a young goat from the flock,

5. Emil Buhrer, *Great Women of the Bible in Art and Literature* (Grand Rapids: Eerdmans, 1994), 91.

but the woman asked for a deposit to ensure that Judah would send payment—his signet ring, cord, and staff (Gen 38:18). Judah gave her what she had asked and had sex with her, and she became pregnant.

After sleeping with Judah, Tamar took off her veil, put on her widowhood garments, and returned to her father's house. Tamar's decision was bold and daring. Her incestuous relationship with her father-in-law and her pregnancy outside of marriage could cost her life, but Tamar took measures to prove who had impregnated her. When Judah sent his friend Hirah to pay the woman and get his deposit back, Hirah did not find her. He found some men who lived in the area and asked them, "Where is the temple prostitute who was at Enaim by the wayside?" (Gen 38:21). The men told Hirah that there was no prostitute in the city. When Hirah relayed this to Judah, Judah stopped the search to avoid being ridiculed by the people of the city.

Three months later, when the news reached Judah that Tamar was pregnant, he was furious. Her infidelity brought shame to Judah's family, so Judah decreed that Tamar should be burned alive for her infidelity. The sentence Judah passed on his daughter-in-law was intended to be a public declaration of Tamar's immorality and a way to restore the honor of his family. Judah did not seek evidence of Tamar's unfaithfulness, nor did he seek the testimony of witnesses who could confirm Tamar's immorality. Her pregnancy was enough evidence for Judah to condemn Tamar to death. When the people in her community prepared to execute Tamar, she identified the father of her child: "It was the owner of these who made me pregnant" (Gen 38:25). She told her executioners to find out to whom the signet ring, cord, and the staff belonged. When Judah recognized that the three items belonged to him, he said, "She is more in the right than I" (Gen 38:26). Judah's declaration served as a public affirmation of Tamar's innocence. He was unrighteous because he deceived Tamar and did not give Shelah to her. Tamar was righteous because she put her life in jeopardy to honor her husband, keep his name alive, and ensure a future for herself.

Tamar was blessed not just with one son, but with twin boys: Perez and Zerah. Although Tamar used deception to become a mother, the Bible does not criticize her behavior. At the end of the book of Ruth, the women of Bethlehem bless Naomi with reference to Tamar: "May your house be like the house of Perez whom Tamar bore to Judah"

(Ruth 4:12). And by becoming an ancestor of David, Tamar also became an ancestor of Jesus (Matt 1:3).

Tamar had to overcome the patriarchal structures of her day, structures that held her subservient to the men in her life, to become a mother and to give an heir to her deceased husband. The men in her life demeaned and dehumanized her. She was the wife of two wicked men, she was accused of being a lethal woman, she was accused of acting like a prostitute, and she was condemned to be burned alive. She was reviled in public for being unfaithful and immoral. Yet Tamar remained faithful to her role as a wife; she persevered through abuse and attained her goal of becoming a mother. Tamar's action reflects her indignation at being dehumanized by her husbands. As Claassens writes, "Even at the point when she is most vulnerable, moments before her death, Tamar's foresight and ingenuity save her from suffering the fate of many women around the world for real or perceived infidelity."[6] With the birth of her two sons, Tamar was no longer the barren woman abused by her two husbands and ignored by her father-in-law. Rather, Tamar proved by her actions what those men refused to acknowledge—that she was a woman of worth and dignity.

6. Claassens, "Resisting Dehumanization," 666.

CHAPTER 36

Rahab: A Prostitute or an Innkeeper?

When the Israelites were preparing to enter the land of Canaan after Moses's death, Joshua sent spies from Shittim, in the land of Moab, to Jericho in order to ascertain the strength of the city's protection against an invasion by hostile forces.

We find Rahab's story in Joshua 2 and 6. According to the story, two spies "entered the house of a prostitute whose name was Rahab, and spent the night there" (Josh 2:1). Rahab received the spies, and when their arrival became known the king of Jericho sent men to apprehend the spies. Rahab, however, hid them and helped them escape through a window of her house. In addition to being a prostitute, Rahab was also in the business of manufacturing linen and engaged in the art of dyeing, since the flat roof of her house was covered with stalks of flax put there to dry (Josh 2:6).

Rahab's house was located on the wall of the city, near the town gate. This location made it convenient for people to come into her house and easy for them to leave the city. Since traders and merchants would frequently pass through Jericho, they probably would patronize the house of Rahab and make it easy for her to be well informed of events outside of Jericho.[1] This could be why she knew of the events in Egypt and what the Israelites had done in their journey toward the land of Canaan.

Rahab is introduced as a *ʾiššâ zônâ*, a "prostitute woman" (Josh 2:1). And since she is also introduced as the head of the household, she may have been a madam. The spies went to Rahab's house because they knew who she was, where she lived, and what her profession

1. Robert G. Boling, *Judges*, AB (New York: Doubleday, 1975), 144–45.

was—the arrival of strangers at the house of a prostitute would not raise much suspicion. Joshua 2:1 says that the spies arrived in Jericho "lodged with" Rahab. The word translated "lodge" means to "sleep with" and may carry a sexual connotation. The same word was used when Potiphar's wife asked Joseph "to lie" with her, or as the NET Bible translates Genesis 39:7, Potiphar's wife said, "Have sex with me" (Gen 39:7 NET).

According to Beatrice Brooks, *zônâ* is one of the many words associated with "women who have been regarded as connected with the fertility cult."[2] It is doubtful, however, that Rahab was a sacred prostitute because sacred prostitutes in the fertility cult were called *qĕdēšâ*, but Rahab is called a *zônâ*, a word used to identify a common prostitute.

Josephus, the Jewish historian, said that Rahab was an innkeeper:

> Now those that met them took no notice of them when they saw them, and supposed they were only strangers, who used to be very curious in observing everything in the city, and did not take them for enemies but at even they retired to a certain inn that was near to the wall, whither they went to eat their supper; which supper when they had done, and were considering how to get away, information was given to the king as he was at supper, that there were some persons come from the Hebrews' camp to view the city as spies, and that they were in the inn kept by Rahab, and were very solicitous that they might not be discovered. So he sent immediately some to them, and commanded to catch them, and bring them to him, that he might examine them by torture, and learn what their business was there.[3]

Josephus's view that Rahab was an innkeeper suggests that she might have been a businesswoman. That is, Rahab was in the business of manufacturing linen and in the business of hospitality. In addition, her skillful negotiation with the spies supports the notion that Rahab was a successful businesswoman. Josephus, however, had reason for

2. Beatrice A. Brooks, "Fertility Cult Functionaries in the Old Testament," *JBL* 60 (1941): 236.
3. Josephus, *Ant.* 5.1–2.

downplaying the fact that Rahab was a prostitute. Rahab played an important role in Jewish history, and according to rabbinic tradition, was an ancestor of the prophet Jeremiah.

Rahab was the first Canaanite person to join Israel as they prepared to enter the land of Canaan. Rahab's decision to protect the Israelite spies stems from a recognition of the divine power behind the Israelites. In her own words (Josh 2:11), she acknowledges that the news of the Israelites' miraculous journey through the wilderness has profoundly impacted her people, causing their hearts to melt with fear and destroying their courage. More importantly, she declares her understanding that Yahweh is the true God of both heaven and earth. This understanding of the God of Israel transforms her from a potential enemy into an ally. Recognizing the overwhelming power of the Israelite God and anticipating their conquest, Rahab chooses to align herself with them.

The writer of the book of Joshua says that the house of Rahab survived in Israel: "But Rahab the prostitute, with her family and all who belonged to her, Joshua spared. Her family has lived in Israel ever since. For she hid the messengers whom Joshua sent to spy out Jericho" (Josh 6:25). This statement clearly indicates that the story of Rahab does not end with the book of Joshua. Rahab became a proselyte and converted to the faith of Israel, and her family survived in Israel. It is possible that the 345 people from Jericho who returned with Ezra from Babylon (Ezra 2:34; Neh 7:36) and the men of Jericho who helped Nehemiah in rebuilding the walls of Jerusalem (Neh 3:2) were descendants of Rahab.

As for Rahab herself, the gospel of Matthew (Matt 1:5) says that Rahab became the wife of Salmon, the son of Nahshon, and the ancestor of Boaz, Jesse's grandfather. Thus, Matthew says that Rahab, through Salmon and Boaz, became the mother of the line from which David's family sprang, and through David, Jesus Christ. As we saw in a previous chapter, Rahab was one of the four foreign women mentioned in Christ's genealogy.

Rahab also appears in the list of the people who lived by faith and who were saved by faith. Rahab is praised as an example of faith: "By faith Rahab the prostitute did not perish with those who were disobedient, because she had received the spies in peace" (Heb 11:31). Rahab is praised for saving the spies and, in the process, finding justification through what she did for the cause of God: "Likewise, was not Rahab the prostitute also justified by works when she welcomed the messengers and sent them out by another road?" (Jas 2:25).

There is no reason to avoid the embarrassment of calling Rahab a prostitute. Rahab stands as evidence of the transforming power of God. By believing in the God of Israel, Rahab, a woman who submitted herself to the desires of men, found forgiveness when she submitted herself to the will of God and was added to a great list of people whose lives were transformed when they believed in God.

CHAPTER 37

Sisera's Mother: The Humanization of the Enemy

Israelite mothers were women of faith who exercised significant influence in their children's lives. They expressed sacrificial love in molding the character of their children to become the leaders of Israel, people who helped build their nation, and instruments in the hands of God to accomplish his work in the world.

Sisera's mother differed from Sarah, Hannah, and the hundreds of mothers in Israel. She was the mother of one of the greatest enemies of Israel. But before we meet this foreign mother and become aware of the pain and loss she experienced, we must meet her son Sisera—the commander of the Canaanite army who fought against Israel.

Sisera, the Canaanite Commander

Sisera commanded the army of Jabin, king of Hazor. Sisera and his army fought against Barak and the army of Israel in a battle that took place in the Valley of Jezreel (see chapter above on Deborah). According to the book of Judges, Sisera lived in Harosheth-ha-goiim, "Harosheth of the Gentiles" (Judg 4:2), the location of which is unknown. It is possible that Sisera was a professional soldier associated with the Sea Peoples, probably with the Philistines. The Sea Peoples arrived in Canaan as part of a group of people who migrated from the Eastern Mediterranean world at the beginning of Iron Age I, around 1200 BC.[1]

After twenty years of oppression by Jabin, (Judg 4:1–2), Deborah and Barak answered God's call to liberate Israel. In the war that ensued, Sisera's army, with nine hundred chariots of iron, far surpassed the

1. Claude F. Mariottini, "Sea Peoples," *MDB* 803–4.

army of Israel, composed of ten thousand men lacking chariots, horses, and weapons of iron.

As the two armies met, Yahweh sent a strong storm that flooded the Wadi Kishon, creating a sea of mud and water that first bogged down the chariots of the Canaanites, rendering them useless in the battle and swept them away. The mighty army and their general collapsed helplessly before Barak. Sisera "got down from his chariot and fled away on foot while Barak pursued the chariots and the army to Harosheth-ha-goiim. All the army of Sisera fell by the sword; no one was left" (Judg 4:15–16).

The Death of Sisera

After Sisera abandoned his chariot, he ran until he came to the tent of Jael, the wife of Heber the Kenite. The Kenites and the Canaanite king were on peaceful terms (Judg 4:17). The Kenites were known for their skills in metalworking, and it is probable that Heber was working for Jabin by repairing his iron chariots. When Sisera came into Jael's tent looking for a place to hide and to rest, she invited him in.

Understandably thirsty, Sisera asked for water, but Jael gave him milk to drink. She even covered him with a rug so that he could sleep in comfort. But after Sisera had fallen asleep from exhaustion, Jael took a tent peg and quietly approached him with a hammer in hand. She drove the tent peg through his temples into the ground. "So Sisera died" (Judg 4:21 GW). The proud commander of the Canaanite army met his death at the hands of a woman, a humiliating end for the strong warrior.

Sisera's Mother

Though Sisera's mother's name is not recorded and we know little about her, we can be certain that, like all mothers whose sons and daughters go to war, she worried over the fate of her son. Judges 5:28–30 records what Deborah thought Sisera's mother was doing while she waited for her son's return. Meanwhile, the readers of the book know that Sisera's army had been defeated and that he had been felled by a woman. Sisera's mother only knew that he was late in returning from battle. "Out of the window she peered, the mother of Sisera gazed through the lattice: 'Why is his chariot so long in coming? Why tarry the hoofbeats of his chariots?'" (Judg 5:28).

The NRSV does not do justice to the anguish in the heart of this mother. The NRSV says that Sisera's mother "peered" and "gazed" through the window. The New Living Translation likewise fails to express her pain and anxiety, "From the window Sisera's mother looked out. Through the window she watched for his return, saying, 'Why is his chariot so long in coming? Why don't we hear the sound of chariot wheels?'" (Judg 5:28 NLT). The NIV ("she cried out") and NAB ("she wailed") do a much better job of communicating the force of the Hebrew verb. Sisera's mother knew that her son was a good soldier who conquered in warfare, but the delay in his arrival indicated that something ominous had happened.

The tears of Sisera's mother show us another perspective on the consequences of war, welcoming us to contemplate a broken heart. Her cry would indicate that she was pacing up and down, anxious to know the fate of her son. In her heart she moans, knowing with a premonition that only a mother can have, that her son was dead and would not return home. Although she refuses to lose hope, her tears bring doubt to her heart, and she fears the worst. Sisera's mother weeps because her heart is telling her that her son has met the fate that the writer of the Song of Deborah desires for all the enemies of Israel: "So perish all your enemies, O Lord" (Judg 5:31).

Her servants tried to reassure her that all was well and that he would return soon, victorious in battle, with the spoils of war. Sisera's mother agreed with their explanation for her son's delay. She tried to reassure herself by saying that he had defeated the enemy and that he was late because there was much spoil to be divided among his soldiers. In her desire to allay her anxiety, she says to herself and to her companions, "Are they not finding and dividing the spoil?—A girl or two for every man; spoil of dyed stuffs for Sisera, spoil of dyed stuffs embroidered, two pieces of dyed work embroidered for my neck as spoil?" (Judg 5:30). These words reflect the tragedy of wars. The expression "a girl or two for every man" (Judg 5:30 NRSV) obfuscates what Sisera's men were doing with the conquered women; the ESV makes it clear: "A womb or two for every man" (Judg 5:30 ESV). This is the language of rape. Her words offer another view of Sisera—he is "a plunderer of Israelite women."[2] That the raping of women and the looting of cities comforts

2. Amy C. Cottrill, "Moral Injury and Humanizing the Enemy in Judges 5," in *Moral Injury: A Guidebook for Understanding and Engagement*, ed. Brad E. Kelle (Lanham, MD: Lexington, 2020), 151.

Sisera's mother is particularly appalling because she knows the pain of loss. Athalya Brenner says that Sisera's mother "is foreign, cruel, and unsympathetic to other mothers or to women in general: she and her ladies expect Sisera and his men to overcome sexually at least a couple of Israelite maidens each and bring them back as war spoil."[3]

The Humanization of the Enemy

The Song of Deborah, with its comments about Sisera's mother and her feelings of anxiety, presents a humane side of Sisera and his mother. The enemy of Israel is a human being who has a caring mother who is anxious for her son's safe return.

In her study of the humanization of the enemy in Judges 5, Amy Cottrill writes that "Sisera is not just an enemy warrior, but is someone with a mother who loves him and awaits his return."[4] This humanizing image invites readers to sympathize even with an enemy of Israel.

Though not part of Israel, like any other mother, Sisera's mother loved her son and cared for his well-being. Like many mothers in both ancient and modern times, she knew the consequences of war and feared for her son's safety. Soldiers on both sides of any conflict have mothers. And sons and daughters on both sides died, leaving mothers across national divides to mourn for the fruit of their wombs. As Tamara Dixon points out, war "leaves a vulnerable world alone, grieving and unprotected—mothers without sons, wives without husbands, children without fathers."[5]

The Talmud states the sound of the shofar is that of a weeping mother (Rosh Hashanah 33b). Mordechai Gafni says that, according to Jewish tradition, the "painful ritual of shofar blowing, the tears of the shofar," is patterned after the tears Sisera's mother shed for her son. According to Gafni, the notes of the shofar's blasts are patterned after the pattern of her tears: "We blow a total of one hundred shofar blasts on Rosh Hashanah because Sisera's mother cried a hundred times."

3. Athalya Brenner, "A Triangle and a Rhombus in Narrative Structure: A Proposed Integrative Reading of Judges IV and V," *VT* 40 (1990): 133.
4. Cottrill, "Moral Injury and Humanizing the Enemy in Judges 5," 151.
5. Tamara Dixon, "'Most Blessed of Women': An Exegetical Study of the Roles of Women Under Patriarchy in Judges 5:24–31," *The Review: A Journal of Undergraduate Student Research* 4 (2006): 10.

The blast of the shophar is compared to the tears of Sisera's mother as an acknowledgment of "the full humanity of our enemies."[6]

The story of Sisera's mother is the story of a nameless woman who loved her son, a woman who wept over her son's death. The death of a child disrupts the life-cycle expectations; no parent should outlive their children. In this way the Song of Deborah humanizes Sisera, the enemy of Israel, by portraying him as a son of a loving mother—as a human being. This nameless enemy of Israel shed tears for all the mothers who have lost sons and daughters in warfare.

Including Sisera's mother in a book about Israelite women of faith offers a profound opportunity to explore themes that transcend tribal boundaries. Her story is a powerful example of what the Bible says about people who lived outside the covenant community. Despite being the mother of Israel's enemy, the Song of Deborah humanizes her. Her character embodies the universal experience of motherhood that cuts across cultural and historical divides. The text reveals an example of maternal love that exists beyond the immediate context of conflict. By highlighting her grief, the text challenges readers to recognize the shared human experience of loss and suffering, even among those traditionally viewed as adversaries. The biblical writer challenges his readers to expand their conception of empathy and shared humanity by including her story.

J. O'Callaghan beautifully expresses the foreboding of Sisera's mother:

The Defeat of Sisera

The mother of Sisera looks out on high,
From the halls of her palace, for evening is nigh:
And the wine-cup is brimmed, and the bright torches burn—
And the banquet is piled, for the chieftain's return.
She cries to her maidens—
"Why comes not my son?
Is the combat not over, and the battle not won?
The steeds of Canaan are many and strong,
Why tarry the wheels of his chariot so long?"
She says in her heart—yea, her wise maidens say—

6. Mordechai Gafni, "Shofar of Tears," *Tikkun Magazine* (September/October 2000): 2–3.

"He takes the spoil—he divides the prey—
He seizes the garment of glittering dyes,
And makes the daughters of beauty his prize!"
But Sisera's mother shall view him no more;
With the warriors of Hazor he sleeps in his gore—
And the bear and the lion his coursers consume—
And the beak of the eagle is digging his tomb.
And the owl and the raven are flapping their wings—
And their death-song is heard in the chambers of kings:
For the sword of the Lord and of Israel lowers
Over Sisera's palace, and Jabin's proud towers.

CHAPTER 38

Jael: A Heroine in Israel

The story of the deliverance of Israel from Canaanite oppression (Judg 4–5) focuses on two women, with a third playing a supporting role. Although Barak commanded the Israelite army in battle, Deborah and Jael played significant roles in Sisera's defeat. A third woman, Sisera's mother, makes an appearance at the end of the story (see 37 above).

When Deborah commanded Barak to fight against the Canaanite army, he was reluctant to go to battle without her. In response, Deborah both affirmed and rebuked Barak. She said: "I will surely go with you; nevertheless, the road on which you are going will not lead to your glory, for the LORD will sell Sisera into the hand of a woman" (Judg 4:9). Readers do not yet realize that Deborah referred not to herself but to a yet unnamed woman, Jael, who appears late in the narrative. Jael was the wife of Heber the Kenite. A form of her name appears in Psalm 104:18 and Job 39:1 and means "a mountain goat" or "a wild goat." In the ancient Near East, women were often named after animals.[1] Heber was the leader of a nomadic clan whose primary occupation was shepherding and metalworking. According to Judges 4:11, Heber—a descendant of Moses's father-in-law—separated himself from the other Kenites to live among the Israelites. He pitched his tent at Elon-bezaanannim ("Oak of the Wanderer"), a place near Kedesh. Since Heber's clan was not Israelite, Heber had maintained a neutral position in the conflict between the Israelites and the Canaanites and had established some kind of peace treaty with Jabin, king of Hazor and the Canaanites. Fewell and Gunn write that Heber the Kenite's livelihood as a metalworker bound him to

1. Blaženka Scheuer, "Animal Names for Hebrew Bible Female Prophets," *Literature & Theology* 31 (2017): 455–71.

King Jabin, whose military power was rooted in his iron chariots (Judg 4:3).[2]

After the struggle between the Canaanites and the Israelites, Barak defeated Sisera. As a result of the flooding of the Kishon River that hindered the movement of the chariots of the Canaanite army (Judg 5:21), Sisera abandoned his chariot and fled on foot, fleeing to the area where Heber lived. When he reached Heber's encampment, he took advantage of the peace that existed between Jabin and the Kenites and asked for the hospitality and protection to which he was entitled under the conditions of their relationship.

Sisera fled to the tent of Jael (Judg 4:17), likely because Heber's tent was separated from Jael or because Heber was not present when Sisera came to Jael's tent. According to the traditions of hospitality that existed in the ancient Near East, Sisera would be safe from Barak and his army because of the inviolability of the protection offered by his host. According to ancient customs, though, it was improper for a man to enter a woman's tent. He did so at Jael's invitation (Judg 4:18), but Sisera's action remained a violation of Heber's family and Jael's honor.

Sisera asked Jael to keep watch at the entrance of the tent and to lie on his behalf to protect his life. Such a request would endanger the alliance that existed between the Kenites and the Israelites and would put the lives of Heber and his clan in danger. By asking Jael to lie and say that there was no "man" in her tent, Sisera was undermining his own masculinity by saying that a warrior who seeks refuge in the tent of a woman is not a man. And since Sisera was the commander of the Canaanite army who sought the protection of a woman in a woman's tent, the writer is casting aspersions on Sisera's masculinity.

Jael offered her hospitality. After Sisera entered and sat down exhausted on the floor, Jael covered Sisera with a mantle, some kind of blanket. Sisera asked for water but, as a good hostess, Jael gave him milk. She did not give him wine because the Kenites did not drink wine (1 Chr 2:55; Jer 35:6). The drink she gave him induced him to sleep and thus enabled her to act against her visitor.

---

2. Danna Nolan Fewell and David M. Gunn, "Controlling Perspectives: Women, Men, and the Authority of Violence in Judges 4 & 5," *JAAR* 58 (1990): 395. See also John Gray, *Joshua, Judges & Ruth*, *NCB* (London: Nelson, 1967), 211–12.

Confronted with Sisera's request for asylum and her pro-Israelite sentiments, Jael made a political decision. When Sisera arrived at her tent, she found herself in a difficult situation. Her husband had aligned himself with the Canaanites, Israel's enemies. Jael was deeply concerned that offering hospitality to Sisera might be perceived as a betrayal of the longstanding relationship between the Kenites and the Israelites. She rejected her husband's alliance with the Canaanites and took the side of Israel in this conflict.[3] While Sisera was asleep from exhaustion, Jael took a tent peg and walked quietly toward him with a hammer in her hand. She hammered the tent peg through his temples into the ground, and thus Sisera died between Jael's feet (Judg 5:27). From the perspective of the writer of Judges, Jael's action was justified. Since Sisera had already violated Jael's honor, Jael's act could be seen as a vindication of her honor. The killing of Sisera was one way by which she eliminated the threat to her clan and avenged the violation of her tent.

In his pursuit of Sisera, Barak came by the place where Jael lived. She led him into her tent, and then showed him where the body of the warrior lay dead. The death of Sisera by the hands of Jael fulfilled Deborah's prophecy that God would deliver Sisera into the hand of a woman (Judg 4:9). And her actions elicited high praise from Deborah afterward:

> In the days of Jael, caravans ceased and travelers kept to the byways. (Judg 5:6)
>
> Most blessed of women be Jael, the wife of Heber the Kenite,
> most blessed of tent-dwelling women. (Judg 5:24)

Israel saw Jael, a Kenite woman, as an instrument God used to strike the last blow against the Canaanites, an act that sealed Israel's victory against Jabin and his army.

What Jael, Deborah, and Barak accomplished was part of the righteous acts of Yahweh (Judg 5:11). The death of Sisera by the hands of Jael is then part of the work of God in liberating the oppressed and defeating the oppressor.

3. Nahum M. Sarna and S. David Sperling, "Jael," in *Encyclopaedia Judaica*, ed. Fred Skolnik and Michael Berenbaum, 2nd ed., 22 vols. (Farmington Hills, MI: Thomson Gale, 2007), 11:58.

Jael is called "most blessed of women." These words seem to anticipate Elizabeth's words to Mary: "Blessed are you among the women" (Luke 1:42). In response, Mary sang a song, the Magnificat, a song that evokes God's victory against Sisera:

> He has shown strength with his arm; he has scattered the proud in the thoughts of their hearts. He has brought down the powerful from their thrones, and lifted up the lowly; he has filled the hungry with good things, and sent the rich away empty. He has helped his servant Israel. (Luke 1:51–54)

CHAPTER 39

Ruth, the Moabite

The book of Ruth is a beautiful love story. It is the love story of a Hebrew man and a Moabite woman. It is the story of forbidden love. The story of Ruth and Boaz is a story of forbidden marriage because the law of Moses did not allow the Moabites to enter the assembly of the Lord: "No Ammonite or Moabite shall be admitted to the assembly of the LORD. Even to the tenth generation, none of their descendants shall be admitted to the assembly of the LORD" (Deut 23:3). The assembly of the Lord refers to the gathering of the people of Israel for worship and for the celebration of festivals. Deuteronomy excludes the Moabites from the assembly of the Lord because of their hostility against Israel and their hiring of the false prophet Balaam to curse Israel (Num 22–24).

The story of Boaz and Ruth is also a story of redeeming love. Boaz was willing to circumvent this prohibition, redeem Ruth, and marry her. One reason Boaz was willing to marry Ruth was because her people were willing to accept Elimelech, Naomi, and their family during their stay in the land of Moab at a time of need and distress caused by the famine in Bethlehem.

Maybe because of the love of Boaz for Ruth or maybe because King David was born out of this forbidden marriage, eventually, this law of Deuteronomy was revoked when Yahweh made a promise to foreigners. Yahweh said, "And the foreigners who join themselves to the LORD, to minister to him, to love the name of the LORD, and to be his servants, all who keep the sabbath, and do not profane it, and hold fast my covenant—these I will bring to my holy mountain, and make them joyful in my house of prayer; their burnt offerings and their sacrifices will be accepted on my altar; for my house shall be called a house of prayer for all peoples" (Isa 56:6–7).

The story of Ruth is set during a specific historical period in the history of Israel—in the days when the judges ruled Israel. The time of the judges was a period of religious and moral depravity in Israel. Joshua and his generation had died and "another generation grew up after them, who did not know the LORD or the work that he had done for Israel" (Judg 2:10). The people's apostasy led to the worship of other gods—"the Israelites did what was evil in the sight of the LORD and worshiped the Baals" (Judg 2:11)—which led to recurring oppression by foreign invaders.

The book of Ruth is named after one of the primary characters in the story, the young Moabite woman named Ruth. Nothing is known about Ruth's family nor about her background.

The book begins with the tragic story of an Israelite family. During the days of the judges, Bethlehem was stricken with a drought that caused a great famine in the land, threatening the family of Elimelech, forcing him, his wife Naomi, and their two sons—Mahlon and Chilion—to become refugees in the land of Moab. Elimelech died in Moab; after his death, Mahlon and Chilion married Moabite women named Ruth and Orpah.

Sometime after their marriage, Mahlon and Chilion also died in Moab, leaving Naomi and the two widows alone and without the support from their husbands. Agnethe Siquans writes, "Without a male head of the family the status of the Israelite woman in Moab as well as the status of her daughters-in-law is no longer assured. Therefore, Naomi decides to return to Bethlehem, probably because she has male relatives there who are obliged to help her."[1] With the loss of the economic support provided by her husband and her sons, Naomi decided to return to her native land, to Bethlehem, the place she was forced to leave because of the famine.

As Naomi prepared to return home, she told her two daughters-in-law to return to their homes. Naomi told them to return to their families so that they could get married again. Orpah decided to return home to her family, but Ruth decided to go to Bethlehem with her mother-in-law. Although Naomi insisted that Ruth return to her family, Ruth decided to follow Naomi to Bethlehem. Ruth said to Naomi, "Do not press me to leave you or to turn back from following you! Where you go, I will go; where you lodge, I will lodge; your people shall be my

1. Agnethe Siquans, "Foreignness and Poverty in the Book of Ruth: A Legal Way for a Poor Foreign Woman to Be Integrated into Israel," *JBL* 128 (2009): 445.

people, and your God my God. Where you die, I will die—there will I be buried. May the Lord do thus and so to me, and more as well, if even death parts me from you" (Ruth 1:16–17).

Ruth's decision to abandon her country, her family, and her god was radical. It indicated that she was making a commitment to the God Naomi served. Ruth was willing to adopt Naomi's people as her people and Naomi's God as her God. Ruth's commitment was a lifetime commitment, "Where you die, I will die—there will I be buried."

Naomi and Ruth arrived in Bethlehem at the time of the barley harvest. Ruth asked Naomi permission to go to the field of anyone who would be kind to her and allow her to gather the grain left behind by the reapers. With Naomi's approval, Ruth went to the fields of Boaz who was a relative of Elimelech, Naomi's husband. Boaz noticed Ruth working in the field and he inquired about her. Once Boaz knew that the woman was a Moabite, related to Naomi, Boaz urged Ruth to remain with the women who were working in his field. Boaz also commanded his servant not to molest her, thus ensuring her safety.

Boaz's action ensured that Ruth would be able to reap safely. Ruth had found favor in the eyes of Boaz. After a successful day of gathering grain, Ruth went back to town. Ruth returned with plenty of food for her and for her mother-in-law. When Naomi saw how much grain Ruth had brought back, Naomi was surprised. Naomi asked Ruth where she had been gleaning. Ruth told her in the fields of Boaz. Naomi uttered a blessing on Boaz saying, "'Blessed be he by the Lord, whose kindness has not forsaken the living or the dead!' Naomi also said to her, 'The man is a relative of ours, one of our nearest kin'" (Ruth 2:20).

Naomi told Ruth that Boaz was one of their close relatives and their *gōʾēl*. A *gōʾēl* was a kinsman or a close relative who could rescue or redeem a family member in times of crisis: "If anyone of your kin falls into difficulty and sells a piece of property, then the next of kin shall come and redeem what the relative has sold" (Lev 25:25). According to the law of redemption in Leviticus, if a member of the family fell into hard times and needed to sell his property, the *gōʾēl* would purchase the land and give it back to the member of his family who had sold his land. Boaz was Naomi's *gōʾēl*. He upheld his duty as Naomi's redeemer by redeeming the land that had belonged to his kinsman Elimelech. By redeeming the land, Boaz also assumed the responsibility to care for Ruth and provide an heir for Mahlon. By marrying Ruth, Boaz would keep the ancestral inheritance in Mahlon's name (Ruth 4:5).

After Boaz married Ruth, she conceived and gave birth to a son. The women of Bethlehem came to Naomi and said to her, "Blessed be the LORD, who has not left you this day without next-of-kin; and may his name be renowned in Israel! He shall be to you a restorer of life and a nourisher of your old age; for your daughter-in-law who loves you, who is more to you than seven sons, has borne him" (Ruth 4:14–15).

In the Old Testament, generally the parents named the child; but in the book of Ruth, the celebrant women of Bethlehem are given this honor. "The women of the neighborhood gave him a name, saying, 'A son has been born to Naomi.' They named him Obed; he became the father of Jesse, the father of David" (Ruth 4:17).

The book of Ruth begins with tragic events. A famine that forced a family from Bethlehem to take refuge in a foreign land. A woman who lost her husband and then her two sons. Behind these tragic events, God was at work to accomplish his work in the world. God used a Moabite woman to show redemption in the land of Israel. Behind the story of Ruth there was the foundation for a greater story of redemption. Ruth became the great-grandmother of David and one of the grandmothers of Jesus Christ: "Salmon was the father of Boaz. Boaz was the father of Obed. Obed was the father of Jesse. Jesse was the father of David" (Ruth 4:21).

Matthew includes Ruth in his genealogy of Jesus: "This is the list of ancestors of Jesus Christ, descendant of David. . . . Salmon and Rahab were the father and mother of Boaz. Boaz and Ruth were the father and mother of Obed. Obed was the father of Jesse, Jesse the father of King David" (Matt 1:1, 5–6 GW).

CHAPTER 40

The Greatness That Was Jezebel

In 1962 H. W. F. Saggs published a book titled *The Greatness That Was Babylon*.[1] The book summarizes the results of years of excavations in Mesopotamia that have produced a vast amount of information about ancient Babylonian civilization. Babylon had a profound impact on the ancient world. The greatness that was Babylon, however, has been diminished by the biblical writers—and for good reason. Jeremiah portrays Babylon as a city of iniquities: "Flee from the midst of Babylon and save your lives, each of you! Do not perish because of her guilt" (Jer 51:6). In the New Testament, Babylon is introduced as a prostitute: "Babylon the great the mother of whores and of earth's abominations" (Rev 17:5).

The same thing happened to Jezebel, the Phoenician princess who married Ahab, the king of Israel. In the Bible, the greatness of Jezebel was diminished by the biblical writers in the same way Babylon was. In this chapter, I study Jezebel from three different perspectives: the defamation of Jezebel, the wickedness of Jezebel, and the greatness of Jezebel.

The Defamation of Jezebel

Jezebel was a great woman in some respects. But because Jezebel introduced the cult of Baal to the northern kingdom, the biblical writers sought every opportunity to defame Jezebel. Take, for instance, the name of Jezebel.

Jezebel's name incorporates the word Zebul, a title for Baal, Jezebel's god. The word Zebul means "exalted," "honored." In the Bible, Zebul was the name of the ruler of the city of Shechem (Judg 9:28). According to Gale A. Yee, the name Jezebel has been changed to defame

1. H. W. F. Saggs, *The Greatness That Was Babylon* (London: Sidgwick & Jackson, 1962).

Jezebel.[2] Yee writes that, as it is written in the Bible, "the name Jezebel is probably a two-layered parody. The original name *ʾîzebul* ("Where is the Prince?") first became *ʾî-zebul* ("No nobility"). Zebul, a title of Baal, was then distorted into *zebel*, "dung." Jezebel's name was "changed in order to show the contempt of the biblical authors."[3] The identification of Jezebel's name with dung is based on a prophecy of Elijah: "The corpse of Jezebel shall be like dung on the field in the territory of Jezreel, so that no one can say, 'This is Jezebel'" (2 Kgs 9:37).

Jehu called Jezebel a whore and a sorcerer. "When Joram saw Jehu, he said, 'Is it peace, Jehu?' He answered, 'What peace can there be, so long as the many whoredoms and sorceries of your mother Jezebel continue?'" (2 Kings 9:22). The "whoredoms" of Jezebel were her promotion of Canaanite religion in the northern kingdom. In the New Testament, the name Jezebel was given to a false prophet who induced Christians to practice sexual immorality: "You tolerate that woman Jezebel, who calls herself a prophet. By her teaching she misleads my servants into sexual immorality and the eating of food sacrificed to idols" (Rev 2:20 NIV).

The Wickedness of Jezebel

The presentation of Jezebel in 1–2 Kings focuses on the evil things Jezebel did because the writers of her story were faithful worshipers of Yahweh who did not agree with her religious views and political policies. As an outsider, Jezebel was judged because of her religion, and the verdict was unfavorable and adverse.

Jezebel was the daughter of Ethbaal, king of Tyre. Jezebel married Ahab, king of Israel, to seal an alliance between the two nations. Jezebel introduced the worship of Baal in Israel. To promote her religion, Jezebel brought to Israel 450 prophets of Baal and the 400 prophets of Asherah (1 Kgs 18:19). Jezebel also ruthlessly persecuted and killed the prophets of Yahweh who opposed her missionary activities (1 Kgs 18:4). To please his wife, Ahab "set up an altar for Baal in the temple of Baal that he built in Samaria. Ahab also made an Asherah pole" (1 Kgs 16:32–33 NIV). Baal was a fertility god who was known by the

2. Gale A. Yee, "Jezebel (Person)," *ABD* 3:848.
3. F. Charles Fensham, "Possible Explanation of the Name Baal-Zebub of Ekron," *ZAW* 79 (1967): 361.

title "Lord of Rain and Dew." During Ahab's reign, Israel experienced a great drought and famine, which the prophet Elijah had proclaimed to show that Yahweh was the true God of Israel.

When Ahab wanted to buy the vineyard of Naboth (1 Kgs 21), Naboth refused because the vineyard was a part of his family's inheritance. Ahab reported this to Jezebel, who responded, "I will give you the vineyard of Naboth the Jezreelite" (1 Kgs 21:7). Jezebel wrote letters in her husband's name and with his seal in which she contrived a legal way to kill Naboth so that her husband could obtain Naboth's vineyard (1 Kgs 21:8).[4]

The people who opposed Jezebel anointed Jehu to put an end to the dynasty of Ahab. After his anointing, Jehu began a religious purge in Israel. Jehu went to Jezreel where Jezebel was living in the palace and killed Jezebel. She was thrown out of a window and her blood spattered against the wall and on the horses. Then Jehu trampled her body under his horses' hooves (2 Kgs 9:33) and the dogs ate the flesh of Jezebel (2 Kgs 9:36).

The Greatness of Jezebel

There is another side of Jezebel that most people who read her story fail to see: her incredible influence over Israelite politics. Athalya Brenner points out that "Jezebel was a real queen, assistant and partner in government to her husband Ahaz. . . . She is aggressive and resourceful, full of political initiative and vigour. . . . [I]t seems that Jezebel enjoyed an exceptional position within [Israelite] society, although biblical writers are loath to admit it."[5]

If Jezebel's story were written from a Phoenician perspective or from the perspective of a worshiper of Baal, her story would be read completely differently. As noted above, Jezebel came to Israel when Omri made an alliance with Phoenicia that was sealed with the marriage between Ahab and Jezebel, the daughter of Ethbaal, the king of Tyre (1 Kgs 16:31). Ethbaal was both a king and a priest in the worship of the goddess Ashtoreth, and his daughter was a high priestess in the temple of Baal. Brenner writes, "A high priestess must be

4. Jezebel had her own royal seal, and it is possible the letters were sealed with it; see N. Avigad, "The Seal of Jezebel," *IEJ* 14 (1964): 274–76.

5. Athalya Brenner, *The Israelite Woman: Social Role and Literary Type in Biblical Narrative*, BibSem (Sheffield: JSOT Press, 1999), 21–22.

educated from birth to govern, for the office requires political expertise and the ability to cooperates with the secular branch of government."[6] As a princess by birth, Jezebel lived in the luxury of the palace and exerted considerable influence in the political, economic, and religious life of Tyre. Jezebel believed that Baal was the source for her prosperous life. When she came to Israel, Jezebel was determined to make her god the god of Israel so that the people of Israel could be as prosperous as the people of her nation.

Jezebel's story is that of a woman determined to be a powerful queen in her new nation. She knew her power as the king's wife and was not afraid to use her position to achieve her goals. Jezebel knew what she believed, and she was determined to defend her beliefs.

When Elijah killed the prophets of Baal, Ahab told Jezebel what Elijah had done. Jezebel did not cry, throw a fit, or run. Jezebel was ready for a fight, and she threatened Elijah. Jezebel sent a messenger to Elijah, saying, "So may the gods do to me, and more also, if I do not make your life like the life of one of [my prophets] by this time tomorrow" (1 Kgs 19:2–3). Elijah was afraid of Jezebel because he knew that she had the power to kill him, so Elijah "fled for his life." Jezebel remained unimpressed by the killing of the prophets of Baal. Elijah's fear reflects the strength of her character as a queen and as a powerful woman. Only a remarkable woman could have dealt with such a critical situation, determined to accomplish her goals.

When Ahab came to Jezebel, upset because Naboth refused to sell his vineyard, Jezebel was willing to fight for her husband and give him what he wanted. Jezebel gave Ahab the vineyard he desired by using her political power. Her action reflects Phoenician politics. Jezebel had a very high view of kingship, and she used the power of the palace to obtain Naboth's vineyard for the king.

When Jehu confronted Jezebel, she remained strong and defiant. Knowing that she was about to die, Jezebel did not flee the city, nor did she disguise herself. Jezebel welcomed Jehu by mocking him, "Is it peace, Zimri, murderer of your master?" (2 Kgs 9:31). Jezebel called Jehu "Zimri" because Zimri became a king by killing his master, the king.[7]

6. Brenner, *The Israelite Woman*, 25.
7. Saul M. Olyan, "2 Kings 9:31. Jehu as Zimri," *HTR* 78 (1985): 203–7.

Jezebel was determined to die with dignity. Before she died, Jezebel "painted her eyes, and adorned her head, and looked out of the window," waiting for Jehu to arrive (2 Kgs 9:30). Jehu himself recognized her determination to die as a queen. After Jezebel was killed, Jehu told his servants, "See to that cursed woman and bury her; for she is a king's daughter" (2 Kgs 9:34).

Jezebel, a Great Woman

If Jezebel was such a powerful political and religious leader in her nation, why does the Bible present such a negative view of Jezebel? The biblical writers were not interested in the greatness that was Jezebel. They were interested in the deleterious role she played by promoting the worship of Baal and Asherah in Israel.

In the patriarchal society of the northern kingdom, the religious and village leaders of Israel would not recognize the power and leadership of a female priest, particularly one who was promoting the worship of a foreign god. To Jezebel, Israel's religion was lacking a female goddess.

I am not promoting or defending Canaanite religion, nor agreeing with the ways by which Jezebel fought for her faith or acted as a queen. Rather, I am looking at Jezebel as a princess and a queen, a strong woman who had strong opinions about her royal role, who took her religion seriously, and who fought for what she believed.

Jezebel's legacy proves to be the legacy of a great woman who lived in the wrong place, at the wrong time, and under the wrong circumstances. Although Jezebel did what was evil in the eyes of Yahweh, she proved that she was a woman of courage, determination, and greatness. Jezebel was definitely a force to reckon with.

If we evaluate Jezebel objectively, apart from the biblical text, Jezebel was a very strong woman who believed that Baal was a great god, and she tried to show that to the people of Israel. Jezebel acted as a queen to help her husband, the king, to get what he wanted.

Jezebel was one of the most influential women of the Bible. At a time when women had few rights or power, Jezebel was a formidable woman who is not remembered as one of the greatest women of her day but as an evil woman who tried to subvert a nation. Notwithstanding the efforts to marginalize Jezebel, there was a kind of greatness in her that cannot be denied: Jezebel was a great-great-great-grandmother of Jesus Christ.

Wickedness Among Faithfulness

In a work dedicated to celebrating the faithful heroines of ancient Israel, the inclusion of Jezebel, perhaps the most notorious female antagonist in Scripture, requires explanation. I offer this defense not to rehabilitate her religious character, which Scripture unambiguously condemns, but to explain why her presence in this study enriches our understanding of female faith in ancient Israel.

Jezebel serves as the essential counterpoint that illuminates true faith by contrast. Jezebel's story provides the dark background against which the radiance of Israel's faithful women shines more vividly. Her narrative offers what theologians call an *argumentum a contrario*—an argument from the opposite—demonstrating through negative example what authentic faith embodies.

The pedagogical value of this juxtaposition cannot be overstated. Jezebel wielded remarkable influence, intelligence, and determination, qualities shared by many biblical heroines. Yet she directed these gifts toward idolatry and injustice rather than covenant faithfulness. By examining how similar capacities for leadership yielded radically different outcomes based on their spiritual orientation, we gain deeper insight into how faith transforms feminine power into redemptive influence. When we contrast the foreigner Ruth with the foreigner Jezebel, and when we compare Queen Esther with Queen Jezebel, we develop a more textured understanding of faithful womanhood.

Jezebel represents a worldview and value system that directly competed with Yahwistic faith in ancient Israel. By understanding the sophisticated Phoenician cultural and religious traditions she embodied—without endorsing them—we better appreciate the genuine spiritual choices facing Israelite women. This contextual understanding transforms our perception of biblical heroines from simple moral exemplars to women who actively chose covenant faithfulness amid compelling alternatives.

Finally, Jezebel's inclusion acknowledges the complex reality that women in Scripture, like all humans, exist on a spectrum of faithfulness. By presenting the stories of faithful women and the story of someone who completely differs from them, this work offers a more authentic representation and presents a more honest portrayal of womanhood in all its moral complexity.

I therefore include Jezebel not to celebrate evil but to deepen our appreciation for good; not to undermine faith but to clarify its distinctive qualities; and not to confuse readers but to sharpen their moral discernment. Her presence in these pages serves as the shadow that defines the light—a pedagogical necessity for any comprehensive study of women's faith in Scripture.

Bibliography

Ackerman, Susan. *Warrior, Dancer, Seductress, Queen: Women in Judges and Biblical Israel*. ABRL. New York: Doubleday, 1998.

Allen, Leslie C. *Ezekiel 1–19*. WBC. Waco, TX: Word Books, 1994.

Angel, Hayyim. "Cut the Baby in Half: Understanding Solomon's Divinely-Inspired Wisdom." *JBQ* 39 (2011): 189–94.

Auld, A. Graeme. *I & II Samuel*. OTL. Louisville: Westminster John Knox Press, 2011.

Avigad, N. "The Seal of Jezebel." *IEJ* 14 (1964): 274–76.

Baden, Joel S. "The Nature of Barrenness in the Hebrew Bible." Pages 13–27 in *Disability Studies and Biblical Literature*. Edited by Candida R. Moss and Jeremy Schipper. New York: Palgrave Macmillan, 2011.

Bailey, Randall C. *David in Love and War: The Pursuit of Power in 2 Samuel 10–12*. JSOTSup. Sheffield: JSOT Press, 1990.

Bechtel, Lyn. "What if Dinah Is Not Raped?" *JSOT* 62 (1994): 19–36.

Ben Zvi, Ehud. "When Yhwh Tests People: General Considerations and Particular Observations Regarding the Books of Chronicles and Job." Pages 11–20 in *Far from Minimal: Celebrating the Work and Influence of Philip R. Davies*. Edited by Duncan Burns and John W. Rogerson. London: T&T Clark, 2012.

Berquist, Jon. *Reclaiming Her Story: The Witness of Women in the Old Testament*. St. Louis: Chalice, 1992.

Blenkinsopp, Joseph. *Isaiah 1–39: A New Translation with Introduction and Commentary*. AB. New York: Doubleday, 2000.

Block, Daniel I. *The Book of Ezekiel, Chapters 1–24*. NICOT. Grand Rapids: Eerdmans, 1997.

Bohmbach, Karla. "Names and Naming in the Biblical Word." Pages 33–39 in *Women in Scripture*. Edited by Carol Meyers, Toni Craven, and Ross Shepard Kramer. Boston: Houghton Mifflin, 2000.

Boling, Robert G. *Judges*. AB. New York: Doubleday, 1975.

Bowen, Nancy R. "The Daughters of Your People: Female Prophets in Ezekiel 13:17–23." *JBL* 118 (1999): 417–33.

Branch, Robin G. *Jeroboam's Wife: The Enduring Contributions of the Old Testament's Least-Known Women*. Peabody, MA: Hendrickson, 2009.

Brenner, Athalya. *The Israelite Woman: Social Role and Literary Type in Biblical Narrative*. BibSem. Sheffield: JSOT Press, 1999.

________. "A Triangle and a Rhombus in Narrative Structure: A Proposed Integrative Reading of Judges IV and V." *VT* 40 (1990): 129–38.

Brooks, Beatrice A. "Fertility Cult Functionaries in the Old Testament." *JBL* 60 (1941): 227–53.

Brueggemann, Walter. *First and Second Samuel*. Int. Louisville: Westminster John Knox, 1990.

________. *1 & 2 Kings*. Smyth & Helwys Bible Commentary. Macon, GA: Smyth & Helwys, 2000.

Buhrer, Emil. *Great Women of the Bible in Art and Literature*. Grand Rapids: Eerdmans, 1994.

Burrows, Millar. "The Origin of the Term 'Gospel.'" *JBL* 44 (1925): 21–33.

Camp, Claudia V. "1 and 2 Kings." Pages 96–109 in *Women's Bible Commentary*. Edited by Carol Ann Newsom and Sharon H. Ringe. Louisville: Westminster John Knox, 1992.

________. "The Wise Women of 2 Samuel: A Role Model for Women in Early Israel." Pages 195–207 in *Women in the Hebrew Bible*. Edited by Alice Bach. New York: Routledge, 1999.

Campbell, Edward F. *Ruth: A New Translation with Introduction, Notes, and Commentary*. AB. New Haven, CT: Yale University Press, 2008.

Caspi, Michael M., and Sascha B. Cohen. *Still Waters Run Deep: Five Women of the Bible Speak*. New York: University Press of America, 1999.

Chankin-Gould, J D'ror, Derek Hutchinson, David H. Jackson, Tyler D. Mayfield, and Leah Rediger Schulte. "The Sanctified 'Adulteress' and Her Circumstantial Clause: Bathsheba's Bath and Self-Consecration in 2 Samuel 11." *JSOT* 32 (2008): 339–52.

Childs, Brevard S. "The Birth of Moses." *JBL* 84 (1965): 109–22.

———. *The Book of Exodus*. OTL. Louisville: Westminster John Knox, 2004.

Claassens, L. Juliana M. "Resisting Dehumanization: Ruth, Tamar, and the Quest for Human Dignity." *CBQ* 74 (2012): 659–74.

Clark, Ronald R., Jr. "The Silence in Dinah's Cry." *RQ* 49 (2007): 143–58.

Clements, Ronald E. *Ezekiel*. Louisville: Westminster John Knox, 1996.

Coogan, Michael D. "Structural and Literary Analysis of the Song of Deborah." *CBQ* 40 (1978): 143–66.

Coogan, Mordechai. *I Kings*. AB. New York: Doubleday, 2001.

Cottrill, Amy C. "Moral Injury and Humanizing the Enemy in Judges 5." Pages 149–60 in *Moral Injury: A Guidebook for Understanding and Engagement*. Edited by Brad E. Kelle. Lanham, MD: Lexington Books, 2020.

Cross, Frank M., Jr., and David Noel Freedman. "The Song of Miriam." *JNES* 14 (1955): 237–50.

Dixon, Tamara. "'Most Blessed of Women': An Exegetical Study of the Roles of Women Under Patriarchy in Judges 5:24–31." *The Review: A Journal of Undergraduate Student Research* 4 (2006): 1–12.

Driver, G. R. "Mistranslations in the Old Testament." *WO* 1 (1947): 29–31.

Edelman, Diana V. *King Saul in the Historiography of Judah*. JSOTSup 121. Sheffield: JSOT Press, 1991.

———. "Ahinoam (Person)." *ABD* 1:118.

Eichrodt, Walther. *Ezekiel: A Commentary*. OTL. Philadelphia: Westminster, 2003.

Eskenazi, Tamara C. "Out from the Shadows: Biblical Women in the Postexilic Era." *JSOT* 54 (1992): 25–43.

Exum, J. Cheryl. "'You Shall Let Every Daughter Live': A Study of Exodus 1:8–2:10." Pages 37–61 in *A Feminist Companion to Exodus to Deuteronomy*. Edited by Athalya Brenner. Feminist Companion to the Bible. Sheffield: Sheffield Academic Press, 1994.

Fensham, F. Charles. "Possible Explanation of the Name Baal-Zebub of Ekron." *Zeitschrift für die alttestamentliche Wissenschaft* 79 (1967): 361–64.

Fewell, Danna Nolan, and David M. Gunn. "Controlling Perspectives: Women, Men, and the Authority of Violence in Judges 4 & 5." *JAAR* 58 (1990): 389–411.

Firth, D. G. "Joshua 24 and the Welcome of Foreigners." *Acta Theologica* 38 (2018): 70–86.

Freed, Edwin D. "The Women in Matthews Genealogy." *JSNT* 29 (1987): 3–19.

Frerichs, Wendell W. "The Birth of Isaac: Genesis 21:1–7." *WW* 14 (1994): 154–61.

Fretheim, Terence E. *Abraham: Trials of Family and Faith*. Columbia: The University of South Carolina Press, 2007.

Frymer-Kensky, Tikva. *In the Wake of the Goddess*. New York: The Free Press, 1992.

________. "Tamar 1." Page 91 in *Women in Scripture*. Edited by Carol Meyers, Toni Craven, and Ross Shepard Kramer. Boston: Houghton Mifflin Company, 2000.

________. *Reading the Women of the Bible*. New York: Schocken Books, 2002.

Gafney, Wilda C. *Daughters of Miriam: Women Prophets in Ancient Israel*. Minneapolis: Fortress, 2008.

________. *Womanist Midrash: A Reintroduction to the Women of the Torah and the Throne*. Louisville: Westminster John Knox, 2017.

Gafni, Mordechai. "Shofar of Tears." *Tikkun Magazine* (September/October 2000): 1–5.

Gaston, Dorothy J. "Matrilineal Background of Genealogies in Genesis." *Semiotics* (1981): 505–19.

Godbey, Allen H. "The Hebrew Mašal." *The American Journal of Semitic Languages and Literatures* 39 (1923): 89–108.

Goldingay, John. *Old Testament Theology*. Downers Grove, IL: IVP Academic, 2009.

Gray, John. *Joshua, Judges & Ruth*. *NCB*. London: Nelson, 1967.

_______. *I & II Kings: A Commentary*. OTL. Louisville: Westminster John Knox, 1970.

Greenberg, Moshe. *Ezekiel 1–20*. AB. New Haven, CT: The Anchor Yale Bible, 1983.

Griffiths, J. Gwyn. "The Egyptian Derivation of the Name Moses." *JNES* 12 (1953): 225–31.

Gruber, Mayer I. "Breast-Feeding Practices in Biblical Israel and in Old Babylonian Mesopotamia." *JNES* 19 (1989): 61–83.

Halpern, Baruch. "Why Manasseh Is to Blame for the Babylonian Exile: The Evolution of a Biblical Tradition." *VT* 48 (1998): 473–514.

Hanson, A. T. "Rahab the Harlot in Early Christian Tradition." *JSNT* 1 (1978): 53–60.

Herbert, A. S. *The Book of the Prophet Isaiah 1–39*. Cambridge: Cambridge University Press, 1973.

Hutchison, John C. "Women, Gentiles, and the Messianic Mission in Matthew's Genealogy." *BSac* 158 (2001): 152–64.

Ilan, Tal. "Huldah, the Deuteronomic Prophetess of the Book of Kings." *Lectio Difficilior* 1 (2010): 1–16.

Jacobson, Diane. "Remembering Tamar." *WW* 24 (2004): 353–57.

Janzen, J. Gerald, and John T. Noble. "Did Hagar Give Ishmael Up for Dead?: Gen 21.14–21 Re-visited." *JSOT* 44 (2020): 517–31.

Japhet, Sara. *I & II Chronicles*. OTL. Louisville: Westminster John Knox, 1993.

Jobling, David. *1 Samuel*. Berit Olam. Collegeville, MN: Liturgical Press, 1998.

Johnson, Benjamin J. M. "What Type of Son Is Samson? Reading Judges 13 as a Biblical Type-scene." *JETS* 53 (2010): 269–86.

Josephus, Flavius. *The Life and Works of Flavius Josephus*. Translated by William Whiston. New York: Holt, Reinhart and Winston, 1961.

Kaiser, Walter C., Jr., Peter H. Davids, F. F. Bruce, and Manfred T. Brauch. *Hard Sayings of the Bible*. Downers Grove, IL: InterVarsity, 1996.

Kass, Leon R. "Educating Father Abraham: The Meaning of Wife." *First Things* 47 (November 1994): 16–26.

Katzenstein, H. Jacob. "Who Were the Parents of Athaliah?" *IEJ* 5 (1955): 194–97.

Keil, C. F. *The Book of Kings*. Biblical Commentary on the Old Testament. Grand Rapids: Eerdmans, 1950.

Klein, Ralph W. "Call, Covenant, and Community: The Story of Abraham and Sarah." *Currents in Theology and Mission* 15 (1988): 120–27.

———. *1 Chronicles*. Hermeneia. Minneapolis: Fortress, 2006.

Klein, Reuven C. "Queen Athaliah: The Daughter of Ahab or Omri?" *JBQ* 42 (2014): 11–20.

Knoppers, Gary N. *1 Chronicles 10–29*. AB. New York: Doubleday, 2004.

Lasine, S. "The Riddle of Solomon's Judgment and the Riddle of Human Nature in the Hebrew Bible." *JSOT* 45 (1989): 61–86.

Levenson, Jon D. "1 Samuel 25 as Literature and as History." *CBQ* 40 (1978): 11–28.

Long, Burke O. *Images of God and Man: Old Testament Short Stories in Literary Focus*. BLS 1. Sheffield: Almond, 1981.

Magonet, Jonathan. "The God Who Hides: Some Jewish Responses to the Book of Esther." *European Judaism* 47 (2014): 109–16.

Mariottini, Claude F. "Onan (Person)." *ABD* 5:21.

________. *Rereading the Biblical Text: Searching for Meaning and Understanding*. Eugene, OR: Wipf and Stock, 2013.

________. "Sea Peoples." Pages 803–4 in *MDB*.

________. "Bathsheba and Her Menstrual Period." July 23, 2019. https://claudemariottini.com/2019/07/23/bathsheba-and-her-menstrual-period/.

McCann, J. Clinton. *Judges*. Int. Louisville: John Knox, 2002.

McCarter, P. Kyle, Jr. *II Samuel*. AB. New York: Doubleday, 1984.

McEntire, Mark, and Wongi Park. "Ethnic Fission and Fusion in Biblical Genealogies." *JBL* 140 (2021): 31–47.

McKenna, Megan. *Not Counting Women and Children: Neglected Stories from the Bible*. Maryknoll, NY: Orbis, 1995.

Meek, Russell L. "The Abishag Episode: Reexamining the Role of Virility in 1 Kings 1:1–4 in Light of the Kirta Epic and the Sumerian Tale 'The Old Man and the Young Woman.'" *BBR* 24 (2014): 1–14.

Mendenhall, George E. "The Shady Side of Wisdom: The Date and Purpose of Genesis 3." Pages 319–34 in *A Light unto My Path: Old Testament Studies in Honor of Jacob M. Myers*. Edited by H. N. Breamet et al. Philadelphia: Temple University Press, 1974.

Meyers, Carol. "The Roots of Restriction: Women in Early Israel." *Biblical Archeologist* 41 (1978): 91–103.

________. "Of Drums and Damsels: Women's Performance in Ancient Israel." *Biblical Archaeologist* 54 (1991): 16–27.

________. "Women and the Domestic Economy of Early Israel." Pages 33–43 in *Women in the Hebrew Bible: A Reader*. Edited by Alice Bach. New York: Routledge, 1998.

De Moor, Johannes Cornelius. *The Elusive Prophet: The Prophet as a Historical Person, Literary Character and Anonymous Artist*. Leiden: Brill, 2001.

Moore, George F. "Fourteen Generations: 490 Years: An Explanation of the Genealogy of Jesus." *HTR* 14 (1921): 97–103.

Moskala, Jiri. "The Mission of God's People in the Old Testament." *Perspective Digest* 16 (2011): 1–21.

Nelson, Richard D. *First and Second Kings*. Int. Louisville: Westminster John Knox, 1987.

Nicol, George G. "The Alleged Rape of Bathsheba: Some Observations on Ambiguity in Biblical Narrative." *JSOT* 73 (1997): 43–54.

Niditch, Susan. "The Wronged Woman Righted: An Analysis of Genesis 38." *HTR* 72 (1979): 143–49.

Nogalski, James D. "Joel." In *The Book of the Twelve: Hosea-Jonah*. Smyth & Helwys Bible Commentary. Macon, GA: Smyth & Helwys, 2011.

Nowell, Irene. "Jesus' Great-Grandmothers: Matthew's Four and More." *CBQ* 70 (2008): 1–15.

Olyan, Saul M. "2 Kings 9:31. Jehu as Zimri." *HTR* 78 (1985): 203–7.

Oswalt, John N. "*bāśar*." Page 135 in vol. 1 of *Theological Workbook of the Old Testament*. Edited by R. Laid Harris. Chicago: Moody Press, 1980.

Preuss, Horst D. *Old Testament Theology*. Volume 2. OTL. Louisville: Westminster: John Knox, 1996.

Reiss, Moshe. "Ishmael, Son of Abraham." *JBQ* 30 (2002): 253–56.

Rendsburg, Gary A. "The Guilty Party in 1 Kings III 16–28." *VT* 48 (1998): 534–41.

Routledge, Robin. *Old Testament Theology: A Thematic Approach*. Downers Grove, IL: IVP Academic, 2008.

Saggs, H. W. F. *The Greatness That Was Babylon*. London: Sidgwick & Jackson, 1962.

Schearing, Linda S. "Abishag (Person)." *ABD* 1:24.

________. "Ahinoam 2." Page 48 in *Women in Scripture*. Edited by Carol Meyers, Toni Craven, and Ross Shepard Kramer. Boston: Houghton Mifflin Company, 2000.

Scheuer, Blaženka. "Animal Names for Hebrew Bible Female Prophets." *Literature & Theology* 31 (2017): 455–71.

Schilling, O. “*bsr*.” Page 315 in vol. 1 of *Theological Dictionary of the Old Testament*. Grand Rapids: Eerdmans, 1975.

Schley, D. G. “Ahithophel (Person).” *ABD* 1:121.

Shearer, Rodney H. “Noadiah (Person),” *ABD* 4:1122.

“Sheerah.” *The International Standard Bible Encyclopedia*. Edited by James Orr. Chicago: The Howard Severance Company, 1915.

Siebert-Hommes, Jopie. “The Female Saviors of Israel’s Liberator: Twelve ‘Daughters’ in Exodus 1 and 2.” Pages 295–311 in *Torah*. Vol. 1.1 in *The Bible and Women: An Encyclopedia of Exegesis and Cultural History*. Edited by Irmtraud Fischer and Mercedes Navarro Puerto. Atlanta: Society of Biblical Literature, 2011.

Siquans, Agnethe. “Foreignness and Poverty in the Book of Ruth: A Legal Way for a Poor Foreign Woman to Be Integrated into Israel.” *JBL* 128 (2009): 443–52.

Skinner, John. *The Book of the Prophet Isaiah Chapters I–XXXIX*. The Cambridge Bible for Schools and Colleges. Cambridge: University Press, 1963.

Smith, George Adam. *The Book of the Twelve Prophets*. New York: A. C. Armstrong and Son, 1902.

Smith, J. Alfred, Sr. “Break the Silence: Justice is Waiting for You to Speak.” *RevExp* 110 (2013): 15–23.

Soggin, J. Alberto. *Judges*. OTL. Philadelphia: Westminster, 1981.

Stökl, Jonathan. “Female Prophets in the Ancient Near East.” Pages 47–61 in *Prophecy and Prophets in Ancient Israel: Proceedings of the Oxford Old Testament Seminar*. Edited by John Day. LHBOTS 531. London: T & T Clark, 2010.

Sussman, Shoshana. “Psalm 68: Echoes of the Song of Deborah?” *JBQ* 40 (2012): 238–40.

Sweeney, Marvin. *I & II Kings*. OTL. Louisville: Westminster John Knox, 2007.

Tate, Marvin E. *Psalms 51–100*. WBC. Dallas: Word, 1990.

Tervanotko, Hanna K. *Denying Her Voice: The Figure of Miriam in Ancient Jewish Literature*. *JAJSup* 23. Göttingen:Vandenhoeck & Ruprecht, 2016.

Torrey, Charles C. “Sanballat ‘The Horonite.’” *JBL* 47 (1918): 380–89.

Trible, Phyllis. *God and the Rhetoric of Sexuality*. OBT. Philadelphia: Fortress, 1978.

________. *Texts of Terror*. OBT. Philadelphia: Fortress, 1984.

Van Seters, John, "The Problem of Childlessness in the Near Eastern Law and the Patriarchs of Israel." *JBL* 87 (1968): 401–8.

Van Wolde, Ellen. "Who Guides Whom? Embeddedness as Perspective in Biblical Hebrew and in 1 Kings 3:16–28." *JBL* 114 (1995): 623–42.

Walton, John H. *The Minor Prophets, Job, Psalms, Proverbs, Ecclesiastes, Song of Songs*. Grand Rapids: Zondervan, 2009.

Weinfeld, Moshe. "The Origin of the Humanism in Deuteronomy." *JBL* 80 (1961): 241–47.

________. *Deuteronomy 1–11*. AB. New York: Doubleday, 1991.

Wright, Jacob L. *Why the Bible Began: An Alternative History of Scripture and Its Origins*. Cambridge: Cambridge University Press, 2023.

Yee, Gale A. "Bathsheba (Person)." *ABD* 1:627.

________. "Jezebel (Person)." *ABD* 3:848–49.

Ziesel, Laura Rogers. "'Like a Weaned Child': Breastfeeding Practices in the Biblical Period." *Wesleyan Theological Journal* 52 (2017): 141–50.

Zimmerli, Walther. *Ezekiel 1*. Hermeneia. Philadelphia: Fortress, 1979.

Index of Scriptures

1 Samuel

2 Samuel

1 Kings

2 Kings

1 Chronicles

2 Chronicles

Ezra

Nehemiah

Esther

Job

Psalms

Proverbs

Isaiah

Index of Authors

Index of Subjects

Index of Hebrew Words